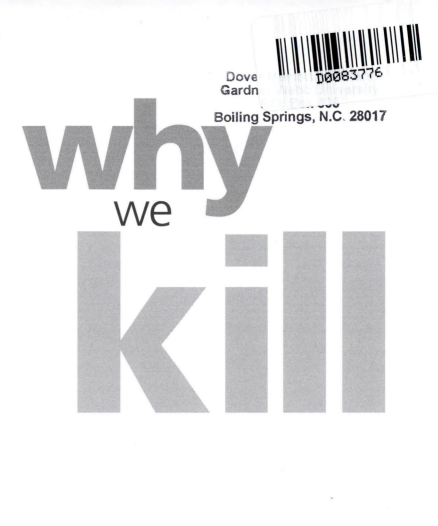

why
we
kill

why we kill

understanding violence across cultures and disciplines

edited by

Nancy Loucks, Sally Smith Holt
and **Joanna R Adler**

**Middlesex
University
PRESS**

First published in 2009 by Middlesex University Press

Copyright © Middlesex University Press

Authors retain rights to individual chapters

ISBN 978 1 904750 42 0

A CIP catalogue record for this book is available from The British Library

Design by Helen Taylor

Printed in the UK by Ashford Colour Press

Middlesex University Press
Fenella Building
The Burroughs
Hendon
London NW4 4BT

Tel: +44 (0)20 8411 4162
Fax: +44 (0)20 8411 4167

www.mupress.co.uk

Acknowlededgments

This book has come together during the course of an extraordinary number of personal and professional challenges for all of us. We would therefore like to thank both our families and especially our participating authors for their tremendous patience, their perseverance, and for their faith in the project. We hope our efforts were worthwhile.

ABOUT THE AUTHORS

Dr Joanna R. Adler is a Principal Lecturer in Forensic Psychology at Middlesex University. She is the Postgraduate Programme Leader for MSc Forensic Psychology and runs Forensic Psychological Services. She has conducted research and published in areas including fear, power, and victimisation in prisons; effects of fear of crime on psychological well-being; intra-familial violence; police stress; the punishment of young offenders; radicalisation of 'at risk youth', post-genocide survival and hate crimes. Recent publications include *Forensic Psychology: Concepts, debates and practice, 2nd Edition* co edited with Jackie Gray and in press with Willan and an entry on genocide in the forthcoming *Cambridge Handbook of Forensic Psychology* (eds. Jennifer Brown and Elizabeth Campbell) with Agnieszka Golec De-Zavala.

Dr Rohan Gunaratna is Head of the International Centre for Political Violence and Terrorism Research, Singapore and Senior Fellow at the Fletcher School of Law and Diplomacy's Jebsen Centre for Counter-Terrorism Studies, Boston. He also holds several honorary appointments including as Senior Fellow, National Memorial Institute for the Prevention of Terrorism, Oklahoma; Member of the Advisory Council, Institute for Counter Terrorism, Israel; and Member, Steering Committee, George Washington University's Homeland Security Policy Institute. Dr Gunaratna holds a Masters in International Peace Studies from the University of Notre Dame, US and a doctorate in International Relations from the University of St Andrews.

Dr Gunaratna is the author of 12 books including *Inside Al Qaeda: Global Network of Terror*, an international bestseller published by Columbia University Press. He also serves on the editorial boards of *Studies in Conflict and Terrorism* and *Terrorism and Political Violence*, the leading counter-terrorism academic journals. Gunaratna has over 25 years of academic, policy, and operational experience in counter terrorism. He led the specialist team that designed and built the UN database on the mobility, weapons and finance of Al Qaeda, Taliban and their Entities. Invited to testify before the 9/11 Commission, he debriefed detainees in Asia and the Middle East including high value detainees in Iraq. A litigation consultant to the United States Justice Department, he served as the US expert in the Jose Padilla trial.

Prof Lawrence M. Hinman is Professor of Philosophy and Director of the Values Institute at the University of San Diego, where he also directs the 'Ethics across the Curriculum' program. He is the author of numerous scholarly as well as popular articles and two books in ethics, *Ethics: A Pluralistic Approach to Moral Theory*, 3rd ed. (Wadsworth, 2002) and *Contemporary Moral Issues*, 3rd ed. (Prentice-Hall, 2003). His website, *Ethics Updates* (http://ethics.acusd.edu) receives over 8,000 visitors a day and has gained numerous awards.

Prof Peter Hodgkinson, BA (Hons), Cert Qual SW, OBE is Founder and Director of the Centre for Capital Punishment Studies (CCPS), Westminster University Law School, London. Prior to joining Westminster in 1989 he was a Probation Officer with the Inner London Probation and Forensic Social Work Advisor at the Denis Hill Secure Unit. He was Honorary Secretary, British Society of Criminology (1978–83); Newsletter Editor, Division of Criminological and Legal Psychology, British Psychological Society (1980–84); Cropwood Fellow, Institute of Criminology, University of Cambridge (1983); Member of the Policy Co-ordinating Group and Council of the Howard League for Penal Reform (1982–99); Editorial Board - Journal of Criminal Behaviour and Mental Health (1989–93); Written Evidence to the House of Commons, Home Affairs Select Committee on The Year and a day Rule & the Mandatory Life Sentence (Howard League 1983); Member of the Steering Committee to the Death Penalty in Commonwealth Africa Project, British Institute of International and Comparative Law (2004–06). Since 1996 he has been Expert and Adviser on capital punishment to the Council of Europe and since 1997 a founding member of the Foreign Secretary's Death Penalty Panel, working closely with governments and NGOs internationally. He is also an advisor to the Council of Europe on prison issues. In 2004 he was appointed OBE in the Queen's Birthday Honours for his work promoting human rights.

Professor Hodgkinson has written and published extensively on capital punishment scholarship and its applied relationship to penal policy and practice including *Capital Punishment: Global issues and prospects.* Hodgkinson & Rutherford, eds., Waterside Press 1996: *Capital Punishment in the USA*, Hodgkinson et al., UK Parliamentary Human Rights Group, 1996 and with Schabas eds., *Capital Punishment: strategies for abolition*, Cambridge University Press, 2003.

Seema Kandelia LLB (Hons), LL.M joined the Centre for Capital Punishment Studies in 2003 as a postgraduate researcher. Her main areas of focus included research into the issues surrounding victims and the death penalty, public reassurance and alternatives to capital punishment. She also monitored capital punishment developments in the USA, the Philippines, the Middle East and Africa, and worked on issues such as juveniles, mental retardation and innocence. Seema now works as a Lecturer and Research Fellow for the Law School at the University of Westminster.

Dr Maria Kaspersson is a Senior Lecturer in Criminology at the School of Humanities and Social Sciences, University of Greenwich. She graduated with a PhD in Criminology from Stockholm University with a thesis on homicide and infanticide in Stockholm. Her current research has involved honour–related violence, the Swedish Prostitution Law and changes in homicide from the 16th to the 20th century. Publications include 'The Great Murder Mystery' in *Comparative Histories of Crime* (Dunstall, Emsley & Godfrey, eds., Willan Publishing, 2003) and 'Homicide and Infanticide in Stockholm 1920–1939' in *Journal of Scandinavian Studies in Criminology and Crime Prevention*, 2003.

Dr Nancy Loucks is Chief Executive of Families Outside, a national charity in Scotland that works on behalf of prisoners' families. During the writing of this book she worked as an independent criminologist, specialising in prison policy and comparative penology. Her work has included extensive research in criminology including the imprisonment of women, aspects of prison discipline and control, violence and bullying, use of drugs and alcohol, suicides and self-injury, and the impact of imprisonment on prisoners' families. Other projects have included research into the employment of people with a criminal record in the European Union, human rights aspects of religious communities in prisons, and risk assessment of serious sexual and violent offenders.

Kay Nooney is a forensic psychologist in HM Prison Service for England and Wales. Her earlier areas of work have included research management and operational research in Prison Service Headquarters. Her work in a London prison specialised in interventions with HIV prisoners, sex offenders and prisoners in crisis. The work in prison was followed by development and evaluation of offending behaviour programmes in prison and the community. She is currently part of the Safer Custody Group in the Prison Service Headquarters, which is concerned with deaths, self-harm and violence in prison custody.

Rupa Reddy LLB (Hons), LL.M was formerly postgraduate researcher at the Centre for Capital Punishment Studies (2002–06) responsible for research on use of the death penalty within the British Commonwealth Caribbean and the Indian subcontinent; as well as research on the issues of gender, race, religion, mental illness and the role of psychiatrists in relation to capital punishment. Rupa also edited the first two volumes of the Centre's Occasional Paper Series journal. She is currently undertaking PhD research at the School of Oriental and African Studies on honour-related violence within UK ethnic minority communities.

Dr Stephen Smith is the co-founder of Britain's first Holocaust Memorial, Beth Shalom, and of the Aegis Genocide Prevention Initiative. He writes and lectures frequently on Holocaust and Genocide studies, and his particular area of specialisation is memorialisation and witness testimony. His awards include an MBE in 2000 and the Interfaith Gold Medallion the same year. Dr Smith edits a continuing series of survivor testimonies (published by Quill Press, 2000–01) and is writer/director of the film documentaries *Wasted Lives* (2000), *Survivors: Memories for the Past, Lessons for the Future* (2001), and *Britain and the Holocaust*

(2002). Recent publications include *Forgotten Places: The Holocaust and the Remnants of Destruction*, *The Holocaust and the Christian World*, and *Making Memory: Creating Britain's First Holocaust Centre.*

During the crisis in Kosovo in 1999, Dr Smith directed the East Midlands Kosovo Appeal. A member of the International task Force on Holocaust Education (Sweden), he works closely with Holocaust projects in Lithuania, Sweden, and the United States. He is Consultant to South Africa's Cape Town Holocaust Memorial Museum.

Dr Sally Smith Holt is an Associate Professor of Religion at Belmont University. She graduated with a PhD in ethics, society and religion from Vanderbilt University. She is interested in sociology of religion and related issues of justice. Recent projects have included research into women's groups and their involvement with fundamentalist religious systems and also research considering just treatment of animals, farming and environmental ethics. Many of the courses she teaches are interdisciplinary, and she has conducted work in the area of capital punishment studies.

Prof Daya Somasundaram is the Professor of Psychiatry at the Faculty of Medicine, University of Jaffna and Consultant Psychiatrist at the Teaching Hospital, Jaffna, Sri Lanka. During his sabbatical leave he worked in Cambodia on a Community Mental Health Programme for the Transcultural Psychosocial Organization (TPO) based in Amsterdam. His research interests include trauma about which he has published papers in international journals and written several books, including *Scarred Minds – the psychological impact of war on Sri Lankan Tamils.* He was instrumental in the adaptation of the WHO manual, *Mental Health of Refugees*, to the Cambodian context as *Community Mental Health in Cambodia* and to the Tamil context as *Mental Health in the Tamil Community.* These manuals are being used to train grass-roots workers in simple psychosocial skills.

Prof Keith Soothill is Emeritus Professor of Social Research and is currently attached to the Centre for Applied Statistics at Lancaster University. His current research interests are in the areas of homicide, sex offending, criminal careers and crime and the media. He taught criminology for over 30 years with well over 200 publications. He wants criminologists to appreciate the links with other disciplines and not to be too narrowly focused. He co-authored the book, *Making Sense of Criminology* (Cambridge: Polity Press, 2002), the monograph, *Murder and serious sexual assault: What criminal histories can reveal about future serious offending* (London: Home Office 2002) and co-edited *Handbook of Forensic Mental Health* (Willan, 2008). His writings on serial killing began with the article, 'The Serial Killer Industry', in the *Journal of Forensic Psychiatry* in 1993, and he has subsequently made several contributions in this area.

Table of Contents

Introduction: Religion, Culture and Killing

Sally Smith Holt, Nancy Loucks and Joanna R. Adler

Whether consciously or unconsciously, people use ethical language every day. We consider what is 'right' and 'good' and think about our 'duty' even if we do not consider specific ethical categories such as virtue ethics, utilitarianism or deontology. We determine how to judge 'bad' or 'wrong' actions and attempt to put together, even if informally, a code of ethics by which to live. In this text, we look specifically at the act of killing by exploring the ethics of this action, taking an interdisciplinary approach to offer the most comprehensive method for discussing the topic. The book deals with a number of types of killing, often considering religious and cultural factors. Throughout, we seek to build up a complex set of answers to the deceptively simple question of why we kill.

Why We Kill may seem a particularly topical book in view of recent world events, not least the attack on the World Trade Center in New York on 11 September 2001, the taking and killing of hostages in Beslan (2004), the terrorist attacks in Madrid (2004), London (2005), and Glasgow (2007). However, planning for the book was well underway before any of these events. They gave an added incentive for publication, but the initial seed had been planted years before, as we thought about how our ethical questions regarding killing could straddle societal and academic boundaries. The questions we ask ourselves and the answers we come to live by should be asked of any era. What wisdom do we draw upon from the past, and how do our contemporary contexts shape us? We believe the answers, or at least the attempt to formulate answers, to such questions are multilayered and complex. Whether the approaches to ethical decision making we use when considering the act of killing are philosophical in orientation or involve a religious component, questions about killing are fraught with difficulty. Let us begin, for example, with the biblical prohibition against killing found in the Hebrew texts.

Virtually every religion and culture has an equivalent to the biblical commandment, 'Thou shalt not kill' – but how consistent is this prohibition? Even within one particular religious or cultural system, some instances seem to allow killing while others do not; confusion and debate exists over when and how killing should occur. For example, 'Thou shalt not kill,' a prohibition found in more than one location within the Hebrew Bible (e.g. Exodus 20:13, Deuteronomy 5:17) does not appear to prohibit all killing. Killing by the state for punishment and warfare are generally condoned throughout this religious

1

text, while the aforementioned prohibition on killing seems to address only outright murder and careless or accidental killing.

In cases of murder and accidental killing, the suggested response is often killing the killer, theoretically because this response restores balance to society. If someone murders, or even kills accidentally, reciprocity demands a response of killing. This may be an act that preserved *imago Dei*, supporting the idea that all life belongs to God. It may have limited blood vengeance: only one life could be taken in response to the killing of an individual. Most biblical scholars concur that both prohibitions against killing and mandates that demand killing are biblical statements that sought to limit vengeance and retaliation and to preserve the idea that life is sacred. Worthy of note is that the Jewish Talmud is very clear that the Sanhedrin took great pains to avoid implementing the death penalty (Mishnah Makkot 1:10).[1] Even within a single religious tradition, conversations about killing are not as clear cut as they may at first appear.

Dr John Kelsay, a noted academic of religious ethics, prefers to translate 'Thou shalt not kill' using the term 'murder' rather than 'kill'. Homicide is certainly the only form of killing that seems to attract universal disapprobation, but as we seek to define homicide or murder, we realise that even here we have problems in identifying the boundaries. Abortion, suicide, euthanasia and capital punishment are among a number of methods of killing that attract titles both of 'murder' and more sanitised nomenclature, depending on the perspective of the audience. Further, should these debates be limited to consideration of human beings? Some animal rights groups apply the idea of homicide to acts against other animals, as demonstrated by the slogan, 'meat is murder'. Noted British theologian and ethicist Andrew Linzey holds that we do not have the right to kill animals because life is not ours for the taking: life belongs to God. What and who determines whether one form of killing is acceptable while another is morally reprehensible?

In this book, we examine specific instances of killing people and analyse these with the intention of informing readers, ideally encouraging an examination of our own ethical beliefs. One may take comfort in separating 'good' people from 'bad' people (Zimbardo 2007), but such separation is not as straightforward as it may at first appear. Zimbardo suggests an alternative conception of evil 'in *incrementalist* terms, as something of which we are all capable, depending on circumstances' (*ibid*.: 7, emphasis in original). He explains that his research into human behaviour in the Stanford Prison Experiment (1972) showed that 'The line between Good and Evil, once thought to be impermeable, proved instead to be quite permeable' (2007: 195).

---

1   "A Sanhedrin that puts one person to death once in seven years is called destructive. Rabbi Eliezer ben Azariah says: Or even once in seventy years. Rabbi Tarfon and Rabbi Akiva say: Had we been the Sanhedrin, none would ever have been put to death." Mishnah Makkot, 1:10

Early experiments such as those by Stanley Milgram (1974) show that virtually all of us are willing to behave in ways we never thought possible, given the right context or authoritative instruction. Events such as the Holocaust and the massacre at My Lai bring this aspect of human behaviour into sharp relief. How many of us can realistically believe that we would never support or facilitate the act of killing? We may not view ourselves as breaking any moral law; we may not go out and kill people we see on the street nor define ourselves as 'killers,' but we can be caught in complex, often confusing social interactions regarding the act.

The topics for this book were chosen specifically to encourage thought about such questions and to deal with such inconsistencies. We invited authors across social science and humanities disciplines to contribute, as we wished to share the approaches of different disciplines and to facilitate trans-theoretical debate. The editors come from distinct theoretical backgrounds and have been motivated to find synergy in drawing on each other's strengths, and on how similar our techniques can be, despite the different language we adopt.

Notwithstanding this, we recognise the complexity of both intra-disciplinary and inter-disciplinary debate, particularly in topics as potentially emotive and politically charged as those we consider here. In defence of such an approach, Zimbardo notes that:

> ...most psychologists have been insensitive to the deeper sources of power that inhere in the political, economic, religious, historic, and cultural matrix that defines situations and gives them legitimate or illegitimate existence. A full understanding of the dynamics of human behavior requires that we recognize the extent and limits of personal power, situational power, and systemic power.
> (2007: x)

We hope that readers will embrace the challenges posed herein and will agree that this varied approach benefits rather than detracts from the text. We believe the book will remain relevant in years to come as the topics and the manner in which they are discussed contribute to present and future debates in this field.

Governments have killed for thousands of years, while at the same time their laws have prohibited individuals from taking similar actions under most circumstances. A report by Amnesty International (1989) called *When the State Kills* – a title later used in other publications on capital punishment including Sarat (2002), emphasised the inconsistency between teaching people that killing is wrong whilst making it an acceptable action when the faceless entity of 'the state' does it for us. How do we deal with these inconsistencies? In the United States, the Supreme Court often cites evolving standards of decency as one way to provide such answers. Its decision in 2005 to prohibit capital punishment for those who were juveniles when they committed their crimes is one example of such action.[2] However the United States is one of the very few Western countries that continues to utilise capital punishment at all. Are further discrepancies at work here?

Another dilemma that did not confront our predecessors involves advances in medical technology. The euthanasia case of Terri Schiavo provides an example that is relatively new to us (see Chapter 5). Medical advances now allow us to keep individuals alive who would otherwise die, so was Schiavo allowed to die or was she killed? Similarly, in France Chantal Sebire petitioned for the right to die due to a rare illness that left her face disfigured and caused extreme pain, yet her government denied her wish. Was this morally correct? Unlike Schiavo, Sebire did not suffer mental incapacitation and reasoned that she had the right to choose death. French law disagreed.

This book examines these and other dilemmas. Why do some people condone abortion yet oppose the death penalty? Why do some condemn suicide yet view the death of suicide bombers as martyrdom? What compels people to take hundreds of schoolchildren and their families hostage in Beslan, draping them in fuse wire and detonators (McAllister and Quinn-Judge 2004)? How could anyone strap explosive devices to two women with learning difficulties and blow them up, along with over 90 bystanders in a crowded Baghdad market (Fletcher 2008)? Why do ordinary people participate in such extraordinary acts of violence and killing as the Rwandan Genocide (www.rwanda-genocide.org)? What does this say about us collectively and individually?

At first glance, the varied types of killing seem largely unrelated, despite the common outcome. We argue that all of us have the potential to kill; many if not most of us probably condone it in some form or another, depending on how we define it and justify it according to our moral code. This is the common thread: something about a moral code, a religious or ethical belief enmeshed within a cultural context, determines one's stance on various types of killing and, indeed, on inhibitors to killing. Further, social context and circumstances can challenge this stance beyond what each individual ever thought possible.

This book intends to address the violence of killing in its contextual, multi-layered and complex manifestations, taking into account how culture plays a pivotal role in understanding violent action yet also remembering the peaceful emphases of various religious and cultural traditions. Each chapter begins with a brief introduction from the editors to help tie the themes together. The

---

2   Roper v Simmons (03-633) 543 US 551 (2005) 112 SW 3d.

chapters discuss various forms of killing and reasons behind these, moving through the spectrum of those which attract universal approbation (for example homicide, serial killing) to those protected by law (capital punishment, abortion) to those that are even venerated (killing in the context of war).

The epilogue draws the themes from the book together, this time with the benefit of the examples put forward in each chapter. We again discuss the common thread we highlighted at the outset: that religious or ethical belief enmeshed within a cultural context determines one's stance on various types of killing and, indeed, on inhibitors to killing. In this attempt to answer the question of why we kill, we do not expect to resolve these differences in moral or religious belief. Rather we hope to increase understanding of them and, in turn, to encourage an examination of our own beliefs.

References

Amnesty International (1989) *When the State Kills: The Death Penalty – A Human Rights Issue, Briefing 1989.* Amnesty International.

Fedler, K. D. (2006) *Exploring Christian Ethics.* Louisville: Westminster John Knox Press.

Fletcher, M. (2008) 'Down's Syndrome bombers kill 91'. *The Times* 2 February 2008, www.timesonline.co.uk/tol/news/world/iraq/article3287373.ece.

Linzey, A. (1999) *Animal Gospel.* Westminster: John Knox Press.

McAllister, J. F. O. and Quinn-Judge, P. (2004) 'Slaughter of the Innocents'. *TIMEeurope Magazine* 4 September 2004, www.time.com/time/europe/html/040913/story.html.

Milgram, S. (1974), *Obedience to Authority; An Experimental View.* New York: Harper and Row.

Roig-Franzia, M. (2005) Schiavo's Feeding Tube Is Removed: Congressional Leaders' Legal Manoeuvring Fails to Stop Judge's Order. *Washington Post*, 19.03.05.

http://www.washingtonpost.com/wp-dyn/articles/A46505-2005Mar18.html (accessed, March, 2008).

Sarat, A. (2002) *When the State Kills: Capital Punishment and the American Condition.* Princeton: Princeton University Press.

Zimbardo, P. (2007) *The Lucifer Effect: How Good People Turn Evil.* London: Rider.

Zimbardo, P. G. (1972) *The Stanford Prison Experiment a Simulation Study of the Psychology of Imprisonment.* Philip G. Zimbardo, Inc.

PROLOGUE: **HOMICIDE**

In Chapter 1, Maria Kaspersson provides an introduction to homicide, as it is perhaps the most universally condemned act of killing. Homicide is not, however, usually a random act by a stranger. Year after year the statistics show we are much more likely to die at the hands of someone we know, more often than not someone in our own household. The chapter outlines three main types of homicide (confrontational, domestic, and other), then discusses domestic homicides – the most common of the three – in more detail. Kaspersson's chapter has been divided into two parts. Part I includes acts of domestic killing such as infanticide and killing in the context of intra-familial violence. Part II then discusses more narrowly culturally defined familial homicide – the so-called 'honour killings' (the killing of someone who is thought to have brought dishonour to a family, such as women who commit adultery or who date or marry outside their own culture) and the practice of suttee, or 'bride burning'.

Cultural factors operate particularly strongly in the realm of domestic violence and homicide. The pattern is evident internationally, though in some cultures the oppression of women is more blatant than in others. Cohen (2001) explains that failure to protect women in such cases does not necessarily mean people are tolerant or accepting of abuse:

> The women do not ignore or condone abuse; nor are they in some psychic state of victim denial. They are trapped in a culture where tolerance is a form of social control, discouraging or even forbidding any acknowledgment of the problem. (They cite the proverb: 'A hidden defeat is better than being disgraced in public.') Not only is the wife blamed for her husband's violence, but her tolerance is a mirage, hiding the fact that passivity ('Why doesn't she tell?', 'Why doesn't she leave?') results not from free choice but lack of choice. (*ibid.*: 52)

Dominant culture can therefore place tremendous pressure on people's response to even the most serious abuse and their ability to prevent it.

Honour killings cross over into the realm of capital punishment in cultures where a woman's 'dishonour' is defined in law. In 2002, 30-year-old Amina Lawal was sentenced in court to death by stoning in Katsina State, Nigeria, for having a child outside marriage. In some countries the act does not even have to be consensual to legitimise killing: in Pakistan in 2002, a court judged a woman raped by her brother-in-law guilty of adultery and sentenced her to death by stoning (Adams 2002). This 'protection' of family honour in the name of religion extends to other forms of killing, such as the culpable homicide of 15 girls in Mecca in March 2002. Religious police prevented male fire-fighters and paramedics from entering the girls' school where a fire had broken out on the grounds that some of the girls' clothing was not appropriate for them to wear in public (Kimball 2002).

In cases such as these, people who believe killing is wrong may believe it to be justified in certain contexts. In this way, they may retain conventional, moral values that killing is wrong, even when they commit such an act. Cohen gives the example of young offenders who '... dispute the conventional meanings attached to their offences or try to evade moral blame and legal culpability. The ubiquity of such accounts shows that conventional values remain salient, even when violated' (2001: 77). They also refuse to '...accept the category of acts to which it is assigned. The equivalent of 'you can't call this stealing' is 'you can't call this torture" (ibid.) – or in the case of honour killings, 'you can't call this murder'.

Kimball emphasises that other members of the same religions will not agree with such extreme actions in their name, nor do these behaviours belong exclusively to the realm of one or two religious groups:

> ...people in all traditions can and do employ horrific means to achieve traditionally accepted goals – not the ultimate goal, but goals that are intentionally or unintentionally elevated and considered sacrosanct. When these result in dehumanizing patterns of behavior towards others – in this case, women within the tradition – something is clearly wrong.... Men and women of faith can and should be at the forefront of the long-overdue struggle to stop religion from being used as a vehicle to oppress and dehumanize groups of people. (*ibid.*: 143)

The overarching point is that religious and cultural views are used as a means to justify the most extreme behaviour – and that all of us may be guilty in some form or another.

References

Adams, S. (2002) 'In Pakistan, Rape Victims are the Criminals.' *New York Times* May 17 2002.
Cohen, S. (2001) *States of Denial: Knowing About Atrocities and Suffering.* Cambridge: Polity Press.
Kimball, C. (2002) *When Religion Becomes Evil.* New York: HarperCollins Publishers Inc.

Chapter 1

'You Always Hurt the One You Love': Homicide in a Domestic Context

Maria Kaspersson

Introduction

If… violence is seen as intentional acts undertaken in order to achieve ends that are deeply embedded in the circumstances of daily life, it becomes an issue for us all, may affect anyone, and is about daily life. (Dobash and Dobash 1999: 141)

Despite homicide being stereotyped as confrontational or, alternatively, as the act of a psychopath, in fact most homicides take place within families (Brookman 2005). This chapter concentrates on these homicides, first in the domestic context generally and then within specific cultural frameworks. These include acts as varied as 'battered wife syndrome', 'extended suicides' and 'honour killings'. To put these into context, a short description of the excluded types of homicide (i.e. mainly public, male-on-male manslaughter) will be given first. This chapter divides homicide into three main groups (Polk 1994: 189–90): confrontational homicide, other homicide, and domestic homicide, based on the relation of victim and offender and on the scene of the crime.

Confrontational and other homicide

Confrontational and domestic are the two dominant types of homicide; 'other' homicides are not as common. Confrontational homicides are described as male-on-male, spontaneous, 'trivial' in origin – but not to the involved parties (Websdale 1999) – connected to alcohol intoxication, committed in public leisure areas (Polk 1994), such as pubs, and honour related (Polk 1999). The cases often have a masculine profile where honour and respect are achieved via the use of violence (Dobash and Dobash 1998). Death is typically caused by assault or stabbing (Brookman 2005). Another important feature is 'victim precipitation', meaning that the victim is the one who precipitates the violence and that both victim and offender are willing participants in the incident (Wolfgang 1958; Campbell 1992; Polk 1999). The deaths are not the result of a premeditated act: the intent is to hurt, not to kill (Brookman 2005).

'Other' homicide is a mixed category. This is a common feature in classifying homicide, since the variety in nature and motive makes the ways of division almost infinite (Wolfgang 1958: 187). This group consists of several types of homicide that are rare but generally receive much more media attention than domestic and confrontational homicide (Campbell 1992; D'Cruze et al. 2006). Lees (1992: 270) points out that this leads to the 'typical' murderer being portrayed as a psychopathic killer. This is because in character they are more spectacular and considered more interesting, often displaying gory and titillating elements, which make them more newsworthy (Reiner 2002). To this group belong such widely different kinds of homicide as homicide committed in connection with other crimes (Polk 1994) – ranging from robbery, hit men and terrorists to serial and multiple killers, sex murderers and 'madmen' (Brookman 2005). Keith Soothill discusses serial killers in Chapter 2 of this text.

What many of these different homicides have in common is that they are instrumental rather than expressive in character. An instrumental homicide is characterised by violence used as a means to gain something else – money, goods, for example – even if it includes killing someone. Instrumental violence is often premeditated (Levi 2002). Another kind of instrumental violence is when homicide is used as conflict resolution. In these cases violence is the ultimate arbiter of the dispute (Polk 1994). Expressive violence, on the other hand, is primarily used to hurt the victim and is more spontaneous in character. Expressive violence can further be seen as emotionally satisfying without economic gain, such as domestic violence or street fights (Levi 2002).

The next sections focus on deliberate killings in a domestic context.

Domestic homicide

> As we as a society try to make sense of domestic homicide, we cannot escape or deny our relationship with it and involvement in it. All the more reason to prevent it. (Websdale 1999: 236)

The World Health Organisation states that, all over the world, more women aged 15–44 die from domestic violence than from cancer, malaria, war or traffic accidents (Almosaed 2004). Though the most frequent form of homicide in most Western countries, domestic homicide is discussed the least. Since patterns of domestic violence and domestic homicide have cross-cultural consistency (Wilson and Daly 1998), this pattern is most likely a worldwide problem. The police have had a tendency to consider domestic violence and domestic homicide as less important (Websdale 1999), and cases of this kind of murder rarely reach the news (Reiner 2002). Their private and sometimes mundane character means they have remained exactly that: private. Until the 1970s, domestic violence – or wife battering, as was the earlier term (Walklate

2001) – was rarely studied or discussed. Private violence within the sanctity of marriage was to be left alone by outsiders. Both Radford (1992c: 258) and Walklate (2001: 114) cite a statement from the Association of Chief of Police Officers in the UK in 1974–5 that illustrates the view of the police: 'We are after all dealing with persons bound in marriage, and it is important for a host of reasons to maintain the unity of the spouses.'

A gendered dimension can be highlighted in cases of domestic homicide in that men not only commit more domestic homicide (and homicide as a whole) than women, but also they commit it for different reasons. Generally it is described in terms that the man's killing is offensive while the woman's is defensive. In other words, men kill for control, while women kill out of despair (Walklate 2001). According to Websdale (1999), a legacy of oppression, discrimination, disadvantage and social despair plays a major role in producing violent interpersonal relationships. Dobash and Dobash (1998) point out that personal exchanges, interactions and daily conflicts are the basis of violent events. They argue that this base is shaped by the cultural context that positions marital partners and often supports men's control and domination over women.

In this context, the term 'femicide' – the misogynous killing of women by men (Radford 1992a; Brookman 2005) – might spring to mind, since many of the forms of homicide are characterised by a context of oppression of women in a patriarchal society. However, in the killings that will be discussed here, not all victims are women, and not all offenders are men. They are, however, often shaped by a gendered context which renders the term appropriate. Different types of domestic homicide are discussed below using cases to illustrate.

Infanticide

Infanticide is the act in which a mother kills her child in the first year of its life because the birth has affected the balance of the mother's mind. Two kinds exist: neonaticide, which takes place within 24 hours of the baby's birth, and infanticide (often labelled manslaughter in the legal process), which takes place within the child's first year (Websdale 1999; Palermo 2002; Brookman 2005). Infanticide is often a premeditated and deliberate act; it is the psychological status of the offender that counts as mitigating and labels it manslaughter (Ward 1999).

Infanticide is very rare; the few cases that occur are committed by women considered to be mentally ill (Palermo 2002). At the same time, cultural differences in the use of contraceptives, abortion, and adoption practices affect the number of cases (*ibid.*). Neonaticide in northern Europe is usually the result of concealed pregnancy and unassisted delivery (Brookman 2005). D'Orban (cited in Brookman *ibid.*: 189) says that women who commit neonaticide usually do not suffer from psychiatric disorder, are young and single and conceal their pregnancy. 'They are often passive personalities who dissociate from the pregnancy and do not seek antenatal care or medical help at the time of birth. They kill the child immediately after birth, usually without any obvious planning or premeditation.' Neonaticide is often the result of a passive rather than active killing.

In November 1999 a 15-year-old girl committed neonaticide. She confessed she stabbed her newborn baby to death after giving birth in secret at home. She had concealed the pregnancy. She pleaded guilty to infanticide and received psychiatric care (Gillan 1999).

Palermo (2002) discusses a multitude of infanticide 'syndromes' such as the 'unwanted child syndrome' and the 'shaken baby syndrome'. In April 2000, Rachel – 23 years, single, depressed, exhausted and non-coping – shook her four-month-old daughter to death. She says herself: 'It was only one shake that I remember and it wasn't even hard or violent. It was more out of frustration than anything. It didn't stop the crying and… then I went to change her nappy… and she stopped breathing.' Questioned at the hospital, she denied shaking the baby: 'The fact that I had caused my baby's death was too much for me to cope with.' She was charged with and convicted of infanticide (Carter 2000).

Pearson (1998) argues that women have been allowed – by men who do not and cannot see women act out of cruelty – to put forward a variety of psychological and medical explanations as mitigating circumstances (see also Brookman 2005; D'Cruze et al. 2006). They most commonly argue postnatal depression and the youth of the mother. Pearson (1998) continues that some of these acts are truly cruel and should be seen and treated as murder, but as Morrisey states: 'Nowhere, it seems, is the presentation of a woman who is both violent and agentic, responsible and human, possible' (cited in D'Cruze et al. 2006: 43). Pearson (1998) believes it is too easy for a mother to get away with infanticide. In other words, some mothers may be mentally ill when committing the act, but not all are.

Filicide

Filicide includes cases where a child or children are killed by a parent or step-parent. Research has shown that step-parents are more common offenders than biological ones, especially in connection with child abuse (Wilson and Daly 1998; Websdale 1999). Likewise, the father or stepfather is the offender more often than the mother or stepmother, but again more female perpetrators are evident than in other homicide categories (Brookman 2005). Websdale (1999: 211) concludes that '…stepfathers often killed boys and girls during periods of extreme rage in which they had become exasperated with them. It seems as if some stepfathers have a lower tolerance for children and less willingness to invest in relationships with them than do natural fathers.' Wilson and Daly (1998) emphasise that mistreatment of stepchildren is a likely source of tension between the step-parent and the biological parent. In one such case, six-year-old Lauren Wright was tortured and finally killed by her stepmother (Coward 2002).

According to Ann Goetting (cited in Websdale 1999: 13), the offenders (parents and step-parents) tend to be undereducated, unemployed, with a previous arrest record, and the relationship between parent and child '…is severed in a rage of impatience and anger at a private residence as a result of beating or shaking.' The sex of the child does not seem to matter (Websdale 1999). Brookman (2005) points out that children can be killed either in a context of prior violence or by a single incident of frustration and aggression.

Child abuse is an issue often connected to the abuse of a partner in the relationship (Wilson and Daly 1998; Websdale 1999). Stark and Flitcraft (cited in Websdale 1999: 25) claim that 'woman battering…is a major context for child abuse' and that the abuse 'represents the extension of ongoing violence.' In a majority of these homicides, the child victims are under two years old. Younger abused children are, naturally, at greater risk of severe injury and homicide (Brookman 2005). In about half of the cases of child homicide the perpetrator had previously used violence against the child (Websdale 1999).

Other cases are the result of child abuse other than direct violence, such as neglect and malnutrition. These children also tend to be less than two years of age (*ibid.*). For example when Ainlee Walker died aged two, her parents were convicted of manslaughter and child cruelty. 'After her death, Ainlee was found to be grossly emaciated, with 64 injuries, including third degree burns' (Wallace 2002).

Child homicide because the children are 'in the way' of a new relationship also occurs. The children are killed either by the mother or the stepfather (Brookman 2005). Websdale (1999) found that stepfathers in such cases saw the child as a hindrance to developing their relationship with the child's mother, while mothers, on the other hand, are less likely to forsake the child if it is older. If it is still a baby, she might turn a blind eye to abuse and neglect since 'the baby is a resented impediment to the new relationship, and the mother has to make a choice' (Daly and Wilson, cited in Websdale 1999: 211). Some mothers feel unable to intervene due to fear, founded in their own victimisation by the partner. According to Websdale, a child may be killed not only because he or she is perceived as hampering a new relationship or because there is no desire to care for another's offspring, a man may, abhorrent as it may be, simply want to establish, 'a coercive regime of patriarchal control within the new family' (*ibid.*).

Another form is cases with motives connected to the child, its behaviour or wellbeing, often called 'altruistic' or 'mercy killings' (Palermo 2002).

Sometimes these killings are also referred to as 'delusional', since the altruism or mercy the offenders act on is delusional rather than factual (Brookman 2005). The offender is the mother, father or both parents. In October 1999, Janquil Turnbull killed her two severely disabled sons, 20 and 23 years old, by suffocating them with a pillow after having given them a drug overdose. She claimed she 'could not cope anymore with looking after the boys' and feared the social services would put them in a home. She was sentenced to three years' probation for manslaughter with diminished responsibility (Guardian 2001).

Children can also be used as 'pawns' or killed in revenge for something the mother or father has done, so called 'spouse revenge filicide' or 'the Medea complex' (Palermo 2002). Daly and Wilson (1998: 225) described a scenario where 'the killer professes a grievance against his wife, usually with respect to alleged infidelities and/or her intending or acting to terminate the marriage'. In February 2002, Steven Wilson murdered his two young sons, seven and eight years old, with a screwdriver in an act of revenge against their mother who had left him after years of abuse. He claimed he wanted to teach his wife 'a lesson she would never forget' (Hull 2003). He was sentenced to life and labelled an 'evil father' by the judge (Branigan 2003a). Five days in to his sentence he hanged himself in his cell (Branigan 2003b). In November 2005, Gavin Hall smothered his daughter Millie, aged three, with a rag soaked in chloroform after he found out his wife was having an affair. He sent a text message to his wife, saying: 'Goodbye, Millie sends her love. She died at 3.32am. Love till death do us part I said and this is what I meant' (Taylor 2006).

Pearson (1998) describes two scenarios with the mother as the offender, either as a revenging Medea, using her children as 'pawns' in punishing the father or as a woman suffering from Munchausen syndrome by proxy. Munchausen syndrome is defined by an unceasing quest for attention from family and doctors. In the syndrome by proxy a person inflicts the injuries on someone else, often a child. The deaths are often masked as cot deaths, or Sudden Infant Death Syndrome (SIDS), and the attention and sympathy given to the grieving mother is the desired outcome. Since it is common that several children die when women suffer from this syndrome, the only way of detecting them is to show a pattern of behaviour. Meadow (1999: 13) sends what he calls a key message: 'Infants … who come from a family in which a previous child has died unexpectedly should raise suspicion.' This lead to the formulation of the so called 'Meadow's Law' that one cot death is tragic, two is suspicious and three is murder unless proven otherwise (D'Cruze et al. 2006). This led to Angela Cannings, whose three babies all died within weeks of their birth, being sentenced to two life sentences for having murdered two of her children in April 2002. They died from cot deaths according to her, but from smothering according to the verdict (Addley 2002). It was seen as too much of a coincidence that all three of her babies died in the same way.

The same circumstance, i.e. that three of her four children died in cot deaths, whose number made them suspicious, brought forward Trupti Patel's prosecution in April 2003 (Payne 2003). In another case, Sally Clark was first sentenced after her two children had consecutively died and the cause of death could not be established. Later, however, it was proven that the second child had died of a virus, and she was freed in January 2003 (Sweeney 2003). She later died in March 2007 from alcohol overdose as she struggled to deal with the experience (Pallister 2007). In August 2005 Professor Meadow lost his right to practise medicine (a decision that was later overturned), since the three women mentioned above were all later released (Batty 2006). The flaw in 'Meadow's Law' is that he erroneously assumed that SIDS is a random phenomenon, when later research has shown that it might run in certain families (Carpenter et al. 2005). Trupti Patel's maternal grandmother came over from India to tell the court that she had lost five of her twelve children in early infancy (Vasagar and Allison 2003). This means that if one cot death occurs in a family, this increases the likelihood that a second child will die from the same reason. This lead to a review of 258 cases of parents convicted of cot deaths (Dyer and Taylor 2004).

Extended suicide

An extended suicide – often called homicide–suicide (Wood Harper and Voigt 2007) – involves an act of killing which is followed by the suicide or attempted suicide of the offender (Starzomski and Nussbaum 2000). The victims are the partner (commonly when the offender is male), children (commonly when the offender is female), or both (almost exclusively with male offenders). The latter type of offenders are called 'family annihilators' and are commonly considered as a type of mass murderer (Wood Harper and Voight 2007). Motives include depression, control, or lack of control such as jealousy (Websdale 1999; Starzomski and Nussbaum 2000) and separation (Johnson 2006). Charles Ewing (in Websdale 1999: 18) notes that 'the typical family killer is more likely to be concerned about losing control over more than just his wife and family. His concern is more often with losing control over all aspects of his life.' Wilson and Daly (1998) paint a scenario in which the killer is a depressed and brooding man who is apprehending disaster for himself and his family and sees extended suicide as the only way out. Polk (1994) notes that with male offenders in extended suicide cases, the victim is part of the suicide plan; the woman is seen as a commodity, and the offender finds it inconceivable that the woman should be left alone to tend for herself. Women avoid abandoning their children via their suicide by killing them as well (Brookman 2005). Another gender difference is that female extended suicides tend to be passive – killings often take place by poisoning – while male are active, using weapons such as knives or guns (Kaspersson 2003b).

In August 2002 Karl Bluestone bludgeoned his wife and two of his four children to death with a hammer. This followed his wife telling him she was leaving him and taking the children after years of abuse and his paranoia regarding her fidelity (Press Association 2001). Peter Stafford bludgeoned his wife and three children with a hammer before killing them with a knife and then hanging himself in October 1999. His brother said 'he was depressed and felt suicidal' (*Guardian* 2000). In April 2006, Alison Davies jumped from the Humber Bridge with her 12-year-old autistic son, killing both (Martin 2006).

Websdale (1999) highlights the fact that press reports usually fail to report a history of woman abuse in cases of extended suicides and notes a need for news coverage that addresses the social context of these killings. McNeill (1992) points out how these cases are described as 'tragedies' – for the man. In cases where the woman was killed after saying she was leaving her abusive husband (as Mrs Bluestone did), reports did not describe the offence as a tragedy for her. In the Bluestone case, the coroner commented upon her decision to leave: 'Whilst it cannot explain the tragedy that subsequently took place it perhaps gives an insight into Karl Bluestone's mind on August 28' (Press Association 2001). Johnson (2006: 458) remarks that cases are depicted as 'acts of frustrated love, rather than acts of extreme and premeditated violence'. McNeill (1992) further argues that the wrongfulness of the man's action is not highlighted, because a man who kills his wife and then himself – regardless of whether he was a wife beater – is the ideal tragic hero. The press reconstructs these femicides – and sometimes familicides – into Shakespearean-style tragedies.

In March 2003 'devoted father' (Stevenson 2003) Keith Young gassed himself and his four young sons, aged three to seven, to death in his car. The reason was he learned his estranged wife – we are told that the marriage had been 'turbulent', she 'got bored' and left him (Loudon and Tozer 2003) – was pregnant by another man. He called her and told her he was going to kill the boys. She alerted the police, but they could not locate him in time, and all five died. Later, she lost the baby she was carrying (Jenkins 2003). The report in the newspaper placed the blame on the mother, even though it acknowledged that 'words could not describe what... she was going through' (Loudon and Tozer 2003). A relative of Young's said: '[She] was the love of Keith's life and he idolised the boys. All he wanted to do was to love her and look after his boys but she took them away from him and did not want to be with him' (ibid.). When it comes to domestic homicide, it is not, as we shall see, uncommon that the victim gets the blame.

Partner homicide: 'Till death us do part'

In partner homicide, typically the man kills his present or ex-partner

(Campbell 1992; Wilson and Daly 1992 and 1998). Female victims are more likely to be victims of intimate partners than are males (Browne et al. 1999). These cases are often part of domestic violence, where the death of the victim is the result of, or a reaction to, the violence (ibid.; Websdale 1999). According to Campbell (1992: 102) 'woman battering routinely precedes femicide'. Wilson and Daly have found that, in all societies, spousal homicide is basically the same: 'most cases arise out of the husband's jealous, proprietary, violent response to his wife's (real or imagined) infidelity or desertion' (1992: 90).

Motives for spousal homicide tend to be gendered, as men kill for control and women kill out of fear of men's potential use of violence against them (Browne et al. 1999). Brookman (2005), looking at the age of the relationship, finds that motives in 'older' relationships are founded in issues around separation, while in 'newer' ones the issues are more about possession. Dobash and Dobash (1998) divide men's motives into four groups: possessiveness, domestic disagreements, right to punish, and power and control.

Possessiveness

Men's possessiveness, their claimed 'ownership' of women, in other words, their 'male sexual proprietariness' and sexual jealousy cause them to kill their partners (Campbell 1992; Lees 1992; Wilson and Daly 1992 and 1998; Websdale 1999: 20). It is not uncommon for killings to follow accusations (founded or unfounded) of adultery or desertion (Campbell 1992; Radford 1992c; Wilson and Daly 1992). In March 2001, Mark Parnham struck his wife more than 70 times with a metal bar over an affair she was having with a work colleague (*Guardian* 2002). Some men felt that they lost control over the woman and threatened to kill her if she wanted to end the relationship. Many men, in turn, followed through with these death threats since they would not give up their 'property rights' over the woman without a fight (Browne et al. 1999; Websdale 1999).

It is not only difficult for a woman to escape a violent relationship, but also very dangerous. Men will often not let 'their' women go, but will track them down and sometimes kill them. More women estranged from abusive partners are killed than are those who still live with them (Lees 1992; Wilson and Daly 1992 and 1998; Johnson and Hotton 2003). This is often expressed in the terms 'If I can't have you, no one can' (Campbell 1992; Lees 1992; Wilson and Daly 1992). Mark Wilkinson suffocated his ex-partner when 'he lost self-control… after she spoke of her plans to start a new life with a boyfriend' (Dyer 2002).

Domestic disagreements and right to punish

Killings can also be the result of disagreements regarding domestic work and resources, where men feel they have a 'right' to punish 'their' women for perceived wrongdoing. Motives for such killings are often given in terms of 'woman blaming' where the wife is accused of neglecting her 'duties', nagging or adultery (Lees 1992; Dobash and Dobash 1998; D'Cruze et al. 2006).

Malcolm Horsman suffocated his wife in December 1998 after her 'drip, drip' of constant and forceful remarks, and her nagging made him 'snap' (Gillan 2000). David Hampson killed his wife with a hammer and hid her death for two years. He claimed that her lack of support and criticism were damaging to his self-esteem and 'very difficult to cope with... I just had to stop her going on and on at me.' He suffered from depressive illness but '[o]nce the source of his depressive illness had been removed in the awful way that it was, he actually got better without further treatment' (*Guardian* 1999).

Power and control

The importance of maintaining power and exercising authority can lead some men to commit homicide (Brookman 2005; D'Cruze et al. 2006). Wilson and Daly found that the most violent husbands were the most controlling ones: many men used violence against women for a long time before killing them to establish control or to reassert control they felt they were losing (Daly and Wilson 1992 and 1998). Hanmer (in Websdale 1999: 207) observes that men's violence against women is 'designed to control, dominate and express authority and power'. Radford (1992c) concludes that masculinity serves to maintain and reproduce power over women. She cites Andrea Dworkin (1992c: 265) who argues: 'Men develop a strong sense of loyalty to violence; men come to terms with violence because it is a prime component of male identity.' Dobash and Dobash (1998: 164) point out that violence and masculinity are connected as 'violent acts may be valorized as signs of masculinity, male authority, power, and control'.

Malcolm Anders, who had fraudulently acted out a wheelchair-bound disability for ten years, stabbed his wife to death in December 2000. The judge said: 'What the evidence indicates to me is that your comfortable lifestyle as an invalid was coming under threat and you resented [your wife's] enjoyment of her work and social life. When matters came to a head you reacted with extreme violence' (Carter 2001).

Battered wife syndrome

The 'battered wife syndrome' refers to cases in which a woman resorts to homicide after years of victimisation (Brookman 2005). The masculine makeup of most partner homicides can equally be highlighted with female offenders: even when women kill men, they are often defending themselves against them (Allen 1987; Faith 1993). Research indicates that self-defence applies in 80% of cases where women kill their partners (Campbell 1992; Lees 1992; Wilson and Daly 1992: 88), consequently termed the 'self-preservation' strategy (Faith 1993; Browne et al. 1999; Websdale 1999). Peterson (1999), in contrast, applies Donald Black's 'self-help' theory of crime, meaning the offender feels wronged, and the killing is an illegal attempt to exact justice.

Pearson (1998), on the other hand, argues that Lenore Walker's views on the battered wife and her concept of 'learned helplessness' – that women are rendered helpless and passive by the randomness of their partners' abuse – are flawed. This concept, Pearson claims, makes sense when explaining why battered women stay in abusive relationships but not when explaining how some women get the energy and strength to 'hit back' or 'escape' by killing the partner. Instead she claims we must be able to see women as aggressors and not only as passive victims. This is crucial in arguing the defence for the battered woman who kills (Brookman 2005). Even if she was violent, this violence was provoked by his long-term abuse, and this abuse is to be seen as at least as provoking as any infidelity or nagging (D'Cruze et al. 2006). On the other hand, it has to be borne in mind that women might kill for other reasons, such as revenge, but still use the defence of previous abuse (Brookman 2005).

After years of violence and sexual degradation, Josephine Smith shot her husband while he was sleeping. She was convicted of murder in 1993, but in January 2002 the UK Criminal Cases Review Commission referred her case to the Appeal Court. Likewise, Sara Thornton killed her drunken and violent husband in 1989. She served five years for murder but was freed after a retrial in 1996 (*Guardian* 2002a).

A gendered nature?

Sex differences are evident in how we look at men and women killing their partners, since they are treated differently. Campbell looks at how men who claim provocation easily get convicted of manslaughter, while battered women get convicted of murder: 'Patriarchal society's fear of women who kill their men is suggested by those manslaughter charges in spite of clear evidence of initial violence by the victim' (1992: 105). Likewise, Websdale (1999) points out that women who kill their partners mostly do so in self-defence, yet they end up serving long prison sentences. Lees (1992) and Radford (1992c) argue this willingness on the side of the court to see men's claims of provocation as mitigation works as a 'licence to kill'. Radford (1992c: 264) argues: 'It is the freeing of wife-killers which issues the licence to kill. Clearly lenient sentencing of violent men overlooks the welfare of women in the wider community.' This 'licence to kill' – others use the less dramatic term 'domestic discounts' (Kaspersson 2003b; D'Cruze et al. 2006) – is only granted to men. Lees (1992: 268) points out that '[n]o such licence to kill is given to women who stand trial for male murder... Even if a woman is raped or has been beaten up, a defence of provocation is rarely upheld.'

In the case mentioned above, David Hampson was sentenced for six years for manslaughter since the judge granted that '…you suffered at the hands of this woman in a variety of ways and… were provoked into doing what you did.' The fact he used a hammer was aggravating, but not, very surprisingly, the fact that for two years he pretended his murdered wife to be alive and claimed her benefits, while he had buried her body in the garden. The judge gave Hampson credit in sentencing for his 'frankness' in admitting his crime to the police (*Guardian* 1999).

This phenomenon of 'victim blaming' is not uncommon in cases where men kill their partners. Campbell (1992) points out that the label 'victim precipitation' has inaccurately been used to blame victims of violence for their own victimisation, and Lees (1992) gives examples of cases where the defence of provocation was accepted on evidence given by the accused or his friends only, with no apparent consideration taken that they might have an interest in maligning the victim. In the Hampson case, the victim's family claimed the 'nagging wife' portrayal distorted the truth. Her brother-in-law said 'We feel [her] character has been virtually destroyed by the way the case has been presented in court. It was as if it was [she] who was on trial… Nobody could speak up for her' (Guardian 1999). Radford (1992b: 231) cites another case in which a woman who had had several relationships was stalked, terrorised and eventually murdered by a former lover. The judge put the blame on the victim, stating 'Those who engage in sexual relationships should realise that sex is one of the deepest and most powerful human emotions, and if you're playing with sex you're playing with fire.'

Culturally defined homicide

The line between domestic homicide and culturally defined homicide is vague. Culturally defined homicides are in many ways domestic, but they are also shaped by cultural aspects. For example, spousal homicides are not uncommonly examples of honour killings (Brookman 2005). Such cases are rarely reported in terms of culture and honour (cf The Gurdip Kaur Campaign 1992 and Southall Black Sisters 1992 for early examples).

Battered woman syndrome cases also have a connection with culturally defined homicide, as some of the women kill because they are trapped by the violence and by their culture and its informal control. For a woman to leave a violent marriage means that she must leave her family completely. She must get away from the disapproving community in which she lives, since granting her freedom would mean dealing with injuries to honour and facing up to the violence inherent in this concept of honour (Gill 2004). This led Kiranjit Ahluwalia to set her husband on fire after ten years of abuse. She was convicted of murder in 1989, but her life sentence was quashed in 1992 when she was freed after a guilty plea of manslaughter was accepted (D'Cruze et al. 2006).

Honour killings

An 'honour killing' is the killing of (usually) a woman because she has brought shame on the family. The shame is usually connected to 'illicit' sexual relationships (Amnesty International, hereafter AI, 1999). Honour killings take place in all countries and in all societies and religions (Almosaed 2004). These killings are about men acting to preserve their honour or social standing. According to Websdale (1999), these killings cannot be explained in terms of culture only; rather, the intersection of culture and broader social structural phenomena provide the fuller context in which they occur. Two factors contribute to honour-related violence towards women: women's 'commodification' and the concept of honour (Almosaed 2004, Gill 2004). Women embody the honour of the men to whom they 'belong', and they have to guard their virginity and chastity. By entering, or having been believed to enter, an 'illicit' sexual relationship, the honour of the family is defiled. The woman's right to life is forfeited as there is no other punishment but death. Since a man's ability to protect his honour is judged by his family and neighbours, he must publicly restore his honour by punishing the one who damaged it. This is why honour killings are often performed openly (Fazio 2004, Gill 2004). According to McWilliams (1998), one reason for this might be that in societies under stress, there are fewer options for women but, more importantly, fewer controls on men. 'Crimes against honour', argues Djabari (1998: 113), 'take no account of the humanity of women as far as the penalty is concerned: the priority is to avoid scandal.'

A woman can consequently defile her family's honour on many grounds, all with a base in the concept of honour and in the commodification of women. The most common causes, which are often interlinked, will be discussed below, illustrated with cases from different countries.

Western lifestyle and independence

A young migrant woman adapting too much to the habits and values of the new country can be seen as threatening. In 1996 a 15-year-old Iraqi-Swedish girl was killed by her brother and cousin because she lived 'in a Swedish way' (Sohlström 2001). The whole Western lifestyle is often seen as threatening, especially when women want the independence and emancipation they see other women enjoy. The Western emancipated woman threatens the traditional concept of honour. The victims often wanted what many women in their situation were not allowed: to live their own lives, choose what to wear, when to go out, decide who to marry, choose whether to study at university or work. Supporters of honour killings say they 'maintain social order in changing times; critics allege that chauvinistic men use the 'family honour' as a pretext for punishing women who want more freedom' (Burke 2000).

Choosing a marriage partner

For a woman to marry, or express a desire to marry, a man of her own choice is seen as a major act of defiance in societies where the father arranges most marriages. The woman damages the honour of the man negotiating the marriage who can expect a bride-price in return for handing her over as a spouse. In European and Hindu traditions, the woman's family provide her with a dowry; in Muslim societies a woman is handed over to her spouse against payment of a bride-price to her father (AI 1999). Bride-prices and dowries are conventions that confirm a woman is a man's property (Mukherjee 1993). Marriage is a trade between families, and if a woman chooses her own partner this can consequently disrupt a financial deal, with her as the property for sale. In 1999 in the village of Begowal, in Indian Punjab, the then 18-year-old Harpreet secretly married 21-year-old Kamaljeet Singh. Harpreet's mother did not approve of the marriage because Mr Singh was poor and had cut his hair, which is against Sikh practice. In April 2000, Harpreet died in mysterious circumstances, which the family claimed was food poisoning. Some weeks before her death she had been forced to have an abortion. She was cremated and her ashes disposed of the same day, breaking Sikh tradition. Mr Singh's mother says she saw bruises on Harpreet's face on the pyre, but there was no post-mortem. Her family claimed there had been no marriage, but Mr Singh contacted the police, provided proof of their marriage and accused Harpreet's family of suppressing and destroying evidence (Chatterjee 2000; Pushkarna 2000). Chatterjee (2000) quotes the lawyer Ranjan Lakhanpal:

> [A] girl wanting to marry a boy of her choice against parental wishes runs the risk of being killed especially if the boy is from another caste, religion, income bracket or community. In the last five years I have dealt with four such cases. None have led to convictions because such cases are almost impossible to prove. All traces of the dead body are spirited away.

In the Western world, cases are about women choosing their own partner or whose partners are not accepted by the family. It is usually a Western man who is not allowed to marry an ethnic minority woman, or the man and woman have different religions. Kurdish–Swedish Fadime Sahindal, who was shot dead by her father in January 2002, told in an interview in 1998 that her Swedish boyfriend had offered to convert to Islam and to do everything – proposal, marriage, wedding party – according to their Turkish–Kurdish culture and tradition:

> Then my parents started to soften, but unfortunately they were persuaded, by my brother and brother-in-law, that a marriage was unthinkable after all... You see, the marriage would have become a precedent and would

have opened the door for mixing the races. And they wonder: 'What will then happen in the long run with Kurdistan, our beloved country, if a lot of half-Swedes run around down there?' (Ekéus 1998)

In January 2003, English–Pakistani Sahda Bibi was stabbed to death by her cousin on her wedding day. He was angry at her decision not to enter into an arranged marriage with one of his relatives, even though Sahda's parents accepted their daughter's choice of husband (Blackstock 2003; Britten 2003).

Refusing an arranged marriage

Honour killings can occur if a young woman refuses to marry a man that her family has chosen. Even if it is often legally stated that she has the right to refuse a husband selected for her, Goodwin (1994: 32) points out that '…familial pressures can be so strong, they may result in her death if she is not acquiescent.'

In the Western world there have been a number of cases where the woman refuses an arranged marriage. Usually the man in question lives in the family's country of origin, and not in the new country. In 1994 a Christian man of Israeli descent, now living in Sweden, killed his daughter when she refused to marry the man he had chosen (Sohlström 2001), and Fadime (above) refused to marry a cousin in Turkey because she would not be 'married off like some kind of cattle' (Gustavsson 1998). Arranged, or rather forced (Labi 2003; Phagura 2003), marriages are real threats for many women and are used as a threat by parents. Afshar (2002: 239) interviewed Asian women in Britain who all confirmed that marriages were arranged for troublesome daughters 'who were likely to behave in a way that could lead to a loss of face.' A Sikh student of mine once confessed that her parents would have killed her if she did not agree to their arranged marriage.

No longer a virgin

The honour of a family is believed to reside in women's chastity and modesty (Pervizat 2002; Fazio 2004). Therefore the woman's virginity until marriage is of utmost importance, and she faces the very real threat of death if she is not a virgin. After the wedding night a sheet with her blood is passed around by her relatives. This causes problems for women who do not bleed, virgin or not, since not all women do at their first intercourse. If the woman is not a virgin, her husband can divorce her immediately and send her home to her parents. The dishonour makes honour killing very likely (Goodwin 1994).

In 2001 a 15-year-old Jordanian boy was sentenced to four years' imprisonment for killing his sister. She was suspected of having lost her virginity when being on the run for a few days from her home. A medical examination proved she was still a virgin, but her brother clubbed her to death and burned the body anyway. He explained he had 'cleansed the family's honour' (*Tidningarnas Telegrambyrå* 2001).

The premarital sex more common or at least accepted in Western cultures is a way of life that causes honour killings since it directly challenges the importance of virginity in arranging marriages and bride-prices. In 1999, Pela Atroshi was shot to death by her uncles in the Iraqi part of Kurdistan. The verdict in Iraq was one year's conditional prison sentence, despite being considered beyond all reasonable doubt that the uncles shot Pela, that it was premeditated, and that it was done with her father's knowledge. It was considered as mitigating and 'honourable' that the father got furious when Pela told him she was not a virgin and therefore could not be married off according to Kurdish tradition (Rönn 2000). One of Pela's uncles simply said: 'If she's not a virgin it's an honour killing' (Rönn and Bergman 2000).

Fadime (above) had sex with her Swedish boyfriend (Gustavsson 1998). In an interview she told about the strict demand that the woman is a virgin when she marries – proven by blood on the sheet, which sheet is then kept as a 'diploma' of the parents' good upbringing of their daughter. This leads to girls contacting gynaecologists to restore the hymen:

> Therefore I didn't have sex myself until a gynaecologist promised she could restore my virginity… So when my mum found out I wasn't virgin anymore the house turned to hell. The shame of the family was enormous and I was labelled a whore (Ekéus 1998).

Hymenorrhaphy, according to Goodwin (1994), is a medical procedure offered in countries throughout the Islamic and Western world. It takes only a few minutes, costs around £200 and is done without anaesthesia, but has to be done three to seven days before the wedding, because the tissue is simply pulled together and the procedure does not last.

Another occurrence that is a threat to chastity and virginity is to have a boyfriend. Young women therefore have boyfriends in secret, and if they have sex they will not even tell their best friends. A Middle Eastern 17-year-old girl living in Sweden explains: 'A girl can in ten years' time tell her friend's husband she wasn't virgin when they married and that she had her hymen restored. Then the marriage is ruined' (Bergsdal 2001). Even if the girls do not have sex with their boyfriends, they are still seen as dishonouring the family by socialising with men while they are not married. A 24-year-old English Muslim woman was killed by her father when he found her with a secret boyfriend in her bedroom (*The Times* 2002). Sonay, a 14-year-old Danish–Iraqi, was found drowned and beaten in February 2002 after her mother found a photograph of a Danish boy in her diary. The parents claimed Sonay had shamed her family by this (Noterius 2002; Edgar 2002).

For adultery

Marriage and fidelity are not matters between husband and wife only: a woman's assumed infidelity reflects the honour of the entire family (Crescentlife 1999). In many countries, men are legally permitted to punish corporally or to kill their wives if the wives are unfaithful. It is considered honour killing and is mitigated. This has led to cases where women have been killed on suspicions only (Goodwin 1994).

In April 1998 a young man in Punjab axed his mother, Ghulam Bibi, to death. She had been traced by her family and brought back home following her supposed elopement with a man. In January 1999, also in Punjab, Ghazala was set on fire by her brother. He suspected she had had an illicit relation with a neighbour. The burned and naked body lay unattended in the street for two hours as nobody wanted to have anything to do with it (Crescentlife 1999). Rukhsana Naz, a British–Pakistani girl was married at the age of 15 to an older man. At the age of 19, she became pregnant by her childhood sweetheart. Rukhsana's mother claimed the child '…was an insult to [her] husband' (Burke 2000). Rukhsana refused to have an abortion and demanded a divorce. Since her marriage she had seen her husband only twice (he lived in Pakistan). She was then invited to a family dinner, during which her brother Shazad strangled her with a skipping rope. Her mother Shakeela helped hold her down (ibid.).

Rape

As a woman's consent – or lack of consent – is irrelevant when it comes to actions defiling the honour of her family, a woman brings shame on her family if she is raped. Rape is experienced not as women's pain, but as male defeat: they 'were too feeble to defend their own property', says McWilliams (1998: 115). Rape is considered adultery, and adultery is one of the biggest sins in most religious traditions. This of course is a huge problem in fighting rape, since women make themselves targets for honour killing if they report a rape since they thereby dishonour their family (AI 1999; Husseini 2002). A woman's legal complaint of rape can be considered a confession of illicit sexual intercourse. Rapists go free, and the victims are prosecuted. Goodwin (1994: 65) interviewed a Mullah (Islamic clergyman) in Pakistan about this, who stated: 'Both the man and the woman should be convicted. And she should be forced to marry the man who has raped her. If she has been corrupted by this man, she must be married to him.' The view that the rapist should marry his victim is held in other countries as well (Goodwin 1994).

In Jordan, 16-year-old Kifaya Hussein was murdered by her elder brother Khaled in 1994. She had been raped by her younger brother and became pregnant. When she told the family what had happened, the younger brother attacked her with a knife. She had an abortion and was later forced to marry a man who was 34 years her senior. He later divorced her and, when she returned to her family, Khaled stabbed her to death. The younger brother was sentenced to 13 years' imprisonment for rape and attempted murder. The older brother's sentence of 15 years imprisonment, however, was halved under article 340 of the Jordanian penal code, which states: 'He who discovers his wife or a female relative committing adultery and kills, wounds or injures one or both of them is exempted from any penalty' (Thomas 1999).

Seeking divorce

If a woman seeks divorce, it is seen as an act of public defiance and therefore calls for punitive action to restore the male honour. Divorce defiles the honour of both the husband and the families involved (AI 1999). Goodwin (1994: 69) quotes a Pakistani doctor whose sister is divorced: 'We try to keep it a family secret. She never goes out. My mother is ashamed of her. It is considered shameful for our family.' Divorces can be threatening to State honour as well, as Afshar (1998: 127) points out: 'The honour of the state is measured in…how obedient [women] are as wives and how dutiful they remain…Disobedient women are seen as a potential source of rebellion and disorder and the destruction of the existing political order.'

Twenty-eight-year-old Samia Imran was shot in April 1999 in Pakistan in the Lahore office of a lawyer who was helping her to seek a divorce from her abusive husband. Her family would not accept a divorce and, according to Samia: 'My parents told me you can get anything you want here, except a divorce' (Goldenberg 1999). It is believed her mother hired the gunman she brought with her into the office. He was later shot dead by a security guard as he left the office, while Samia's family managed to escape (Galpin 1999). The public outrage, however, focused more on the lawyers and the organisers of the women's shelter who were helping Samia. In the local newspaper an advertisement announced a demonstration against '…a dirty conspiracy against Islam, Pakistan, family life as we know it' (Goldenberg 1999). The Chamber of Commerce in Peshawar and several religious organisations demanded the lawyers be arrested for '…misleading women in Pakistan and contributing to the country's bad reputation abroad' (AI 1999: 8).

Cases like these take place in Western Europe as well. An Iraqi–Kurdish family arrived in Gothenburg, Sweden, in the early 1990s. Shortly afterwards the husband was sentenced for abuse of his wife, and they later divorced. In revenge for the dishonour the woman caused in reporting her husband to the police and in divorcing him, the eldest son stabbed her to death in the street in 1998 (Söderhjelm 2002; Rundkvist 2002).

Explaining the concept of honour and honour killings

Honour in Western Europe today is very much an individual concept, while in cultures in which honour killings take place that concept is collective

(Websdale 1999). This means that Western men claiming 'honour' as the cause behind violence are threatened as individuals, not as a collective. The woman 'shames' him personally, not his and/or her whole family (Kaspersson 2003a). As women have become more aware of their rights and have taken steps to do something about it, the number of honour killings has risen (AI 1999).

Offenders explaining their motives for honour killings can illustrate this concept of collective honour. In 1999 in Jordan, 34-year-old Sarhan was sentenced to six months' imprisonment for having killed his sister Jasmine, 20, after she had been raped by a family member. He explains:

> If I hadn't killed my sister it would be like killing my whole family…People would look down on me and think I'm not a real man…I loved my sister but my family and the society forced me to kill her…I wish I had risked the death penalty. Then my family wouldn't have pressed me to kill my sister since I would have been killed myself. (Husseini 2002)

Faqir Mohammed killed his daughter in Manchester when he found her secret boyfriend in her bedroom. He told the police: 'According to the law it was not right, but according to religion it was right. It is out of the question that a man can go with an unmarried woman in her bedroom' (*The Times* 2002).

One of Pela's uncles (above) said: 'He [Pela's father] discussed with us the topic how to get rid of her, and in that way to enable him to hold his head high again in public and save the honour of the family' (Bergman 2000).

Fadime's father (above) in his confession explained:

> I felt I had to shoot…I have never hurt anyone in my whole life, but my daughter was horrible, she did a lot of evil things. I ended up on TV and people found out a lot of things…She reported my own son to the police and he was imprisoned for seven months…There was no other solution. I didn't feel well. Since five–six months back I had those thoughts. It was my last option. That's why I shot her. (Hååard 2002)

In court he added: 'You know she acted like a whore. She did terrible things to me, you know, every day she was with a boy' (Kadhammar 2002b). Fadime's sister (above), who witnessed the murder, stated in court that her father blamed Fadime for everything that had gone wrong in the family. He had said: 'Everything is Fadime's fault. One should kill her' (Kadhammar 2002a). Fadime herself illustrated the view that blood is the only payment for dishonouring the family. In an interview in 1998 she said: 'I know it itches in my brother's hands to get me – it would increase his status in the family to kill me' (Gustavsson 1998).

Twenty-five-year-old Mohammed Merheban in Liverpool killed his brother-in-law when he suspected him of having an affair with his wife. He told the court he committed the murder because his honour had been insulted. A family member emphasised the importance of action: if he had not acted, '…he would not be allowed to live within that society. That is how people are brought up' (Burke 2000). Samia Imran's father, Sarwar (above), said regarding honour: 'Everyone must have honour. Everyone must possess honour' (Goldenberg 1999).

Women embrace the honour culture as well, even if some are themselves victims of this tradition. Rukhsana's mother (above) explained why her disobedience and behaviour meant she had to die: 'We did not want to kill her. But it was written in her fate' (Hall 1999). Zarina and her lover Suleiman were killed in Pakistan in August 1999 by her brothers. Her mother said: '…there is no grief in honour, it was right to kill them. They saw them together and they killed them' (Crescentlife 1999). Aminat and her alleged lover Azizullah were killed by her brothers and brothers-in-law in Pakistan. Her mother-in-law said, 'We saw them together all the time…I have been robbed, my honour has been robbed, I have been violated. This was injustice against me. So we axed her' (*ibid.*).

Suttee: 'the most virtuous act of a woman'

Sati [pronounced su-thi], or suttee, is the Hindu tradition of burning widows on their husbands' pyre. It also refers to a woman who has died in this way. Opinions differ as to which term to use (Leslie 1991); this section uses 'suttee' for the burning of widows, and 'sati' for the woman who dies in the act.

Suttee can be seen either as a form of domestic homicide or as a form of (sometimes coerced) suicide. Parrilla (1999) points out the different perspectives: one traditionalist view is that a woman committing suttee grants her husband's spiritual salvation. Feminists, political leaders and many rural and elite parts of the population, however, see the practice of suttee as a national disgrace and an immoral act. Leslie (1991) states that suttee – whether enforced by men or 'embraced' by women – is an act of violence against women that can only arise in a society that is male dominated and woman demeaning. The main question is not that some women 'choose' to commit suttee, but why they make this choice.

History of suttee

Birodkar (n.d.) explains that in Hindu mythology, Dakhsha's wife Sati was so distraught at his death that she immolated herself on his funeral pyre. Since then her name has been given to the self-immolation of widows and means 'a virtuous woman'. The sati was worshipped as a goddess, temples were built in her memory and hero-stones commemorating brave satis were erected and worshipped (Kamat 1997).

The origins of the suttee practice is debated, with some scholars dating the origins to the Veda period (circa 3500 BC), others to the origins of the caste system in the first century AD. The first documented instance of suttee was that of Haggadetomma's widow Balakka in 908 AD (Kamat 2001). Hindus considered suttee praiseworthy, but it was never obligatory, and most widows did not undergo it. Suttee often took place in connection with wars when women either killed themselves to honour their husbands who had died on the battlefields or to protect their own honour from invading enemies (Birodkar n.d.; Kamat 1997; Parrilla 1999).

During the British reign in India, suttee was mainly practised in Bengal, particularly around Calcutta. Suttee was said to be rampant because of inheritance laws that entitled widows to a share of the husband's property, as well as large deprivation resulting from colonialism (Abraham 1997; see also Oldenburg 2002 for the effects of British colonialism). Between 1815 and 1824, 6,632 suttees were recorded in Bengal, Bombay and Madras, 90% of which took place in Bengal. The practise of suttee in Rajastan was revived as a consequence of the huge expansion of commercial returns of the Sati temple in Jhunjhunu (Abraham 1997). Since independence, the number of suttees in the state has increased: of 40 suttees in India after 1947, 28 took place in Rajastan (see also Harlan 1994).

Stein (1992) emphasises that even if these figures are horrifying in absolute numbers, suttee was only committed by a small minority of widows. Suttee, and the significance of it, can best be understood in terms of what the sati was valued for and what the alternatives were for her, as well as the normative place of women in the Indian society. Kelkar (1992: 118) states, 'The subordinate role of women in the family is duplicated in the society as a whole.'

Several attempts were made to abolish suttee, but not until the British period and the 1829 Suttee Regulation Act was it declared illegal. This was done neither easily nor without friction. Indians complained the suppression of suttee was an attack on their culture and customs (Toynbee 2001). According to historian John Keay (in Harding 2002), Lord Bentinck, the evangelical British governor-general who outlawed suttee, is said to have been less concerned with saving lives than with demonstrating the superiority of Christianity to Hinduism. However, as McWilliams (1998: 124) points out, 'by attempting to impose their own "superior" morality, colonialists may have outlawed practices that involved forms of gendered violence. Such colonial intrusions may have helped reduce violence against women in some instances.' When the British left India, the independent government reaffirmed the illegality of suttee, but it took many large-scale social reforms by, among others, Mahatma Gandhi actually to stop the practice. Despite official abolition, however, suttee still occurs, and sati remains an ideal (Leslie 1991; Kamat 1997).

Cases

In 1987, Roop Kanwar, a young widow, was burned in suttee in the state of Rajasthan, stirring a social debate on the topic. Was it suttee or murder? Her family claimed she had informed her father-in-law of her intention of becoming sati and prayed piously while burning to death, others that her husband's family forced her and first had drugged her with opium and shoved her back to the pyre when she tried to escape. Her waving arms were interpreted in two ways: as blessings on the villagers or as pleading for assistance. People who assisted Roop in the suicide were arrested, and her father-in-law and brother-in-law were charged with murder. Roop was idolised and attained deity status. In 1996, the Indian Court freed the relatives who assisted – or forced – Roop. (Bajpai 1987; Oldenburg 1994; Abraham 1997; Parrilla 1999; Kamat 2001; Harding 2002)

Abraham (1997) portrays reactions of hostility towards anti-suttee laws and quotes defenders as saying that suttee is a part of Hindu faith, and if a woman wants to become sati she should not be deprived of the option. She also highlights that murder charges were not investigated even though Roop had been dragged to the pyre and set on fire by her 15-year-old brother-in-law. According to Leslie (1991), Roop made a conscious choice not to become a widow. By becoming sati she would grant salvation to her husband and, regardless of their actual behaviour, to generations of the two families. She would also be worshipped in her community. Leslie concludes: 'This is the empowerment of [suttee]: a strategy for dignity in a demeaning world' (1991: 190).

In Tamoli, in the north Indian state Madhya Pradesh, Kuttu Bai entered the funeral pyre of her deceased husband Mallu Nai in 2002 in order to commit suttee. Her sons are said either to have tried to stop her, or to have encouraged her in order to gain from the donations that follow cases of suttee. The elder son lit the pyre, as is the tradition. Police that came to the place were chased away by an audience consisting of around 1,000 people. Afterwards, Kuttu's two sons were arrested (Harding 2002). Police spokesperson Savita Shoney said: 'We suspect them of pushing their 65-year-old mother into this because they simply wanted to grab her property', which consisted of six acres of land (Spillius 2002; Vidlund 2002). However, a team from India's National Committee of Women concluded that nobody had forced Kuttu to do anything: 'She wanted to kill herself. It wasn't because of pressure from the family' (Harding 2002). Fifteen other villagers were also arrested on charges of, among other things, conspiracy and illegal gathering. Most of them, including the sons, were released on bail. The general belief was that there would be no punishments, and the police have been criticised for failing to prevent the suttee despite being warned it was going to take place (Harding 2002). Police afterwards guarded the village to prevent glorification of the event. However, worshippers came as soon as the police had gone (Spillius 2002; Harding 2002).

The position of widows

Suttee cannot be understood without understanding the position of Hindu widows in India. Leslie (1991) points out that in Sanskrit religious law the concept of woman is almost always negative. The only answer in religion to being female is to become the perfect wife, i.e. a devoted wife (Parrilla 1999). A widow denotes a woman who has chosen to live on without her husband, and it is implied that she should live an ascetic life in celibacy since she has chosen not to become sati. Stein (1992) claims it is not difficult to see why death might be preferred to widowhood. Prescriptions for widows instruct that she should eat only one plain meal a day, not sleep in a bed, avoid leaving the house and wear only the plainest clothes. This is necessary for the sake of her husband's soul and to avoid for herself being reborn as a female animal. Among the Brahmins and other higher castes, the heads of widows were shaven, and they had to wear red or white saris without ornaments. They were not allowed to take part in public family functions, and nobody cared about their death. Independence from Britain meant the dress taboo for widows was abolished, but widowhood is still considered a curse and, especially in the lower social strata, families often do not support widows (Kamat 2002; Mukherjee 1993). Stein (1992: 64) quotes a Portuguese chronicler who states, '…their relations speak to [the widows], advising them to burn themselves and not to dishonour their generation.' In *The Jewel in the Crown*, Scott (1966: 230) portrays the same phenomenon:

> …poor Shalini was still childless. Her husband…spent most of his time with prostitutes. He died some years later of a seizure in the house of his favourite. 'Imagine,' Shalini wrote to her brother at that time, 'Prakash's sisters actually suggested I should become [sati] to honour such a man and acquire merit for myself!'

Kamat (2002) points out that obvious gender discrimination has existed – and still exists – among Hindus. A widower could remarry as many times he liked, but a widow could not remarry irrespective of her age. Since Indian independence in 1947, widows are allowed to remarry, but it is still uncommon. Child-marriages were allowed until early twentieth century, and child-widows were particularly discriminated against. Their mere existence, or seeing their faces, was a bad omen (Birodkar n.d.).

Another problem with widows is that girls marry at a very young age, not uncommonly under the legal age of 18, to men often considerably their seniors (Mukherjee 1993). This means a number of women of childbearing age are widowed. Add to this the difficulty for these widows to remarry and their difficulties in supporting themselves or in finding support from their families becomes apparent. Mukherjee therefore finds it hardly surprising some of these young widows were burned to become sati, in order to reduce their number and the burden of maintaining them. Stein (1992: 64) cites early Tamil literature that states that 'if a widow is chaste and young, she is so infected by magic power that she must take her own life.' Childless widows, like 18–year-old Roop, become absolute threats (Abraham 1997). Sociologist Susan Visvanathan says: 'Widows are ostracised and not allowed to participate in rituals. She [Kuttu, above] would have assumed her life would be one of isolation and despair and shame and suffering' (Harding 2002).

By committing suttee, women avoid becoming widows. So, as Leslie (1991) points out, one important point is missing when suttee is referred to as 'widow-burning' or 'the self-immolation of the widow': a sati is a wife who chose not to become a widow at all.

The sati ideal

'She had an aura about her. She was calm as the flames enveloped her', said an eyewitness to Roop Kanwar's suttee (cited in Bajpai 1987: 123). A Hindu woman said:

> In every Rajput family, it is something drilled into you from earliest childhood. Your husband is supposed to be a sort of godlike figure, and sati is the ultimate achievement for a girl. You're almost hypnotized into thinking this thing (*The New York Times*, 1987.09.19, cited in Leslie 1991: 182).

Leslie (1991) cites an eighteenth-century Sanskrit Manual, which claims that the proper role of women includes the practice of suttee. This is not for every woman, but only for those who aspire to the highest ideal. Suttee is never compulsory, but she who chooses not to become a sati faces the hardships and indignity of life as a widow. Suttee is a ritual you perform if you want the rewards accrued to the act and, practised by a devoted wife, confers great blessings on both wife and husband as it takes away her own sin as well as that of her husband (Parrilla 1999).

The Sanskrit Manual gives examples of the virtuosity connected with suttee: 'Just as the snake catcher drags the snake from its hole by force, even so the virtuous wife snatches her husband from the demons of hell and takes him up to heaven' (quoted in Leslie 1991: 185). Likewise: 'Even in the case of a husband who has entered into hell itself…even then a woman who refuses to become a widow can purify him: in dying she takes him with her' (*ibid.*). Neither does it matter whether the woman commits suttee voluntarily or coercively: 'Women who…perform the ritual act of dying with their husbands when the time comes – whether they do this of their own free will, or out of anger, or even out of fear – all of them are purified of sin' (ibid: 186).

Whatever the past deeds of wife and husband, the sacrifice in suttee purifies them both. By burning, the woman, her husband and her and her husband's family will be in paradise for 35 million years, regardless of how sinful they might have been (Leslie 1991; Stein 1992). The ideal of the devoted wife can be achieved in three ways. First, a woman dies before her husband and then waits patiently for him in heaven. If she is not that lucky and he dies first – by sin in the present or a previous life – she can commit suttee. The third way is to live on as a widow, leading an ascetic life in celibacy for the rest of her days. Since it is considered much harder (for a woman) to lead an ascetic life, suttee is considered far easier and far safer than the path of the celibate widow. Suttee is based on the belief that a woman is sexually unreliable by nature and incapable of leading a chaste life if she is not controlled by her husband. The fear is the young widow will fall into immoral practices (Birodkar n.d.; Leslie 1991; Stein 1992).

Is suttee murder?

Leslie (1991: 180) asks whether we can dismiss every case of suttee as murder. She says, 'Are not some cases, most perhaps, in some sense 'voluntary'?' West (1965) classified suttee as an altruistic type of suicide, according to Durkheim's classification, characterised by individuals who sacrificed themselves to society out of a sense of duty or honour.

The case of Roop Kanwar in 1987 turned out to be an embarrassment for the then Prime Minister Rajiv Gandhi. Forced into action he rushed through a new act on suttee threatening anyone who abetted suttee with the death penalty or life imprisonment (Harding 2002). The glorification of suttee through public rituals, processions and the collection of funds was made a criminal offence, whether the suttee was voluntary or not (Leslie 1991). Abraham's (1997) analysis of the 1987 Commission of Sati (Prevention) Bill that took effect from January 1988 found it to be seriously flawed. The Act states that suttee is comparable to suicide, defined as the burning or burying alive of a widow. Suttee is not equated with murder, despite the social reality that suttee is not always voluntary. Abraham claims the Gandhi government's opportunism is evident in the act. They would not say suttee was voluntary, which had been the practice until Roop's case, nor would they say suttee is murder. Abraham therefore calls the Act 'decorative' and serving no real purpose.

The problem with Abraham's argument is her categorical statement that suttee is *always* murder, ignoring the fact that the social reality in India may make widows *choose* suttee. Parrilla (1999) points out that simply enacting laws cannot change deeply held and cherished traditions. Social change must challenge the fact that women are culturally conditioned to consider their own lives worthless after the husband's death and reverse centuries of female oppression. As Leslie (1991: 190) states: 'This is the empowerment of [suttee]: a strategy for dignity in a demeaning world. The tragedy is that Roop Kanwar could find no other. For in such a world, for most women choice itself is a fiction.'

As mentioned above, the Commission of Sati (Prevention) Act criminalises the glorification of suttee, even if it does not tackle the continuing worship offered in various sati temples across India, especially in Rajastan. The state government can remove sati temples and stones, but not if they are 20 or more years old. Abraham (1997) states the act has been totally ineffective in curbing the religious and commercial significance of suttee worship in Rajastan. The case of Roop Kanwar proved that suttee was good business, as her village became a pilgrim spot that prospered with the regular stream of visitors.

The district's senior bureaucrat, B. R. Naidu, tried to explain Kuttu's suttee (above): 'I think [this was] because of backwardness, illiteracy and superstition. People in their psyche still want to glorify this act. There were so many present and yet nobody tried to stop it' (cited in Harding 2002). Local people were proud of Kuttu's suttee. They boasted of previous incidents before independence in 1947 as well as one in the 1950s. The villagers in Kuttu's village believed suttee was a sacred practice and that her death would persuade the gods to send rain to end the drought they had suffered (ibid.).

Pro-suttee groups, such as the Committee for the Defence of the Religion of Sati, demand their right to commit, worship and propagate suttee as Hindus and as women, and claim suttee is a fundamental part of their traditions (Parrilla 1999). Indian feminists, on the other hand, argue that suttee is a deplorable act and a crime against women. For these feminists, the glorification of Roop Kanwar, and the portrayal of her as a chaste and devoted wife who sacrificed her life for her husband, exemplified the oppressive status of women (ibid.). They also find it disturbing that those women actively support organisations and activities that limit their own rights – something also found with honour killings.

Leslie (1991: 181) claims that, for Indian feminists, suttee 'is only one symptom of a deep-seated hatred for women throughout India'. Parallels are drawn with dowry deaths (see Birodkar n.d.; Mukherjee 1993), female infanticide and an increase in abortions of female foetuses. Venkatrami (1986: 125) points out that 'India is one of a handful of countries where female infant mortality exceeds that of the male.' Likewise, 90% of suicide cases in India are committed by women, but as a female Indian police officer said, 'It is very difficult to decide whether a burn case is suicide or murder. In both cases the victim is doused from head to toe in kerosene and severely burnt. We feel that 80% of these cases... are suicides. The husband and in-laws are certainly culpable because it is their harassment which drives the person to this act' (cited in Kelkar 1992: 120).

Dowry murder

Oldenburg (2002: xi) does not think that suttee is the main problem. For her, the far more common dowry murders are her main concern. She sees suttee as suicide but claims that dowry murder is murder 'culpable on social, cultural, and legal grounds, executed privately, and often disguised as an accident or suicide'. Newlywed young women are burned to death by their husbands or his family if her dowry is considered insufficient and the bride's family is unable to contribute more (Rastogi and Therly 2006). The practice of dowry – even though outlawed in 1961 – is still flourishing in India as women are heavily dependent on remaining married. It is shameful to be divorced (or unmarried) and causes financial difficulties due to prejudice towards and discrimination against divorcees. If the woman's family cannot live up to the husband's demands, he might arrange an 'accident' – often in the shape of burnings caused by the volatile kerosene cookers generally used – so he can marry someone else with a better dowry. Many of these dowry murders are masked as accidents and suicides, and the reporting and investigation of them is minimal (Oldenburg 2002).

The dowry system discriminates against women as they – or rather their families – are the ones who provide the dowry. Also, poorer parents have to marry their daughters to 'cheaper' men, i.e. often older or otherwise less desirable ones. The system is financially draining, and some parents avoid the future costs by 'selecting' male offspring. Daughters are not regarded as highly as sons, get less education, have less influence and power in society and continue to be dependent on fathers and husbands. Oldenburg (2002) claims that current legislation is not enough. Indian women need to be empowered and laws need to be just, as well as enforced, so people have faith in them.

Conclusion

Homicide is a rare crime, but generally – independent of time and place – considered the most serious. In looking at one specific type of homicide – those committed in a domestic context – it appears that even though they make up about half of all homicides, they are far from the ones receiving most interest. The private and seemingly 'mundane' character is often not considered very newsworthy.

At the same time, the number of female victims and female offenders is greater for domestic homicide than for other types. Likewise, it has been shown that men and women kill for different reasons. Men kill for control of their wives, their daughters' chastity, or their ex-partners new lives, while women kill to defend themselves from men. This means that domestic homicide is a gendered phenomenon when it comes to motives, but also when it comes to how we look at and treat the cases.

Apart from the gendered character, another prominent theme is oppression of women by men. Men kill unfaithful women, disobedient daughters, wives whose families cannot provide more dowry, or innocent children as revenge, but they have also created a social order where women cannot leave their partners and husbands, whether violent or not, and where suttee is considered a better option than widowhood. What seems to be important is not only to highlight the violence that takes place behind closed doors or within tight communities but also to highlight the gender and power dimensions within them. Only by bringing these processes into the open can we work to understand and prevent domestic homicide.

References

Abraham, S. (1997) 'The Deorala Judgement Glorifying Sati'. *The Lawyers Collective* 12, 4–12. Addley, E. (2002) 'The baby killer'. *Guardian*, 18 April.

Afshar, H. (1998) ''Disempowerment' and the Politics of Civil Liberties for Iranian Women'. In H. Afshar ed. *Women and Empowerment. Illustrations from the Third World.* Basingstoke: Macmillan, 117–33.

Afshar, H. (2002) 'Marriage and family in a British Pakistani community'. In S. Jackson and S. Scott, eds., *Gender. A Sociological Reader.* London: Routledge, 238–40.

Allen, H. (1987) 'Rendering Them Harmless: The Professional Portrayal of Women Charged with Serious Violent Crimes'. In P. Carlen and A. Worrall, eds., *Gender, Crime and Justice.* Milton Keynes: Open University, 81–94.

Almosaed, N. (2004) 'Violence Against Women: A Cross-cultural Perspective'. *Journal of Muslim Affairs* 24, 67–88.

Amnesty International (1999) Pakistan. *Honour Killings of girls and women*, ASA 33/18/99, http://www.web.amnesty.org/ai.nsf/index/ASA330181999 (accessed 2002.03.05).

Bajpai, R. (1987) 'Thousands Visit Indian Village Where Bride Died by Suttee'. *San Fransisco Chronicle*, 17 September. (Reprinted in J. Radford and D. E. H. Russell, eds. (1992) *Femicide. The Politics of Woman Killing.* Buckingham: Open University Press, 123–4).

Batty, D. (2006) 'Q & A: Sir Roy Meadow'. *Guardian*, 17 February.

Bergsdal, G. (2001) 'Jag måste vara oskuld tills jag gifter mig' [I have to be virgin until I get married]. *Svenska Dagbladet.* 11 December.

Birodkar, S. (no date) *Hindu Social Customs: Dowry, Sati and Child Marriage.* http://www.hindubooks.org/sudheer_birodkar/hindu_history/practices1.html (accessed: 11.11.2002).

Blackstock, C. (2003) 'Police fear suspect in bride killing has fled country'. *Guardian*, 14 January.

Branigan, T. (2003a) 'Boys killed in revenge by 'evil' father'. *Guardian*, 26 March.

Branigan, T. (2003b) 'Man who killed sons found hanged. Prisoner uses shoelaces on fifth day of life sentence'. Guardian, 31 March.

Britten, N. (2003) 'Murdered bride refused arranged marriage'. *Daily Telegraph*, 14 January.

Brookman, F. (2005) *Understanding Homicide.* London: Sage.

Browne, A., Williams, K. R. and Dutton, D. G. (1999) 'Homicide Between Intimate Partners'. In M. D. Smith and M. A. Zahn, eds. *Studying and Preventing Homicide. Issues and Challenges.* Thousand Oaks: Sage Publications. 55–78.

Burke, J. (2000) 'Love, honour and obey – or die', *Observer*, 8 October.

Campbell, J. C. (1992) ''If I Can't Have You, No One Can': Power and Control in Homicide of Female

Partners'. In J. Radford and D. E. H. Russell eds., *Femicide. The Politics of Woman Killing*. Buckingham: Open University Press, 99–113.

Carpenter, R.G., Waite, A., Coombs, R.C., Daman-Willems, C., McKenzie, A., Huber, J. and Emery, J.L. (2005) 'Repeat sudden unexpected and unexplained infant deaths: natural or unnatural?' Lancet 365(9453), 29–58.

Carter, H. (2000) 'It was just one shake'. *Guardian*, 18 October.

Carter, H. (2001) 'Wheelchair fraudster gets life for killing wife'. *Guardian*, 22 November.

Chatterjee, P. (2000) '"Honour killing" casts medieval shadow over India', *Guardian*, 20 November.

Coward, R. (2002) 'Teacher abuse'. *Guardian*, 2 July.

Crescentlife (1999) *Violence Against Women in the Name of Honour*, http://www.crescentlife.com/articles/honor2.htm (accessed 2002.10.02).

D'Cruze, S., Walklate, S. and Pegg, S. (2006) Murder. Cullompton: Willan Publishing.

Djabari, L. (1998) 'The Syrian Woman: Reality and Aspiration'. In H. Afshar ed. *Women and Empowerment. Illustrations from the Third World*. Basingstoke: Macmillan, 110–116.

Dobash, R. E. and Dobash, R. (1998) 'Violent men and violent contexts'. In R E Dobash and R. Dobash, eds., *Rethinking violence against women*. Thousand Oaks: Sage, 141–68.

Dyer, C. and Taylor, M. (2004) 'Cot deaths: law in disarray as 258 cases of convicted parents to be reviewed'. *Guardian*, 20 January.

Edgar, J. (2002) 'Pappan misstänks för hedersmord på 14-åring. Flickans kropp funnen i vattnet – nu är fadern anhållen' ['Father suspected of honour killing of 14-year-old. The girl's body found in the water – now the father is arrested']. *Aftonbladet*, 20 June.

Ekéus, C. (1998) 'Är det kultur att låsa in unga tjejer?' ['Is it culture to lock young girls up?']. *Aftonbladet*, 4 August.

Faith, K. (1993) *Unruly Women. The Politics of Confinement and Resistance. Vancouver:* Press Gang Publishers.

Fazio, I. (2004) 'The family, honour and gender in Sicily: models and new research'. *Modern Italy* 9, 263–80.

Galpin, R. (1999) 'Woman's 'honour' killing draws protests in Pakistan'. *Guardian*, 8 April.

Gill, A. (2004) 'Voicing the Silent Fear: South Asian Women's Experiences of Domestic Violence'. *The Howard Journal* 43, 465–83.

Gillan, A. (1999) 'Girl, 15, stabbed her baby to death after secret birth'. *Guardian*, 12 November.

Gillan, A. (2000) 'Millionaire given life term for killing wife'. *Guardian*, 2 June.

Goldenberg, S. (1999.) 'A question of honour'. *Guardian*, 27 May.

Goodwin, J. (1994) *Price of Honour. Muslim Women Lift the Veil of Silence on the Islamic World*. London: Warner Books.

Guardian (1999) 'Six years' jail for hammer killing of nagging wife'. 29 October.

Guardian (2000) 'Man killed wife and three children, then hanged himself'. 1 February.

Guardian (2001) 'Mother killed sons in "living nightmare"'. 27 February.

Guardian (2002) 'Teacher jailed for killing wife over affair'. 12 January.

The Gurdip Kaur Campaign (1992) 'Fighting for Justice'. In J. Radford and D. E. H. Russell, eds., *Femicide. The Politics of Woman Killing*. Buckingham: Open University Press, 306–11.

Gustavsson, C. (1998) 'Rana, 23: "Min familj ska döda mig"' ['Rana, 23: "My family will kill me"']. *Aftonbladet*. 4 February.

Håård, L. (2002) '" Skjut mig – inte Fadime."' Mammans sista desperata försök att hindra mordet' ['"Shoot me – not Fadime."' The mother's last desperate attempt to prevent the murder]. *Aftonbladet*, 7 March.

Hall, S. (1999) 'Life for "honour" killing of pregnant teenager by mother and brother'. *Guardian*, 26 May.

Hall, S. (2001) 'Mother kills son, 4, before turning gun on herself'. *Guardian*, 12 June.

Harding, L. (2002) 'The ultimate sacrifice'. *Guardian*, 23 August.

Harlan, L. (1994) 'Perfection and Devotion: Sati Tradition in Rajastan'. In J. S. Hawley, ed., *Sati, the Blessing and the Curse. The Burning of Wives in India*. New York: Oxford University Press, 79–99.

Hull, L. (2003) 'Boys "were butchered by their father to spite wife who left him"'. *Daily Mail*, 11 March.

Husseini, R. (2002) 'Jasmine, 20, våldtogs – därför sköts hon ihjäl' [Jasmine, 20, was raped – therefore she was shot to death]. *Aftonbladet*, 16 March.

Jenkins, R. (2003) 'Father said: when you find me the boys will be dead.' *The Times*, 17 September.

Johnson, C. H. (2006) 'Familicide and Family Law: A Study of Filicide-Suicide Following Separation'. *Family Court Review* 44, 448–63.

Johnson, H. and Hotton, T. (2003) 'Losing Control. Homicide Risk in Estranged and Intact Intimate Relationships'. *Homicide Studies* 7, 58–84.

Kadhammar, P. (2002a) 'Systern – ljuset i en mörk historia. Vi var lite fnissiga, sa hon om kvällen då hon, modern och Fadime träffades' ['The sister – the light in a dark story. We were a little giggly, she said about the night when she and the mother met Fadime']. *Aftonbladet*, 13 March.

Kadhammar, P. (2002b) 'En människas liv på fyra sidor' ['A person's life in four pages']. *Aftonbladet*, 14 March.

Kamat, J. (1997) *The Tradition of Sati in India*. http://www.kamat.com/kalranga/hindu/sati/htm (accessed 11.11.2002).

Kamat, J. (2001) *The Tradition of Sati Through the Centuries*. http://www.kamat.com/kalranga/women/sati/timeline.htm (accessed 11.11.2002).

Kamat, J. (2002) *The Widows of India*. http://www.kamat.com/kalranga/women/widows/ (accessed 11.11.2002).

Kaspersson, M. (2003a) 'Honour Killings as Hate Crimes'. Paper presented at the *Hate Crime Conference* in Nottingham, 21–22 February.

Kaspersson, M. (2003b) 'Homicide and Infanticide in Stockholm 1920–1939'. *Journal of Scandinavian Studies in Criminology and Crime Prevention* 3, 135–153.

Kelkar, G. (1992) 'Women and Structural Violence in India'. In J. Radford and D. E. H. Russell, eds. *Femicide. The Politics of Woman Killing*. Buckingham: Open University Press, 117–22.

Labi, A. (2003) 'Culture Clash. Forced Marriages. The Runaway Bride'. *Time*, 5 May, 42–45.

Lees, S. (1992) 'Naggers, Whores and Libbers: Provoking Men to Kill'. In J. Radford and D. E. Russell eds., *Femicide. The Politics of Woman Killing*. Buckingham: Open University Press, 267–288.

Leslie, J. (1991) 'Suttee or Sati: Victim or Victor?' In J. Leslie, ed., *Roles and Rituals for Hindu Women*. London: Pinter Publishers.

Levi, M. (2002) 'Violent crime'. In M. Maguire, R. Morgan and R. Reiner eds. *The Oxford Handbook of Criminology*. Oxford: Oxford University Press, 795–843.

Loudon, A. and Tozer, J. (2003): 'Gassed to death. Their father couldn't bear it when their mother became pregnant by another man. So he killed them...and himself'. *Daily Mail*, 28 March.

Martin, L. (2006) 'Fathers who kill their children'. *Guardian*, 5 November.

McNeill, S. (1992) 'Woman Killer as Tragic Hero'. In R. E. Dobash and R. Dobash eds. *Rethinking violence against women*. Thousand Oaks: Sage, 178–83.

McWilliams, M. (1998) 'Violence Against Women in Societies Under Stress'. In R. E. Dobash and R. Dobash, eds. Rethinking violence against women. Thousand Oaks: Sage, 110–40.

Meadow, R. (1999) 'Unnatural sudden infant death'. *Archives of Disease in Childhood* 80, 7–14.

Mukherjee, P. (1993) *Hindu Women. Normative Models*. Second revised edition. London: Sangam Books.

Noterius, M. (2002) '14-årig flickas död kan vara "hedersmord"' ['The death of 14-year-old girl can be an "honour killing"']. *Aftonbladet*, 12 February.

Oldenburg, V. T. (1994) 'The Roop Kanwar Case: Feminist Responses'. In J. S. Hawley, ed. *Sati, the Blessing and the Curse. The Burning of Wives in India*. New York: Oxford University Press, 101–30.

Oldenburg, V. T. (2002) *Dowry Murder. The Imperial Origins of a Cultural Crime*. New York: Oxford University Press.

Palermo, G. B. (2002) 'Murderous Parents'. *International Journal of Offender Therapy and Comparative Criminology*. 46: 123–43.

Pallister, D. (2007) 'Solicitor wrongly jailed for killing sons died from excess alcohol'. *Guardian*, 8 November.

Parrilla, V. (1999) Sati: Virtuous Woman Through Self-Sacrifice. http://www.csichico.edu/~cheinz/syllabi/asst001/spring99/parrilla/parr1.htm (accessed: 11.11.2002).

Payne, S. (2003) 'Mystery of why mother "murdered three of her babies"'. *Daily Telegraph*, 30 April.

Pearson, P. (1998) *When she was bad. How women get away with murder*. London: Virago Press.

Pervizat, L. (2002) "Honour Killings' in Turkey'. *Monitor*. 15: 18–20.

Peterson, E. S. L. (1999) 'Murder as Self-Help: Women and Intimate Partner Homicide'. *Homicide Studies* 3, 30–46.

Phagura, S. (2003) 'The trials of an Asian bride'. *The Sunday Times*, 16 February.

Polk, K. (1994) *When Men Kill. Scenarios of Masculine Violence*. Cambridge: Cambridge University Press.

Polk, K. (1999) 'Males and Honor Contest Violence'. *Homicide Studies* 3: 6–29.

Press Association (2001) 'PC killed wife and children with hammer. Daughter, aged six, told neighbour of frenzied attack'. *Guardian*, 7 November.

Pushkarna, V. (2000) 'A death and a row. Punjab: Was SGPC chief Bibi Jagur Kaur responsible for her daughter's death?'. *The Week*, 7 May.

Radford (1992a) 'Introduction'. In J. Radford and D. E. H. Russell eds., *Femicide. The Politics of Woman Killing*. Buckingham: Open University Press, 3–12.

Radford (1992b) 'Retrospect on a Trial'. In J. Radford and D. E. H. Russell eds., Femicide. *The Politics of Woman Killing*. Buckingham: Open University Press, 227–32.

Radford (1992c) 'Womanslaughter: A Licence to Kill? The Killing of Jane Asher'. In J. Radford and D. E. H. Russell, eds., *Femicide. The Politics of Woman Killing*. Buckingham: Open University Press, 253–66.

Rastogi, M. and Therly, P. (2006) 'Dowry and its Link to Violence Against Women in India'. *Trauma Violence & Abuse* 7, 66–77.

Reiner, R. (2002) 'Media made criminality: the representation of crime in the mass media'. In M. Maguire, R. Morgan and R. Reiner, eds. *The Oxford Handbook of Criminology*. Oxford: Oxford University Press, 376–416.

Rönn, C. (2000) '"Bröderna planerade mordet tillsammans med pappan'. I dag börjar rättegången om "hedersmordet"' ['"The brothers planned the murder together with the father.' The trial of the " honour killing" starts today']. *Aftonbladet*, 14 December.

Rönn, C. and Bergman, Y. (2000) '"Jag tittade bort när Hana sköts". Hanas 37-årige farbror om mordet: "Jag är oskyldig."' ['"I looked away when Hana was shot." Hana's 37-year-old uncle on the murder: "I'm innocent"']. *Aftonbladet*, 19 December.

Rundkvist, F. (2002) 'Slog och brände sin dotter – fick fängelse. Idag kom domen mot kurdiska flickans pappa och bror' [Hit and burned his daughter – got jail. The verdict of the Kurdish girl's father and brother given today']. *Aftonbladet*, 28 February.

Scott, P. (1966) *The Jewel in the Crown*. London: Panther Books.

Söderhjelm, S. (2002) 'Pappa och son inför rätta för dödshot' [Father and son prosecuted for death threats]. *Aftonbladet*, 18 February.

Sohlström, P.-I. (2001) '18-årig flicka skalperades – av sin bror. Familjen tyckte hon träffade fel pojkvän' ['18-year-old girl scalped – by her brother. Her family disapproved of her boyfriend']. *Aftonbladet*, 16 December.

Southall Black Sisters (1992) 'Two Struggles: Challenging Male Violence and the Police'. In R. E. Dobash and R. Dobash eds. *Rethinking violence against women*. Thousand Oaks: Sage, 312–16.

Spillius, A. (2002) 'Sons face trial after mother commits suttee'. *Daily Telegraph*, 8 August.

Starzomski, A. and Nussbaum, D. (2000) 'The Self and the Psychology of Domestic Homicide-Suicide'. *International Journal of Offender Therapy and Comparative Criminology* 44, 468–79.

Stein, D. K. (1992) 'Women to Burn: Suttee as Normative Institution'. In J. Radford and D. E. H. Russell, eds. *Femicide. The Politics of Woman Killing*. Buckingham: Open University Press, 62–66.

Stevenson, S. (2003) 'Father kills four sons at beauty spot'. *Metro*, 28 March.

Sweeney , J. (2003) 'The love that put doctors' claims on trial'. *Observer*, 2 February. *The Times* (2002) 'Muslim murdered daughter in a rage', 19 February.

Taylor, M. (2006) 'Distraught father suffocated daughter after wife's affair'. *Guardian*, 3 November.

Thomas, K. (1999) 'Jordan's women fight to repeal honour killing law'. *Guardian*, 7 September.

Tidningarnas Telegrambyrå (2001) 'Pojke dömd för hedersmord i Jordanien' ['Boy sentenced for honour killing in Jordan']. *Svenska Dagbladet*, 20 November.

Toynbee, P. (2001) 'Limp liberals fail to protect their most profound values'. *Guardian*, 10 October.

Vasagar, J. and Allison, R. (2003) 'How cot deaths shattered mother's dreams'. *Guardian*. 12 June.

Venkatrami, S. H. (1986) 'Female Infanticide: Born to Die'. *India Today*, 15 June. (Reprinted in J. Radford and D. E. H. Russell, eds. (1992) *Femicide. The Politics of Woman Killing*. Buckingham: Open University Press, 125–32).

Vidlund, S. (2002) 'Kvinna levande bränd av sina söner. Femton gripna efter änkebränning i Indien' ['Women burnt alive by her sons. Fifteen arrested after widow burning in India']. *Svenska Dagbladet*, 7 August.

Walklate, S. (2001) *Gender, Crime and Criminal Justice*. Cullompton: Willan Publishing.Wallace, W. (2002) 'Vicious victims'. *Guardian*, 25 September.

Ward, T. (1999) 'The Sad Subject of Infanticide: Law, Medicine and Child Murder, 1860-1938'. *Social & Legal Studies*. 8, 163–80.Websdale, N. (1999) *Understanding Domestic Homicide*. Boston: Northeastern University Press.

West, D. J. (1965) *Murder Followed by Suicide*. London: Heinemann.

Wilson, M. and Daly, M. (1992) 'Till Death Us Do Part'. In J. Radford and D. E. H. Russell, eds. *Femicide. The Politics of Woman Killing*. Buckingham: Open University Press, 83–98.

Wilson, M. and Daly, M. (1998) 'Lethal and Nonlethal Violence Against Wives and the Evolutionary Psychology of Male Sexual Proprietariness'. In R. E. Dobash and R. Dobash eds. *Rethinking violence against women*. Thousand Oaks: Sage, 199–230.

Wolfgang, M. E. (1958) *Patterns in Criminal Homicide*. Philadelphia: University of Pennsylvania.

Wood Harper, D. and Voigt, L. (2007) 'Homicide Followed by Suicide. An Integrated Theoretical Perspective'. *Homicide Studies* 11, 295–318.

PROLOGUE: SERIAL KILLING

In Chapter 2, Keith Soothill explores some of the more unusual types of homicide such as serial killing, mass murder, and killing by those with co-occurring mental health diagnoses or personality disorders. The sometimes bizarre and highly unusual nature of these acts means that they attract more media attention, yet they are the rarest and arguably the most difficult to comprehend within mainstream cultural explanations. This is where a multi-disciplinary approach bears most fruit: studies of serial killers usually focus on individual pathology such as psychopathy to explain acts of this nature. Soothill, on the other hand, explores the possibility that other factors may be at work, such as wider sociological and societal influences.

Few other authors have taken this approach,[3] though looking beyond individual pathology reveals some fascinating patterns of behaviour. One of the more dramatic examples of killing as a result of the evolution of social belief systems was not the work of a serial killer but the mass killing of people in a series of attacks with poison gas on subways in Japan in 1994 and 1995. The attacks were carried out by followers of Asahara Shoko who had devised an extreme strand of Buddhism called Aum Shinrikyo. Like other believers in a 'doomsday' scenario, Asahara believed 'time was short and the future of the world hung in the balance. The end he envisioned justified any means, including coercion and violence' (Kimball 2002: 81). Asahara used force against followers who tried to leave (reminiscent of other extremists such as Jim Jones with his followers at the People's Temple in Guyana) and against people who opposed him. His beliefs and actions were not a form of terrorism in the sense of fighting for a particular cause, but more from a belief in an imminent global crisis – a 'catastrophic war' (*ibid.*, 82) – which eventually led him to develop what he considered to be a '"compassionate" rationale for violence' (*ibid.*).

What seems especially striking is how Asahara claimed his beliefs were rooted in Buddhist teachings, yet 'Anyone who stepped outside this [Aum] faith and interpretive framework that legitimized violence faced the harsh reality that one had in fact committed what Buddhist teaching regards as the greatest sin – destroying life' (Michiko 2001:192). Professor Soothill eloquently explains how such changes in social constructs can have an impact upon individual behaviour, even such extreme behaviour as killing.

---

3   Eisner (2003) gives a fascinating description of changes in rates of recorded homicides over the centuries in Europe and the social concepts that seem to affect these. D'Cruze, Walklate, and Pegg (2006) also take this alternative approach, looking at 'murder and murderers' from social and historical perspectives.

References

D'Cruze, S., Walklate, S., and Pegg, S. (2006) *Social and historical approaches to understanding murder and murderers*. Devon: Willan Publishing.

Eisner, M. (2003) 'Secular Trends of Violence, Evidence and Theoretical Interpretations.' In M. Tonry, ed., *Crime and Justice: A Review of the Research*, vol. 30.

Kimball, C. (2002) *When Religion Becomes Evil*. New York: HarperCollins Publishers Inc.

Michiko, M. (2001) 'When Prophecy Fails: The Response of Aum Members to the Crisis.' In R. Kisala and M. Mullins, eds., *Religion and Social Crisis in Japan*. New York: Palgrave.

Chapter 2

Serial Killing

Keith Soothill

Introduction

Popular and academic interest in serial killing has mushroomed over the last decade. Serial killing has become big business, with various state and private interests having vested reasons for keeping serial killing in the news (Soothill 1993). This growth of interest needs to be seen in the context of notable shifts in public reaction to sex crime since the Second World War.

Since the crimes of Jack the Ripper in 1888 in London, serial killing has largely been seen as the sexualised murder of women by men in modern Western society. However, the murders of Jack the Ripper were not immediately recognised as a series of *sex* crimes, and there is no necessary connection between serial killing and sex crime. Nevertheless, the link is usually made. Indeed, Caputi argues powerfully that the seemingly unprecedented crimes of Jack the Ripper 'essentially invented modern sex crime. We might think of him as its "father"' (1988:4).

What happened was that, with the activities of this still anonymous killer, serial killing seemed to emerge as a new criminal genre. This is misleading, for plenty of evidence of earlier examples of serial killing exists. The crucial point is that the phenomenon of Jack the Ripper arose in a new age – 'at the end of the nineteenth century, coincident not only with a powerful movement of Western feminism, but also with the rise of the popular press and mass media, the invention of the camera, the mass production and distribution of pornography, the medical inventions of gynaecology and psychoanalysis, and the technologizing of weaponry' (*ibid*.:12). Feeding off the speculation and fiction surrounding Jack the Ripper, serial killing generates more myths than most crimes. Separation of fact from hyperbole, whilst also recognising its importance, is very difficult. Caputi, for instance, maintains that 'serial sex murder is in fact a form of twentieth-century terrorism, an outrage against women analogous to the anti-witch crazes of the middle ages' (*ibid*.: back cover). This is a strong claim to make, but the claim underpins the central issue of this chapter: are serial killers simply aberrant beings, separate from the rest of us, or do they and their activities somehow represent some of the critical tensions within society?

Serial killing as a social problem

In most countries serial killing has not been a serious problem. However, the emergence of a serial killer can quickly change that perception as fear and anxiety sweep through a community. In Britain since the Second World War, concerns have shifted regarding sex crime and only comparatively recently returned to concerns about serial killing. In the 1950s there were particular concerns about prostitution on the streets, but soon the focus shifted to homosexual activity – more specifically towards decriminalising homosexual activity between consenting adults in private, which was given legislative effect in the 1960s.

The 1970s had the new-wave women's movement starting in the United States and identifying rape as a matter of grave concern. The 1980s in Britain will mainly be remembered by the focus on inquiries about child sex abuse, but there was a return to the issue of prostitution on the streets characterised by a concern about 'kerb-crawling', whereby men in cars sought prostitutes. However, in the late 1970s and early 1980s a series of killings of prostitutes, reminiscent of the Jack the Ripper killings of the previous century, focused attention on serial killing. The problems associated with catching the perpetrator, Peter Sutcliffe, known as the Yorkshire Ripper, focused specific attention on the shortcomings of the police in dealing with this kind of crime. In brief, interest in the phenomenon re-awakened and was reinforced by a remarkable rise in films and television productions relating to fictional and factual portrayals of serial killing.

Fictional representations tend to emphasise stereotypes, but sometimes truth can be stranger than fiction. It was certainly a shock to the British public at the start of this century that the person who is probably the most prolific serial killer in British history and sometimes headlined as 'the world's most prolific serial killer' was a general practitioner from a singleton practice in Market Street, Hyde, near Manchester. Harold Frederick Shipman was convicted at Preston Crown Court on January 31, 2000 of the murder of 15 of his patients while he was working as a doctor. The subsequent inquiry suggested that Shipman killed 215 people – mostly elderly women (171 women and 44 men) – and the Chair, Dame Janet Smith, had suspicions about the deaths of another 45 of his former patients, making a total of some 260 people. Shipman was sentenced to life imprisonment but ultimately took his own life while serving his sentence at HMP Wakefield in January 2004.

Despite a lengthy inquiry (Smith 2005), why Shipman committed his crimes remains a puzzle. Soothill and Wilson (2005) tried to confront this puzzle and to move beyond the usual individualistic explanations of serial killing towards a wider analysis that embraces a more structural approach whereby we can begin to understand the meaning of serial killing at a societal level. In brief, they argue that the actions of serial killers, sadly but usefully, identify social breakdowns. Quite simply, serial killers prey on the vulnerable. While the Shipman case reveals how the stereotype of the serial killer needs to be continually revised, the victims were still the vulnerable. In fact, Shipman's murders escaped attention for so long because ultimately inadequate social protection existed for the group on which he preyed, namely the elderly, and mostly women.

More recently, the serial killing of five women who worked as prostitutes – what became known as the Ipswich killings – in the last three months of 2006 produced yet another unhappy reminder of the Jack the Ripper murders in the late nineteenth century. Even compared with the Yorkshire Ripper case in the 1970s, a major difference was the more sympathetic attitude of the public and the more ready response of the police which comparatively quickly produced a defendant in court accused of the murders. Nevertheless, the case also demonstrates the persistent vulnerability of young women involved in prostitution. Wilson, following Soothill and Wilson's theme (2005), highlights the people as being most at risk from such predators as 'elderly people, women involved in prostitution, gay men, runaways, 'throwaways' and 'children moving from place to place' (2007: back cover). As Grover and Soothill (1999) claim, the vulnerability of certain groups of victims 'shows the limitations of current societal organisation' (1999:13). They ask us to recognise that the victims of serial killers not only reflect wider social relations, but also that they may be victimised because they are living outside the moral order of capitalist society.

However, one needs to go beyond thinking about one society, such as Britain, for the differences in numbers between countries are stark. Caputi (1988) quotes FBI statistics to show how serial murders increased dramatically over two decades: in 1966 an estimated 644 such murders took place in the US, compared to an estimated 4,118 in 1982, or nearly eighteen per cent of all murders that year. While these figures seem somewhat inflated, the contrast with England and Wales is remarkable. Between 1960 and 1995 evidence exists of only 15 trials involving 17 serial murderers in England and Wales (Grover and Soothill 1999). While different definitions and a focus on trials may explain some of the variation, the scale of serial killing in the United States is of a different order.

The higher volume of serial killing in the United States is due, at least in part, to the larger population of the United States (around 265 million) as compared to that of England and Wales (around 52 million). A more meaningful comparison is between the crime *rates* of the two countries. Interestingly, Langan and Farrington note that 'whether measured by surveys of crime victims or by police statistics, serious crime rates are not generally higher in the United States than England' (1998: iii). However, the major exception to the pattern of higher crime rates in England is the murder rate. The 1996 US murder rate, for example, is nearly six times higher than in England. Equally there is no doubt that serial killing is much more prevalent in the United States.

One serial killer can generate massive distress and outrage within a community, but in reality, differences in the numbers of serial killers at different times and in different countries are worthy of note. This point relates directly to the types of explanation that one needs to call upon. However, before considering serial killing in detail, we first need to recognise other forms of multiple killing that have recently raised concern.

Definitions of multiple killing

The homicide case that received the most media coverage in Britain during the last quarter of the twentieth century was not perpetrated by a serial killer but by a mass killer. In a study of the coverage of homicides in *The Times* for the period 1977–99, 13 homicide cases dominated the coverage – two cases involving mass killers, five cases involving serial killers and six cases involving single homicides (Soothill et al. 2002). The Dunblane Primary School massacre easily outstripped the other cases in terms of the amount of coverage: on 13 March 1996 Thomas Hamilton walked into Dunblane Primary school and shot dead 16 pupils and one teacher. He also injured many others before shooting himself. Various reasons have been presented to explain this atrocious act, but the dominant theory appears to be revenge on the community he felt taunted him. In fact, this outrage also tuned in with more general and widespread concerns about the issue of paedophilia, as the perpetrator had had such allegations made against him. The similarity underpinning the public concerns surrounding multiple killing and paedophilia is that the media reporting tends to highlight the dangers posed by strangers rather than intimates and the dangers posed in public space rather than in the private sphere. In fact, most danger involves intimates in the private sphere (see Chapter 1), but this aspect tends to be overlooked in media coverage. Egger maintains that 'mass killers generally target people they know (family members or co-workers), often for revenge' (2001: 278).

There have been similar kinds of outrage elsewhere. In April 1999 in the United States, two students killed 12 of their classmates and a teacher at Columbine High School in Littleton, Colorado, before killing themselves. In April 2002, in the worst school shooting in Europe since the Dunblane tragedy, 17 people were killed after a gunman – a former pupil – opened fire in a school in Erfurt, eastern Germany. He then turned the gun on himself. Within a more explicitly political context, the suicide bombers of Palestine deliberately perpetrate mass killing on Israeli citizens in response to Israeli provocation (see Chapter 8).

However, multiple killings may not just take place within one day. On Wednesday 2nd October 2002, Captain Barney Forsythe, director of the major crimes unit of Montgomery County Police Department in Maryland reported, 'Chief, we have a homicide… and it's a little out of the ordinary.' A middle-aged white man had been shot in the back. However, there was just one unusual detail, for it appeared that a high-powered rifle had been used, making a small entrance wound and a large exit wound. The next morning a call came in about a second shooting. A man had been killed while mowing the lawn in front of a Dodge dealership in Bethesda. Then a call came in reporting another fatal shooting, at a Mobil gas station in Rockville – three unusual deaths in one evening and one morning. This was the start of the largest manhunt in American police history. As Police Chief Charles Moose in charge of the investigation later commented, 'It was the worst thing any police officer can encounter – he was killing at random' (*Guardian*, 15 October 2003). The case, known as the Washington Sniper, involved ten sniper victims killed in Maryland during a three-week killing spree. There was growing public impatience and fear during these three weeks. The arrest of the defendants by 50 police officers, as they slept at a lay-by in a car that had been converted into a sniper's hide, produced a national sigh of relief. 'In the control room, there was no applause. There was no shouting. There were no high-fives. Just a sense of relief' (*ibid.*).

So what are the differences between these various kinds of multiple murder? Indeed, one of the most difficult tasks in any study of serial killers is actually defining what this means. Egger notes that 'prior to the 1980s, individuals who killed more than one victim were referred to as mass murderers' (2001: 278). He suggests that social scientists began to appreciate the need to distinguish between those who killed their victims in a single event and those who killed over a period of time. In other words, two types of multiple murders were separated out. Author and former FBI profiler Robert Ressler is often credited as the first to introduce the term 'serial killer' to distinguish the latter group from the former. However, the terms are social constructions, and delineating the boundaries is sometimes problematic. The term 'spree killing' – usually referring to homicides occurring in multiple locations over a more extended period of time than a mass killing – is often added in an attempt to clarify, but confusions still abound. Some definitions suggest that serial murders must occur over a time period of more than 30 days, while the term 'spree killing' covers killings conducted over a shorter span.

Shifts do occur. So, for example, the distinction between killings by terrorists and multiple killings with no evident political motive is becoming increasingly blurred. In the United States, one of the defendants in the Washington Sniper case, John Allen Muhammad, was reported to be tried under an untested statute that likens murder to acts of terrorism: 'legal analysts say the provision obviates the need to prove Mr. Muhammad's finger was on the trigger of the Bushmaster rifle that was used in most of the killings' (*Guardian*, 15 October 2003).

Mass homicide is now usually defined as the killing of multiple victims in one place at one time. In fact, the two essential elements that distinguish mass homicide from other forms of multiple victim homicide are those of location and time. While the terms can be used wrongly, particularly by the media, the boundaries of the definitions are difficult to police. So, for example, Petee points out that 'Howard Unruh, one of the first high profile mass murder cases in the United States, moved from store to store when he killed 13 people in downtown East Camden, New Jersey in 1949' (2001: 270). Similarly, the time dimension can be extended so that when murderers kill their victims over a period of several hours, such as in hostage situations, this is still likely to be regarded as a mass murder.

The number of homicides needed to qualify as a multiple homicide – either in its 'serial' or 'mass' variety – is another source of contention. As Petee (2001) points out, the choice is largely between having four victims as the cut-off point (e.g. Levin and Fox 1985; Dietz 1986) or three (e.g. Holmes and Holmes 1994; Kelleher 1997; Petee et al. 1997). As stated earlier, these categories are social constructions, and the choice is somewhat arbitrary.

There seem to be many more multiple homicides in the United States than elsewhere: Petee suggests that 'mass murder seems to be largely an American phenomenon' (2001: 270). While the US also seems to have had large numbers of serial killers, most countries have experienced the problem in some form. Although the numbers of such events outside the US remain comparatively small, one should not underrate the very real and understandable concerns that a reporting of multiple killings sets off in a community. The task of this chapter is not to deny the importance of the concern but to challenge the nature of much of the focus. In brief, some questions are being highlighted, while perhaps even more important questions are being neglected.

The definition of a serial killer

Even after separating out serial killing from mass homicide, there are still important issues to confront. The Federal Bureau of Investigation (FBI) simply defines a serial murderer as 'someone who has murdered three or more victims, with a cooling-off period in between each of the homicides' (Griffiths 1993, quoted in Egger 2001). Others have tried to identify more components.

Egger (1984) originally suggested a six point identification of the serial killer: there must be at least two victims; there is no relationship between perpetrator and victim; the murders are committed at different times and have no direct connection to previous or subsequent murders; the murders occur at different locations; the murders are not committed for material gain; and subsequent victims have characteristics in common with earlier victims (in Gresswell and Hollin 1994: 3). In fact, most of the components of this definition could be challenged. For example, to assert that 'there is no relationship between perpetrator and victim' is a stringent condition and would certainly exclude some perpetrators, such as Dennis Nilsen and Fred and Rosemary West, whom most in Britain would regard as serial killers. Of course, what constitutes a 'relationship' is problematic, but I would argue that Egger is too restrictive in his conceptualisation of 'relationships'.

The assertion that murders have to take place in different locations to be classified as serial killing also seems unnecessarily restrictive. It seems curious to disqualify a killer who lures or forces his or her victims to a specific location to be killed from being labelled as a serial killer. Fred and Rosemary West, who killed at least nine young women (non-familial victims), retain the label of serial killers despite committing the known offences at the same address in Gloucester, England (Sounes 1995).

Egger has made other attempts at pointing to the components of a serial killing scenario (e.g. Egger 1998), but these should all be regarded as likely ingredients rather than of any definitional status. Nevertheless, reservations about Egger's efforts should not mask the point that his work begins to provide some clues as to how one might consider serial killing as a distinctive sub-set of 'multiple murder'. No one has, or is likely to, set down a completely satisfactory definition for all purposes (Jenkins 1988). There will, for example, be the person who commits one murder and is caught, convicted and sentenced, but who fully intended to continue killing. Such a person would be excluded from any of the academic studies using the conventional definition.

Counting the number of serial killers as well as the number of their victims can be regarded as hazardous. Nevertheless, there are enough known serial killers to make some observations about classification. In brief, the crimes and methods deployed by serial killers make placing them into neat categories difficult: every assertion seems to have an exception. However, it still seems fair to say that serial killers in most Western countries tend to be white, male and in their 20s when they begin to murder. Despite this, there are female serial killers (such as Aileen Wuornos in the United States, who was sentenced to death for killing six middle-aged men, and Beverley Allitt in England, who killed four children whilst working as a nurse), and there are black serial killers (such as Wayne Williams, who killed 26 young black boys in Atlanta, and Carlton Gary, who was involved in a series of rape–murders of elderly white women in Columbus, Georgia.

Age, gender, and ethnicity are unlikely to identify a serial killer, but the *modus operandi* (MO) or 'signatures' are often crucial in establishing links between crimes:

The ritual aspect of the crime... which is conceived of fantasy and endlessly rehearsed in the offender's mind before he kills for the first time – is his 'signature', his mark, and it is principally this 'signature' which enables a series of crimes to be linked through behavioural analysis' (Wilson and Seaman 1997: 33).

Serial killers tend to choose a certain type of victim: some focus exclusively on women, others on men and yet others on children. Jack the Ripper seemed to target prostitutes specifically, and the sobriquet 'Ripper' soon becomes attached to serial killers with the same predilection (e.g. the Yorkshire Ripper in England). Alternatively, the sobriquet can be used in relation to Jack the Ripper's tendency to take certain internal organs of his victims. As another example of collecting 'trophies', one can cite how Jeffrey Dahmer kept his victims' skulls.

The choice of victim, 'signatures', and 'trophies' may help identify links between various killings and to develop a psychological profile, but they also underline the point that serial killers and their crimes can be very different. Ressler and Schachtman (1993) made an early attempt to divide the killers into two major groups, recognising that some plan their deeds carefully whilst others seem much more haphazard in their actions. This led to the influential distinction Ressler and Schachtman make between organised and disorganised serial killers:

> The major attribute of the organised offender is his planning of the crime. Organised crimes are premeditated, not spur of the moment. The planning derives from the offenders' fantasies... [which] have usually been growing in strength for years before he erupts into covert antisocial behaviour.... With the organised killer, the victims are personalised, the offender has enough verbal and other interchange with the victims to recognise them as individuals prior to killing them.... the killers' logic displayed in every aspect of the crime that is capable of being planned.... The disorganised killer doesn't choose victims logically and so often takes a victim at high risk to himself, one not selected because he/she can be easily controlled. (1993: 183–4)

In the event, the distinction between organised and disorganised killers produces a continuum rather than a dichotomy, for the evidence from the activities of most serial killers suggests that both organised and disorganised components may co-exist. Certainly these early insights have heralded a variety of ways of trying to capture the range of behavioural patterns serial killers display.

Holmes and DeBurger (1988) categorised three types of serial killers based on behavioural patterns and the motives that seem to predominate:

(i) *Visionary type* includes the serial killers who commit their homicides as a result of 'visions' or 'voices' telling them to do so

(ii) *Mission-oriented type* believes that they have a mission to rid the world of what they perceive as an undesirable group of people

(iii) *Hedonistic type* focuses on the killings that are for the maintenance of pleasure.

They identify four variants within this:

a) *Lust-oriented*, where there is a 'central focus on sexual gratification'

b) *Thrill-oriented*, where the homicidal act is primarily the outcome of seeking thrills and excitement

c) *Comfort-oriented*, where the aim seems to be for the serial killer to enjoy life, which is being '[in] control of immediate circumstances so that 'the good life' can be attained' (1988: 78)

(iv) *Power/control oriented type. The search for power and control is common to many serial killers. Holmes and DeBurger describe it thus: '…the fundamental source of pleasure is not sexual, it is the killer's ability to control and exert power over his helpless victim' (1985: 32).*

As Leyton (2000) stresses, Gresswell and Hollin (1994) are among those who have been critical of Holmes and DeBurger's categories. The lack of mutual exclusivity between the types sometimes makes distinguishing clearly one from another difficult. Secondly, the categories are neither exhaustive nor consistent. For example, contract killers are excluded because their motivation is deemed financial, yet they include such practical motives as killing for insurance. Finally, the typology does not account for killers whose motivations may change over time (Leyton 2000: xxiii). In brief, as with many typologies, the 'types' are static rather than dynamic or, as Gresswell and Hollin more elegantly state, the need for a typology recognises 'there is a process to multiple murder' (1994: 5).

Explaining serial killing: individual and structural approaches

The suggestion that some questions are being highlighted while perhaps even more important questions are being neglected is particularly important in relation to the possible explanations of serial killing.

In trying to identify serial killers – which is obviously crucial for their detection – there is largely an appeal to psychological explanations. If, as seems likely, there will be an increasing appeal to biological or genetic explanations about criminal behaviour, such explanations remain at the individual level. The questions of why more serial killers seem to exist in some historical times than others and in some countries but not others may be difficult to confront using explanations which have meaning only at the individual level. Perhaps more recourse to explanations at the societal or structural level is necessary, but these have tended to be neglected.

The greater focus on individual approaches is understandable. Certainly any recent attempts to 'combat' offences involving serial killers have been at the individual level: psychological profiling, DNA testing and offender databases are all necessarily linked to the offender as an individual, with the primary focus in trying to develop psychological profiles through offender profiling or biological profiles through DNA testing. In essence, these reflect laudable attempts to improve detection.

There have also been attempts at the psychological level to explain, rather than simply to describe, serial killing. The case of Kenneth Bianchi (more popularly known as the Los Angeles 'Hillside Strangler') illustrates some of the controversies. John Watkins (1984) saw Bianchi as a consultant in 1979. Under hypnosis, Bianchi manifested what appeared to be a multiple personality. An underlying personality, 'Steve', whose existence was apparently unknown to Bianchi, claimed responsibility for the two murders in Bellingham and those in Los Angeles. Another consultant, Martin Orne, would not accept the diagnosis of multiple personality and made the diagnosis of 'Antisocial Personality Disorder with Sexual Sadism', claiming that Bianchi was a clever malingerer. Orne and colleagues (1984) argue strongly that the case of Kenneth Bianchi highlights the limitations of clinical diagnostic procedures in a forensic setting. They stress that the stakes are so high in terms of potential punishment (including death in the United States) that multiple killers are likely to mislead deliberately. Indeed, they suggest that 'under these circumstances the assumption that what the defendant says necessarily reflects his phenomenal experience is no longer justified' (p.426). Hence, in suggesting that the oral evidence from multiple killers may be suspect, Orne and his colleagues undermine much of what psychologists and psychiatrists use as evidence.

Despite these reservations, Gresswell and Hollin point out that the literature has identified a number of common background, cognitive, and behavioural variables, including 'histories of sexual and physical abuse, abandonment, failure to bond with parents, bedwetting, torturing animals, firesetting, a pervasive sense of isolation, alienation, use of sadistic sexual fantasy, compulsive masturbation, lack of acquired inhibitions against violence, depersonalisation of victims, and a belief that the use of violence against others is legitimate (McDonald, 1963; Brittain, 1967; MacCulloch, Snowden, Wood & Mills, 1983; Levin & Fox, 1985; Burgess et al., 1986; Holmes & DeBurger, 1988; Ressler, Burgess & Douglas, 1988; Norris, 1990)' (1992: 441).

The important point to recognise is that these variables are not limited to multiple killers but are shared with many other offenders as well as those who have not entered the criminal justice process. In short, as Gresswell and Hollin rightly say, these variables 'are best viewed as relating to a "set" or propensity for criminal behaviour that requires a specific trigger to be realised in a particular form' (1992: 441). Indeed, they appropriately stress, 'it is unwise to assume that multiple murderers are a homogeneous population' (*ibid*.). In other words, it seems likely that the 'trigger' will vary enormously from individual to individual.

David Canter, in his account of psychological profiling as a science using behavioural rather than forensic evidence, proclaims that a new level of understanding is needed – 'a theory about what drives a person beyond the bounds of socially acceptable aggression into the realms of criminal violence' (1995: xiv). He argues that the actual events – 'those actions and locations which are the focus of police attention must be the building blocks of any fruitful theory of interpersonal violence' (*ibid*.). This approach, using the variations in the violent actions themselves as clues to a criminal's personality and identity, has been very popular over the past decade and has undoubtedly been an important catalyst in re-appraising detection techniques. However, it seems to make few inroads into why the actions were committed in the first place. In short, the dominant individualistic discourse arguably fails to meet the challenge of causation satisfactorily, and we need to consider explanatory frameworks that are more ambitious in their scope. Certainly the main result of psychologising and medicalising causes of crime is that it ignores its historical and cultural specificity. So what are the questions that cannot so readily be answered by an approach at the individual level?

One of the problems is that the so-called 'experts' in the area of serial killing are largely psychologists or psychiatrists who tend to individualise social problems. They look for the cause of aggression within the individual and tend to regard the source of the problems as wrapped in some form of psychopathology. However, this cannot explain why there are significant variations in the rates of serial killing over time and between societies.

An explanation at the structural level

Canadian anthropologist Elliott Leyton (1986) has probably provided the most useful insights beyond an individualistic analysis of this apparently increasing social problem. In his book, *Hunting Humans: The Rise of the Modern Multiple Murderer*, he argues that the multiple murderer is in many senses the embodiment of the central themes in his (and, much more unusually, her) civilisation as well as a reflection of that civilisation's critical tensions. The implications of his analysis, published in the mid-1980s, were quite simply political dynamite. In a world in the 1980s when the 'American dream' was being glorified as the Communist Bloc was so dramatically crumbling, Leyton posed a fundamental challenge to that dream. Perhaps the dream may be a precursor to a nightmare: the vast and increasing numbers of multiple murderers in the United States suggested that American society might provide the key to the development and existence of cultural forms which actually fed this nightmare. There has largely been an 'ostrich response' to this provocative thesis, which was less likely to excite the interest of capitalist news media than the hint of a criminal gene.

The important questions essentially focus on time and place: is serial killing quintessentially a modern phenomenon? Why in some countries and not others? The work in trying to answer these questions calls upon disciplines other than psychiatry and psychology.

Is serial killing quintessentially a modern phenomenon?

Is serial killing something that has happened largely since the sensational Jack the Ripper murders, or is there an earlier history of the phenomenon? There is no definitive answer to this. However the historian, Bernard Capp, argues that 'human nature changes very slowly and we can find cases in some ways parallel as far back as the seventeenth century' (1996: 21). In fact, reflecting British interest in the Gloucestershire serial killings by Fred and Rosemary West discovered in 1993, Capp points out that 'by an extraordinary coincidence, one [in the 17th century] even featured another Gloucester couple running a cheap lodging house. *The Bloody Innkeeper* (1675) described how the remains of seven men and women had been dug up in the backyard of an alehouse at Pultoe, near Gloucester' (*ibid.*). The pamphlet was written before the couple came to trial, and the outcome remains unknown. However, Capp maintains that 'the bloody innkeeper and his wife were by no means unique' (*ibid.*: 22) but, as Capp himself acknowledges, 'these seventeenth-century cases do not correspond exactly to modern equivalents. None appears to have been motivated by perverted sexual drives; there are no Stuart equivalents of the Wests or "Yorkshire Rippers"' (*ibid.*: 26). In fact, most of the cases he cites 'originated in domestic tensions and quarrels in alehouses and taverns', characterised by the motivational account of greed, and poison was the favoured technique of killing. In probing the past, one is of course limited by the type of serial killing that is more likely to be detected. Nevertheless, Capp maintains that 'multiple murders and serial killings were probably no rarer in seventeenth-century England than today' (*ibid.*: 22).

Leyton (1986) points to earlier examples – how Sawney Bean in fifteenth-century Scotland murdered to steal the possessions of passers-by and ate their bodies, and how in France the Baron Gilles de Rais, born in 1404 into one of the greatest fortunes of France, allegedly murdered between 141 and 800 children, mostly boys, during the last eight years of his life. He would take the local children to his castle and, after raping and violating them in some way, would torture and kill them. In replying to the court interrogators the baron admitted that he committed the crimes 'entirely for my own pleasure and physical delight', so displaying all the hallmarks of the modern serial killer.

Hunting Humans (Leyton 1986) is a seminal work on the sociology of multiple killing. One of the insights of this early book about American serial killers was that they are rarely drawn from the ranks of the truly oppressed. Or, more specifically, they are rarely women and almost never black. In fact, while serial killers are drawn from what Leyton calls 'very different social niches', they are largely from the aspiring lower-middle and working classes. What he suggests is that a proportion of these men began to fantasise about revenge 'and a tiny, but ever-increasing, percentage of them began to react to the frustration of their blocked social mobility by transforming their fantasies into a vengeful reality'. He further stresses that what is important is that these feelings of revenge developed in a cultural milieu which glorified violence as an appropriate and manly response to frustration. Hence, he argues that one has to look beyond the individual to the society, and in particular the social structures in which he or she lives if one is to explain multiple killing more fully. To develop his thesis, Leyton identifies three broad historical periods and argues that in these three periods the social genesis of multiple killers and their victims are socially specific. Table 1 summarises his historical configurations and shows the broad socio-economic background of the serial killers and their victims. The Table suggests significant changes in the socio-economic background of killers and their victims between the historical epochs. In broad terms, the socio-economic background of the serial killer has 'fallen' from that of aristocracy in the pre-industrial period to upper-working/lower middle class in the modern era. The socio-economic background of the victims has, again broadly speaking, 'risen' from being peasantry in the pre-industrial era through the 'lower orders' in the industrial period, to that of the middle classes in the modern era.

Table 1: Historical epochs, serial killers and their victims

	Pre-industrial (pre-late 19th century)	Industrial (late 19th century – 1945)	Modern (post-World War II)
Killer	Aristocratic	Middle-class (e.g. doctors, teachers)	Upper-working/lower-middle class (e.g. security guards, computer operators)
Victim	Peasant	'Lower-order' (e.g. prostitutes, housemaids)	Middle-class (e.g. university students)

Source: adapted from Leyton (1986: 269–5)

While Table 1 presents an elegant and interesting classification, the crucial issue of why differences exist between historical epochs still needs to be addressed. Leyton explains the changes through the concept of 'homicidal protest'. Through this concept he suggests that in each of the historical periods the configuration of the social structure is such that some persons, when faced with challenges to their position in the social hierarchy, react to those challenges through the 'protest' of killing members of the threatening group. Homicidal protest can take differing forms, and one can identify examples from each of the three periods (Grover and Soothill 1999).

In placing multiple murder in historically located social structures and relationships, Leyton constructs a useful framework for the analysis of serial killing. However, Leyton's thesis is not unproblematic. Categorisations of historical periods are always difficult to make and, as Grover and Soothill stress, the three distinctive periods 'could be criticised, on the one hand, for being too broad in their time spans, and, on the other hand, being too rigid at their boundaries' (1999: 6). In focusing upon social change, one needs to recognise that change is likely to be more gradual than the highly definable shifts which Leyton's analysis seems to imply.

Grover and Soothill (1999) use the Leyton framework to examine the experience of Britain since the 1960s. In this 'modern' era (post-1960), following Leyton, one might expect that British serial killers would be drawn from the upper working class and lower middle class, and that victims would be predominantly from the middle classes. In fact, the evidence broadly supports the Leyton thesis but becomes much more problematic when the *victims* of British serial killers are considered. The victims are *not* from the relatively powerful middle classes, but are from relatively powerless and vulnerable groups: children and young adults; gay men; women (particularly those vulnerable through their work in the sex industry or on account of the breakdown of familial relations); and pensioners. In fact, the general *absence* of persons from relatively powerful positions is especially noticeable. Evidence from the relations of capitalism (class), central to Leyton's conception of 'homicidal protest', seems to be lacking in the British context.

Grover and Soothill identify the dilemma: in the light of the British experience, should we dismiss or try to modify the Leyton approach? These commentators choose to modify it on the basis that there is an unnecessary narrowness in defining protest simply in terms of class. They suggest the focus of social relations be widened to those beyond class relations to include other social relations, such as patriarchy. Indeed, it needs to be recognised that Britain is both a capitalist *and* a patriarchal society. Widening the analysis in this way provides scope for classifying a greater variety of serial killers. In recognising patriarchal relations, it becomes clearer why serial killers often murder women and children: it is an expression of power through which men are able to dominate and oppress. The construction of masculinity is central to this. In the case of Yorkshire Ripper Peter Sutcliffe, for example, Lucy Bland argues that he was able to carry out his murderous attacks for so long because of his male 'normalness'. In other words, Sutcliffe reflected 'a normal male culture of drinking, prostitution and violence' (1987: 206–7). Indeed, violence against women was a central feature of the environs in which he circulated: it can be argued that Sutcliffe's systematic murder of women was inextricably bound in the patriarchal nature of society through which men are able to maintain their position of relative power and authority through various strategies, which includes violence against women (Walby 1990).

Feminists have tended to avoid a focus on serial killing, but three books – Caputi (1988), Cameron and Frazer (1987), and Radford and Russell (1992) – have bucked the trend. Their general argument is that serial killing is a function of patriarchal society. Caputi (1988: 6) argues that serial killing should be seen as a 'ritual of male sexual dominance', communicating messages to both male and female members of society, re-establishing the 'truths' of patriarchal society, that women are inferior, weak and loathed by the only members of society that matter – men.

Radford and Russell argue that femicide should simply be seen as one extreme in a continuum of sexual violence that exists to further the aims of patriarchal society. Cameron and Frazer also stress that serial killing is deeply rooted in social relations. Society, they suggest, 'gets the crimes it deserves' (Cameron and Frazer 1987: 34). In brief, feminist analysts argue that the behaviour and attitudes of 'normal' men back up the idea that serial killing is an element of patriarchal society (Ashburner and Soothill 2002: 96).

The most contentious issue in relation to Leyton's work, however, is how far it is generalisable. Where he focuses on the contemporary scene, his focus is on American multiple murderers – four serial killers and two mass murderers. However, in the concluding chapter of his book, where he develops his socio-structural account of multiple killing, he switches dramatically from the specific focus of his earlier chapters to a more generic focus on worldwide multiple murder. It is this leap from the nation-specific focus of the USA to a wider, international focus that perhaps produces the main critique of Leyton's thesis. Thus, we need to consider why there is such variation in serial killing in different countries.

Why serial killing in some countries and not others?

The differences between countries in terms of the numbers of serial killers can be quite striking. Certainly the contrast between England and Germany in the 1930s is thought provoking. As far as can be ascertained, no serial killers were captured or at large in Britain during this time, whereas at least a dozen examples were recorded in Germany.

Essentially sociologists are concerned with both structural and cultural explanations of phenomena, and in Germany in the 1930s curious cultural and structural arrangements came together rather dangerously. Certainly the structural conditions were problematic for some groups. The aftermath of the First World War produced new stresses and tensions in Germany, particularly for the aspiring lower middle and working classes. Recruitment into Hitler's Brown Shirts and various Fascist groups was one solution for many of the frustrated and disenchanted. However, we are concerned here with serial killing and sexual murder.

Tatar's book, *Lustmord: Sexual Murder in Weimar Germany* (1995), produces some fascinating clues as to what happened in Germany between the Wars which may have had a bearing on the phenomenon of serial killing. In focusing on the politically turbulent Weimar Republic, she produces evidence of one of the most disturbing images of twentieth-century Western culture: the violated female corpse. The images abound in painting, literature and films of the time, but Tatar argues that this history has remained a closely guarded secret. She points, for example, to 'the sheer number of canvases from the 1920s with the title *Lustmord (Sexual Murder)*' and which, she argues, 'ought to have been a source of wonder from Weimar's cultural historians long before now' (p.4).

In examining these images of sexual murder, she produces a powerful study of how art and murder have intersected in the sexual politics of culture in Weimar Germany. She suggests male artists and writers, working in a society consumed by fear of outside threats, visualise women as enemies who can be contained and mastered through transcendent artistic expression. In fact, Tatar shows male artists openly identifying with real-life sexual murderers: George Grosz posed as Jack the Ripper in a photograph with his model and future wife as the target of his knife. Further, there are the corpses of disembowelled prostitutes in Otto Dix's paintings. So, for example, Otto Dix's painting entitled *Sexual Murder* (1922) 'freezes a moment right after death – the blood is still trickling from the body and gathering in pools. The killer has had sufficient time to make his getaway.' (Tatar 1995: 15) Another Otto Dix painting – *Sex Murderer: Self-Portrait* (1920) – actually shows the murderer. '[T]he artist portrays himself here as a murderer, slicing body parts in a moment of savage homicidal frenzy. Notwithstanding the cartoon-like, surreal style, the painting conveys both the rage of the assaulter and the terror of the victim.' (*ibid.*: 16)

Tatar has a complex argument, but she essentially suggests that 'violence against women reflects more than gender trouble and can be linked to the war trauma, to urban pathologies, and to the politics of cultural production and biological reproduction' (dust cover). This recognition of the importance of both structure and culture is an important contribution towards helping us to understand why some societies provide the conditions under which serial killing flourishes.

Towards a conclusion

Modern society continues to be fascinated by serial killers, both real and fictional. This chapter has tried to place the study of serial killing within a wider context. It focuses on a series of questions, but the underlying thrust of the argument is that understanding why one individual becomes a serial killer while another will not requires a combination of individual and sociological approaches. Similarly, explaining why there are more serial killers at some time periods and in some countries rather than others requires a similar recourse to a variety of explanations.

The chapter has particularly stressed consideration of background structural and cultural factors. So, for example, Elliott Leyton's structural approach is seductive but problematic. In analysing serial killing as a cultural phenomenon, Mark Seltzer points to the United States as an information society characterised by 'wound culture'. Selzer's book presents a complex argument about forms of public violence in our culture and goes on to explore what he regards as the central components in the inner logic of serial killing. Selzer notes how serial murder and its representations 'have by now largely replaced the Western as the most popular genre-fiction of the body and of bodily violence in our culture' (1998: 1). He sees modern culture portraying a different response to the spectacle of the wounded body since the start of the 20th century: 'the wound … is by now no longer the mark, the stigmata, of the sacred: it is the icon, or stigma, of the everyday openness of every body' (*ibid.*: 2). In brief, he regards compulsive killing as not only 'a collective spectacle but also one of the crucial sites where private desire and public cultures cross' (*ibid.*: 109). Or, as he powerfully argues, 'the convening of the public around scenes of violence has come to make up a *wound culture*: the public fascination with torn and opened private bodies and torn and opened psyches, a public gathering around the wound and the trauma' (*ibid.*). Selzer talks of the emergence of a pathological public sphere that he seems to define as 'the breakdown between psychic and social registers – the breakdown between inner and outer and 'subject' and "world"' (*ibid.*: 260). It is a bleak world in which the serial killer operates.

There is still some way to go before we clarify ways of integrating some of these approaches. There is a danger that, to date, theorists have largely neglected the area of gender. Serial killing powerfully illustrates the nature of gender relations within Western culture. However, feminist theories and texts have tended to focus solely on men murdering women; such approaches need to be extended to cover the whole spectrum of serial killing, whether it involves heterosexual or homosexual relations, male or female killers (Ashburner and Soothill 2002). It may be dangerous to assume that any theory can cover the whole spectrum of serial killing, but many cases do have a common denominator: sexuality. Perhaps we must look to the social construction of sexuality in order to understand sexual murder, regardless of what it involves. There is evidence, for example, that the Yorkshire Ripper, Peter Sutcliffe, was very much a part of his culture:

> The Sutcliffe killings certainly implicate Sutcliffe's sexuality in particular and male sexuality in general. Far from 'deviating from the norm', Sutcliffe was an exaggeration of it. Violence and aggression form central components of male sexuality as it is socially constructed. (Bland, in Radford and Russell 1992: 252)

A fairly familiar argument is that the fusion of sex and violence as created by cultural apparatuses produces confusion for the incipient serial killer. The usual scapegoat is pornography. However, mainstream entertainment also produces a masculine sexuality that links sex and violence, with women portrayed as objects to be used however men desire (Ashburner and Soothill 2002: 97). Yet this type of analysis produces a problem. If the society that Sutcliffe and others are living in is as misogynistic as is sometimes suggested, then why are there not even more men committing these kinds of acts? There seems little doubt that one needs both cultural and individualistic approaches to explain why one individual becomes a serial killer while another will not (see Ashburner and Soothill 2002).

Jefferson (1994), writing on the construction of masculinity, draws on the work of Lacan to argue that entry into the language of the 'social' is the founding point of self-identity, and therefore that subjectivity (and actions) are ultimately a combination of both individual experiences and social influences. So, as Selzer argues, 'by 1900 a new kind of person has come into being and into view, one of the superstars of our wound culture: the lust-murderer or stranger-killer or serial killer' (1998: 2); the notion of 'serial killer' can thus increasingly be seen as an option open to individuals within our society. Whether individuals choose to take up or identify with this depends upon their experiences, desires and fantasies, which are ultimately influenced by social or cultural factors. Only some individuals will internalise destructive messages, and even fewer will act upon them, depending on their life experiences or 'desires'. The important point is that the cultural messages linking sex and violence are in no way limited to masculine heterosexuality and can be internalised by anyone depending on his or her experiences. For example, the female serial killer, Aileen Wuornos, is believed to have been physically and sexually abused for much of her childhood and therefore would have been receptive to ideas that sex and violence are deeply intertwined.

Female violence is increasingly seen as a major problem, especially among juveniles. This may be a precursor to more females becoming serial killers. As more and more women incorporate violence into their sexuality, some may, at the extreme, eroticise the act of murder and become serial killers. Certainly it seems unlikely that serial killing as a phenomenon will remain constant. However, understanding and explaining serial killing is more complicated than most are willing to acknowledge. As Ashburner and Soothill stress:

Recognising a view of society and psyche as ultimately separate but also intertwined, and so allowing one to combine sociological and individual approaches, is probably the way forward in trying to explain the phenomenon of serial killing. (2002: 97)

References

Ashburner, E. and Soothill, K. (2002) 'Understanding serial killing: how important are notions of gender'. *The Police Journal* 75, 93–99.

Bland, L. (1987) 'The Case of the Yorkshire Ripper: Mad, Bad, Beast or Male?' In P. Scraton and P. Gordon, eds., *Causes for Concern: British Criminal Justice on Trial?* Harmondsworth: Penguin.

Brittain, R. P. (1967) 'The sadistic murderer', *Medicine, Science and the Law* 10, 198–207.

Burgess, A. W., Hartman, C. R., Ressler, R. K., Douglas, J. E., and McCormack, A. (1986) 'Sexual homicide: a motivational model', *Journal of Interpersonal Violence* 1, 251–272.

Cameron, D. and Frazer, E. (1987) *The Lust to Kill*. Cambridge: Polity Press.

Canter, D. (1995) *Criminal Shadows*. London: HarperCollins.

Capp, B. (1996) 'Serial Killers in 17th Century England'. *History Today*, 46 (3): 21–26.

Caputi, J. (1988) *The Age of Sex Crime*. London: Women's Press.Dietz, P.E. (1986) 'Mass, Serial and Sensational Homicides'. *Bulletin of the New York Academy of Medicine* 62: 477–91.

Egger, S. A. (1998) *The Killers Among Us: An Examination of Serial Murder and Its Investigation.* Englewood Cliffs, NJ: Prentice-Hall.

Egger, S. A. (2001) 'Serial Homicide'. In C. D. Bryant, ed., *Encyclopaedia of Criminology and Deviant Behaviour*, Volume II. Philadelphia: Brunner-Routledge, 278–80.

Gresswell, D. M. and Hollin, C. R. (1992) 'Towards a New Methodology for Making Sense of Case Material: An Illustrative Case Involving Attempted Multiple Murder', *Criminal Behaviour and Mental Health,* 2, 329–41. (Reprinted in Leyton, E. H. (2000) *Serial Murder: Modern Scientific Perspectives*. Dartmouth: Ashgate).

Gresswell, D. and Hollin, C. (1994) 'Multiple Murder: A Review'. *British Journal of Criminology* 34, 1: 1–14.

Grover, C. and Soothill, K. (1999) 'British Serial Killing: Towards a Structural Explanation'. *The British Criminology Conferences: Selected Proceedings*. Vol. 2. www.britsoccrim.org/bccsp/vol02/08GROVE.HTM

Holmes, R. and DeBurger, J. (1985) 'Profiles in terror: the serial murderer'. *Federal Probation*, XLIX (September), 29–34.

Holmes, R. and DeBurger, J. (1988) *Serial Murder*. Thousand Oaks, CA: Sage.

Holmes, R. M. and Holmes, S. T. (1994) *Murder in America*. Thousand Oaks, CA: Sage Publications.

Jefferson, T. (1994) 'Theorising Masculine Subjectivity'. In T. Newburn and E. Stanko, eds., *Just Boys Doing Business*. London: Routledge.

Jenkins, P. (1988) 'Serial Murder in England, 1940–1985'. *Journal of Criminal Justice* 16, 1–15.

Kelleher, M. D. (1997) *Flash point: The American Mass Murderer*. Westport, CT: Praeger.

Langan, P. A. and Farrington, D. P. (1988) *Crime and Justice in the United States and in England and Wales, 1981–96*. Washington: US Department of Justice.

Levin, J. and Fox, J.A. (1985) *Mass Murder: America's Growing Menace*. New York: Plenum.

Leyton, E. (1986) *Hunting Humans: The Rise of the Modern Multiple Murderer.* Toronto: McClelland and Stewart.

Leyton, E., ed. (2000) *Serial Murder: Modern Scientific Perspectives.* Aldershot: Ashgate, Dartmouth.

MacCulloch, M. J., Snowden, P. R., Wood, P. J. W. and Mills, H. E. (1983) 'Sadistic fantasy, sadistic behaviour and offending.' *British Journal of Psychiatry* 143, 20–29.

McDonald, J. M. (1963) 'The threat to kill', *American Journal of Psychiatry* 120, 125–130.

Norris, J. (1990) *Serial Killers.* London: Arrow.

Orne, M. T., Dinges, D. F. and Orne, E. C. (1984) 'On the Differential Diagnosis of Multiple Personality in the Forensic Context', *International Journal of Clinical and Experimental Hypnosis* 32, 118-69. (Reprinted in Leyton, E. H. (2000) *Serial Murder: Modern Scientific Perspectives.* Dartmouth: Ashgate).

Petee, T. A., Padgett, K. G. and York, T. S. (1997) 'Debunking the Stereotype: An Examination of Mass Murder in Public Places'. *Homicide Studies* 1: 317–37.

Petee, T. A. (2001) 'Mass Homicide'. In C. D. Bryant, ed., *Encyclopaedia of Criminology and Deviant Behaviour*, Volume II. Philadelphia: Brunner-Routledge, 270-72.

Radford, J. and Russell, E. H., eds. (1992) *Femicide: The Politics of Woman Killing.* Buckingham: Oxford University Press.

Ressler, R. K., Burgess, A. W. and Douglas, J. E. (1988) *Sexual Homicide: Patterns and Motives.* Lexington, MA: Lexington Books.

Ressler, R. K. and Schachtman, T. (1993) *Whoever Fights Monsters.* London: Pocket Books.

Selzer, M. (1998) *Serial Killers: Death and Life in America's Wound Culture.* London: Routledge.

Smith, J. (2005) Shipman: The final report. www.the-shipman-inquiry.org.uk/reports.asp (accessed 26.1.08)

Soothill K (1993) 'The serial killer industry', *The Journal of Forensic Psychiatry*, Vol. 4, No. 2, September, 341–54.

Soothill, K., Francis, B., Pearson, J. and Peelo, M. (2002) 'The Reporting Trajectories of Top Homicide Cases in the Media: A Case Study of The Times'. *Howard Journal of Criminal Justice*, 41, 5, December, 401–21.

Soothill, K. and Wilson, D. (2005) 'Theorising the puzzle that is Harold Shipman', *Journal of Forensic Psychiatory and Psychology*, Vol. 16, No. 4, 685–98.

Sounes, H. (1995) *Fred and Rose.* London: Warner Books.

Tatar, M. (1995) *Lustmord: Sexual Murder in Weimar Germany.* Princeton: Princeton University Press.

Walby, S. (1990) *Theorising Patriarchy.* Oxford: Blackwell.

Watkins, J. G. (1984) 'The Bianchi (LA Hillside Strangler) Case: Sociopath or Multiple Personality'. *International Journal of Clinical and Experimental Hypnosis* 32, 67–101. (Reprinted in Leyton, E. H. (2000) *Serial Murder: Modern Scientific Perspectives.* Dartmouth: Ashgate).

Wilson, C. and Seaman, D. (1997) *The Serial Killers: A Study in the Psychology of Violence.* London: Virgin Publishing Ltd.

Wilson, D. (2007) *Serial Killers: Hunting Britons and Their Victims.* Winchester: Waterside Press.

PROLOGUE: CAPITAL PUNISHMENT

Capital punishment as a form of killing is more controversial than many. Most Western societies have abolished it, with the notable exception of the United States. Even after abolition, however, many people in these societies continue to support the death penalty, and elsewhere it remains standard practice. Peter Hodgkinson, Seema Kandelia and Rupa Reddy take this debate forward through a discussion of the politics of capital punishment, religious perspectives, and the rights and responses of primary and secondary victims.

The focus on secondary victimisation in this chapter is a particularly interesting one. Most discussions of capital punishment weigh the rights of the victim against the human rights of the perpetrator and the morality of killing in the name of the state. However, few of these discussions acknowledge that capital punishment creates new victims in the form of the partners and families of the perpetrator. This group attracts less sympathy than the families of the victims of crime (see for example Condry 2007), but they too are innocent and lose a loved one at the hands of someone else – in this case, state authority. What new perspective does this put on our definitions of killing?

References
Condry, R. (2007) *Families Shamed: The consequences of crime for relatives of serious offenders.* Cullompton: Willan Publishing.

Chapter 3

Capital Punishment: Creating More Victims?

Peter Hodgkinson, Seema Kandelia and Rupa Reddy

Introduction

This chapter examines the issue of why we kill in the context of capital punishment. In particular, it will look at justifications for the death penalty that revolve around addressing the needs of victims in homicide cases. Our major contention is that the death penalty, whilst purporting to help victims' families to achieve 'justice' on behalf of the deceased, and 'closure' for themselves after the trauma of homicide, in fact creates a form of 'secondary victimisation'[4] (Goodey 2005: 157) and further victims, including the families of the condemned. Far from usefully addressing the aftermath of homicide for victims' families, this chapter argues that the death penalty and its processes, from the initial prosecution to the end of the lengthy appeals process, reproduce and widen the scope of victimisation.

Key to this is the question of who constitutes a 'victim'. In homicide cases the 'primary victim' is the deceased, and therefore for the purposes of our argument when referring to the category of 'secondary victim' we mean the families of the deceased, sometimes known as 'co-victims' or 'survivors' (Hodgkinson 2004: 335). However, we also argue that the families of the offender in capital cases should be considered to fall within the category of secondary victims. Both sets of families are affected by the original crime and have to endure the capital process. However, whilst the needs of survivors are to some extent being acknowledged and addressed, the needs of the families of offenders are not (Sharp 2005).

The first section of this chapter examines the theoretical and practical role of victims in the criminal justice system, specifically in capital cases. We will show that although in Anglo–American jurisdictions the right to punish has theoretically been all but completely passed into the power of the state, the

---

4   A term often used by rape victims when they refer to the 'aggressive and embarrassing cross-examination' to which they are subjected by police and at trial.

participation of victims has been gradually increasing. Whilst this has largely been in the area of 'service rights' dealing with their material and psychological needs, they have also had increasing input into the procedural aspects of capital cases. The second section argues that, although seemingly helpful to victims, problems relating to procedural participation have contributed greatly to further secondary victimisation of victims' families. Furthermore, we argue that as well as aggravating the experiences of the families of homicide victims, the death penalty also creates new victims in the form of the families of offenders, who therefore should be included in the category of secondary victims. We conclude by examining restorative justice as one possible means for overcoming some of these problems.

The experience of the family of the homicide victim in capital punishment

The criminal justice system attempts to fulfil a number of aims in relation to prevention of crime and protection of the public. Sentencing is only one aspect of this system. Broadly speaking, in Anglo–American legal systems the right to punish an offender has been removed from the individual victim to the state. The reasoning for this is based on social contract theory and posits that citizens in a sovereign state give up their personal right to punish those that have harmed them; in return the state acts as a 'proxy retaliator' and protects law and order on behalf of the citizen (Ashworth 2005: 71; Garland 2001: 109–10). A major reason for enforcing this social contract revolves around the protection of the rule of law, and the need to ensure that decisions which may affect individual rights, such as punishment, are taken impartially and independently rather than by individuals with an emotional involvement in the decision (Ashworth 2005).

As well as ensuring fair treatment of suspects and offenders, the removal of punishment from the private sphere also prevents social disorder in the form of vigilantism or reprisal killings (Ashworth 2002; Kanwar, 2001). An extreme example of the potential results of the breakdown of the rule of law in this respect are the long running 'blood feuds' found in certain regions of Albania. In the latter jurisdiction, the Kanun legal code enshrined customary practices dating back to the fifteenth century, including principles relating to personal honour. According to this code, violations of honour such as the killing of an individual often result in reprisal killings of male members of the killer's family, triggering a blood feud, which can continue for many years.[5]

However, it does not follow from this reasoning that the victim, or in the

---

5   Ismail Kadare, one of Albania''s most eminent authors, provides an authoritative analysis of the Kanun system through the vehicle of fiction in *Broken April* (1991). See also Albanian Human Rights Group (2000–2001).

case of homicide, secondary victims, should have no role in the criminal justice system. At its most basic, in capital cases the right to some level of involvement arises from the fact that they are forced into the involuntary role of victim as a result of the homicide. Secondary victims may also have a vested interest in ensuring that the oft-stated aims of punishment are fulfilled, namely deterrence, incapacitation and retribution. The death penalty incapacitates offenders, thus protecting potential future victims. Perhaps more relevant is the issue of whether the death penalty acts as a general deterrent to murder. Although the harm they have already suffered cannot be reversed, many victims' family members may still have an interest in ensuring that others do not suffer a similar trauma. The ongoing debate as to the deterrent value of the death penalty has been fraught with methodological disagreements; yet despite a lack of conclusive evidence as to its effectiveness, deterrence continues to be cited as a primary justification for the death penalty (Hodgkinson 2004). As Hood (1996) argues, in utilitarian terms:

> The issue is not whether the [death penalty] deters some people, but whether, when all the circumstances surrounding the use of capital punishment are taken into account, it is a more effective deterrent than the alternative sanction: most usually imprisonment for life or very long indeterminate periods of confinement. (p.1)

There are also principled arguments against the deterrence justification based on Kantian desert theory, which argues that the offender's sentence should be determined only in relation to the crime committed, rather than for other reasons such as the potential future deterrent effect.[6] Desert theory is highly relevant to secondary victims since it incorporates legitimate desire for revenge for the harm inflicted into a more impartial assessment of the punishment based on proportionality. It is also important because its analysis of crime creates an imbalance between the law-abiding citizen and the offender, thus giving an unfair advantage to the offender which can only be redressed through punishment (Clarkson et al. 2007).

In relation to victims of serious crimes such as homicide, critics of desert theory have questioned whether any punishment can adequately redress the harm caused by the offence and whether the theory differs significantly from the more emotional impetus of revenge (Lacey 1988). In the context of the death penalty, victims' groups have also used the desert justification to lobby for harsher punishment, as opposed to a more impartial assessment of sentence based on proportionality. Thus, one reason why the right to punish has been

---

6   See Von Hirsch (1976) for further discussion of the basis of the debate around desert theories of punishment.

removed from victims in the state model described above is to ensure that the desire for private revenge is tempered by an impartial and independent assessment of the resultant punishment. In this sense desert theory acts as a limitation upon the victim's participation in the punishment process.

Addressing victim needs: participation in capital punishment

Although the justifications for limiting the formal role of victims and their families is important, nonetheless the victim, and in the case of homicide the victim's family, has always taken some part in the prosecution of such cases, largely through their evidence as witnesses during the trial. The question becomes not *whether* the victim or secondary victim should participate in the prosecution of the offence, but exactly *what level* of involvement they can or should have. The latter has changed significantly in recent years in all criminal cases, including homicide cases. This has taken the form of two levels of participation. The first, and probably most significant, is an increase in 'service rights', including the right to be kept informed of the progress of the case, the status of the offender, and the right to receive appropriate support throughout the legal process (Sanders and Young 2007: 657). The second is an increase in procedural rights, namely the ability to give a statement on the impact or harm which the offence has caused. The question of what influence such statements have on sentencing is discussed in greater detail below.

Worldwide research on secondary victims of homicide shows an overall deficiency of support services (Hodgkinson 2004). The organisation Victim Support in the UK offers a range of material and psychological support services to secondary victims,[7] and this issue has been a prominent aspect of political lobbying on behalf of victims in the USA. However, most countries appear to have very little in the way of service provision for crime victims in general and none for the families of homicide victims and the condemned. The Jamaican government, despite problems of infrastructure and funding, provides a victim support unit, which also provides a service for the families of homicide victims and a recently drafted victims' charter which provides rights to information and service provision in relation to victims' involvement with the criminal justice system.[8] In Trinidad and Tobago, an independent victim support service has been set up by the non-governmental Caribbean Centre for Human Rights.[9]

---

7   See http://www.victimsupport.org.uk/vs_england_wales/index.php for further information on this government- funded but independent organisation.
8   Available at http://www.jis.gov.jm/victims_charter.pdf
9   The CCHR Victim Support Project started in November 2006 and has already shown tremendous progress with counsellors identified, volunteers recruited and trained, and a sample of homicide victims' families contacted and surveyed. As of June 2007, the VSP has made over 60 calls to families affected by homicide, identifying them from newspapers or from word of mouth. Nine families have been referred for counselling despite the stigma attached to counselling in Trinidad & Tobago.

Increases in victim participation in the criminal justice system are often presented in the form of a balance between the rights of offenders and victims, whereby 'the rights of victims and offenders are posited as being diametrically opposed' (Edwards 2004: 970), and any extension of victims' rights must come at the cost of a concurrent incursion into the rights of the defendant. This is not necessarily accurate in the case of service rights, since unless the conflict lies in an allocation of scarce resources, services to assist victims do not detract from the due process rights afforded to defendants. However, the increasing procedural role of victims may have a more significant effect on the treatment of offenders.

In England and Wales, the Crown Prosecution Service's Code of Practice states that the consequences for the victim and the views of the victim or their family must be taken into account when making the decision to prosecute.[10] Sentencing reports already take account of the harm caused to victims and wider society in determining the retributive severity of the sentence and the level of incapacitation required to protect victims (including potential future victims; Ashworth 2005). The Victim Personal Statement scheme allows victims to convey information to the court on how the crime has affected them (*ibid.*). However, the statement does not necessarily have to be taken into account in determining the sentence, and a lack of consistency is evident in relation to the circumstances in which this occurs (*ibid.*). In a more recent pilot scheme launched in five courts in England, the families of homicide victims have been given the opportunity to present the court with a statement on the effect of the crime on them, between conviction and sentence, which may possibly have more influence on sentencing outcomes.[11]

In the USA, advocacy by individual victims and groups of victims (including secondary victims) has had some success in increasing the participation of victims at a number of stages of the legal process. The level of formal participation has largely taken the form of the use of Victim Impact Statements at the sentencing stage of capital trials, an issue first raised in the Supreme Court in *Booth v. Maryland*,[12] where such evidence was declared inadmissible. Since then, the Supreme Court in the case of *Payne v. Tennessee* has deemed the introduction of certain types of victim impact evidence as

---

Assistance is provided in a number of ways, for example, by providing emotional support, referrals to counsellors and supermarket hampers. The VSP has recruited the support of one psychiatrist and 17 psychologists and has a number of doctors they can call upon to advise them when necessary. Projects at the planning stage include working with the families of the condemned, the prison system, victims in jail, and the development of restorative justice initiatives.

10 See http://www.cps.gov.uk/victims_witnesses/codetest.html

11 See the government consultation which launched this pilot scheme, available at http://www.dca.gov.uk/consult/manslaughter/manslaughter.htm. See Sweeting et al. 2008 for the findings of the evaluation of that pilot scheme http://www.justice.gov.uk/docs/research-victims-advocates.pdf

12 *Booth v. Maryland* 482 US 496 (1987)

admissible.[13] This comprises information on, firstly, the victim's character and contribution to society and, secondly, the impact of the murder on their family (Hoffmann 2002–3). A third type of evidence concerning the opinion of the secondary victims about the sentence was not ruled on in the case and thus remains inadmissible (*ibid.*).

Conflict continues in the academic and political debate on this issue, with some arguing that the benefit of victim impact evidence is that it helps the victim's family in homicide cases to gain 'closure' from the trauma caused by the crime.[14] In the context of analogous evidence in the UK, Erez (1999) argues that such participation empowers victims by making them more visible within the criminal justice system, which has two effects: it is both cathartic, even if it does not necessarily have the desired level of impact, and it has a beneficial influence on assessing proportionality of sentence by fully informing the court of the effects of the crime. Hoffmann acknowledges that whilst there may be some negative effects to admitting such evidence, such as influencing the impartiality of the sentence or further victimisation of the secondary victims, the benefits outweigh these. Specifically, he argues that the jury in US capital cases are currently left to assume (in the absence of further information) that 'the survivors would prefer to see the defendant sentenced to death' (Hoffmann 2002–3: 540) and that if survivor opinion evidence were allowed in very strictly constrained circumstances, at least the intellectual dishonesty this situation caused would be alleviated (*ibid.*: 542). Indeed, secondary victims who advocate less harsh punishment would be incorporated into the system, which is currently not the case.[15] Therefore it could be argued that a demonstrably positive effect exists in allowing the family to inform the court of the harm caused by the crime and its ongoing effect.

The participation of victims in sentencing decisions is not a recent development in other legal jurisdictions, and the other end of the spectrum is demonstrated by the example of *Shari'ā* systems.[16] In these, although the state still takes on the overall role of regulating crimes, as in Anglo–American systems, the role of the victim is very different. Of the three categories of crime contained in the *Shari'ā*, the *Qesas* principles provide a number of options for dealing with crimes such as homicide. One is the talionic 'eye for an eye' punishment which gives the victim 'the right to inflict or have inflicted upon the perpetrator the same harm as the victim suffered', including death (Bassiouni 2004: 182). The second option is victim compensation (*diyya*),

---

13 *Payne v. Tennessee* 501 US 808 (1991)
14 See Mosteller (2002–3) for a discussion as to the use of concepts of 'closure' and 'catharsis' to justify the use of victim impact evidence in the USA.
15 See Hodgkinson (2004) for a more detailed analysis of this issue.
16 See Bassiouni (2004) for a detailed discussion on all aspects of the death penalty in relation to the *Shari'ā*.

which is encouraged in part to avoid reprisal killings leading to longstanding 'blood feuds' that could result from the first option (Bassiouni 2004). The third option is set out as the most preferable: forgiveness by the victim and their heirs instead of the infliction of further harm or compensation (*ibid.*). In practice, a number of Islamic jurisdictions[17] have enacted criminal law provisions which have the effect of restricting the availability of the death penalty to specific types of premeditated murder circumstances, thus diminishing the facility of the victim's family to dictate the sentence of the offender (*ibid.*). The state in these jurisdictions thus takes a more prominent 'sovereign state' role in dealing with the offender, albeit not to the same degree as Anglo–American systems.[18]

The issue of what level of participation victims should take in sentencing relates to the issue of the rule of law, and the desire for an independent and impartial assessment of the sentence an offender should receive. One major point which arises from the discussion of both the American and *Shari'ā* systems is that in capital cases this level of procedural participation by secondary victims inevitably leads to inconsistency and arbitrariness. The type and severity of sentence is determined by how merciful or retributive the secondary victims are in each individual case rather than by a set of predetermined sentencing rationales (Hoffmann 2002–3; Hodgkinson 2004; Ashworth 2005). This may be exacerbated by the finding that the fate of the defendant is determined not necessarily on the facts but on just how articulate and persuasive the secondary victims are (Hoffmann 2002–3). The sentence is assessed using other factors besides the aims of sentencing, such as 'just deserts' or deterrence.[19]

Unintended consequences of capital punishment: the phenomenon of secondary victimisation

Beyond the issue of the treatment of offenders and the rule of law, a major problem with increasing the rights of victims to participate in the legal process is that they may misinterpret the importance of their role. For example, if their participation proves to be less influential than they were led to expect, they

---

17 Bassiouni (2004) cites Algeria, Egypt, Iraq, Jordan, Lebanon, Morocco, Syria and Tunisia as examples.

18 An interesting consequence of this level of influence by the family of homicide victims in certain *Shari'ā* systems has been noted in relation to so-called 'honour killings', where the murder of a female family member is often carried out by members of her own family (see Chapter 1). This leads to a situation where the offender is simultaneously a secondary victim. If the offender not only belongs to, but was indeed sanctioned by the victim's family to commit the offence, then the latter may be more concerned with representing the interests of the offender than seeking 'justice' on behalf of the deceased victim. For a detailed exposition of this issue in relation to the law in Pakistan see Warraich (2005).

19 Nadler and Rose (2002–3) examine in detail the effects of victim impact testimony on juror assessment of punishment in capital trials in the USA.

could experience a type of 'secondary victimisation' (Edwards 2005). In the case of the victim's family, the powerlessness they experience at the involuntary and violent loss of their loved one may to some extent be compounded if the court then ignores their opinion on whether the death penalty should be used (Hoffmann 2002–3). In this way, victim personal statement schemes can raise and then dash the hopes of the victim's family and exclude them whilst ostensibly seeming to empower them (Sanders and Young 2007; Ashworth 2005).

Hoffmann suggests that in capital cases this could be alleviated if victims' families are clearly informed of the role of their evidence from the outset, and that it will only be one of numerous considerations in determining sentence (Hoffmann 2002–3; Ashworth 2005). This would also reduce the potential for further arbitrariness and inconsistency in sentencing, since all parties would be clearly aware of the role of victim impact evidence from the outset. Compounding the potential for inconsistency and further victimisation of family members is discrimination between victims, with courts at times giving precedence to the views of those whom they see as more 'worthy' than others. Often, the exercise of this discretion is based on how retributive the victims' family are and thus can further victimise those not deemed to satisfy this standard (Hodgkinson 2004).

One of the primary reasons governments give for retaining the death penalty is that it is necessary to address the needs of crime victims in attaining 'closure' after the trauma of homicide (Hodgkinson & Schabas 2004). Yet Kanwar (2001: 215) argues in the context of the USA that although 'nothing expresses the impossibility of closure more dramatically than the death penalty', nonetheless 'a feeling of closure for the secondary victims has become, at least implicitly, an independent justification for the retention and enforcement of the death penalty' (ibid.: 216). The case of Timothy McVeigh, the Oklahoma City bomber who drove a truck loaded with explosives into a federal office building in April 1995, killing 168 people, demonstrates that this is a complex issue for those affected by murder. After witnessing McVeigh's execution, Kathleen Treanor, whose daughter died in the bombing, stated 'It's a demarcation point…it's a period at the end of a sentence. It's the completion of justice and that's what I'll remember about today' (CNN.com 2001b). A survey carried out by ABC News/Washington Post in April 2001 reported that 60 per cent of the US population surveyed think that the death penalty is fair because it gives satisfaction and 'closure' to the families of the victims (Langer 2001).

However, not all victims' families find that retribution, in the form of execution of the criminal, gives them 'closure'. In contrast to Kathleen Treanor's view, Bud Welch stated that he would not find closure 'by taking Timothy McVeigh out of his cage to kill him. It will not bring my little girl back' (CNN.com 2001a). The relief secondary victims feel when the offender is executed at the end of the lengthy appeals process is often short-lived. Kanwar (2001) gives the example of Linda Kelley, the first secondary victim to view the execution of an offender in Texas in 1996, and describes how her responses developed from the belief that viewing the execution of the murderer of her two children would help give her 'closure'; happiness after the execution mixed with anger at the offender's last words; ambivalence that he had escaped further suffering; then an eventual questioning of whether witnessing the execution had in fact given her 'closure' in any real sense, since it had not changed the fact that her children were still gone. This shows that the belief that the process of capital punishment can achieve 'closure' is largely illusory.[20]

Creating more victims: families of the offenders

The death penalty not only impacts on the family of the victim, but also the family of the offender, yet the latter is almost always overlooked in any discussion on the death penalty. Both families experience suffering as a result of the homicide, one through loss of a loved one, the other through the loss by execution, and neither through any 'fault' of their own. Both sets of families have similar needs and concerns and therefore, we argue, should be recognised as 'victims'. Even though both sets of families experience significant trauma following the murder, the response from the community, from the media, most victim groups, the state and the criminal justice system differs significantly, with most sympathy reserved for the families of the victim.

While justifications of deterrence and retribution underpin continued strong support for capital punishment, it is very important to be aware of the 'incidental' or 'collateral' affects of the death penalty in its application. One aspect of this concerns the offenders' families who, due to their marginalisation and the hostility directed to them as well as to their family member, the suspect, express a deep level of hurt and anger that the state wants to kill their loved one. It is difficult for the families of the condemned to understand how the state, which is meant to be protecting all of its citizens from harm, can be responsible for the death of their loved one – there is no one 'on their side' (Sheffer and Cushing 2006: 15).

A number of studies have examined the impact that the death penalty has had on offenders' families. Many of these focus on the individual stories outlining the experiences of the family. They document the shock and distress that families of offenders experience upon learning of the crimes committed

---

20 See Lithwick (2006) and Domino and Boccaccini (2000) for a further discussion on whether killing brings 'closure' to victims' families.

by their loved ones. They highlight feelings of pain, loss and depression, similar to those experienced by family members of the victims. Offenders' families also suffer psychiatric and physical problems such as Post-Traumatic Stress Disorder, weight gain/loss, and addiction to alcohol or drugs, as well as having to bear the financial burden of having a loved one facing a capital trial. Further to this are feelings of profound guilt and anxiety about a capital trial and the possibility of execution (King 2005; Sharp 2005; King 2004; Beck et al, 2002; Vandiver 1989; Smykla 1987).

While members of the victims' family are critical of the criminal justice system, this seems to be much more prominent for family members of the offender. In many cases, the lack of compassion from police, prosecutors, defence attorneys, judges and society as a whole can compound the distress of the offender's family (Beck et al. 2002; Eschholz et al. 2003). However, anecdotal evidence suggests that differences in the criminal justice system's treatment of families are not only a question of degree; there also is a qualitative difference. Beck highlights a case in which the mothers of two offenders were 'instructed to refrain from crying or showing emotion. They compared this to the treatment of the victim's family members, who were given tissues and breaks when they were overcome with emotion' (Beck et al. 2002: 401). In another example of differential treatment, the victim's family was placed prominently in sight of the jury, whereas the offender's relative was deliberately placed out of their sight (*ibid.*: 401). In addition, the offender's family's history of violence and abuse can be brought into the public sphere ostensibly as part of the mitigating process though actually further stigmatising the offender's family in the eyes of the jury.

In some jurisdictions, family members are not afforded a basic right to know when their loved one will be executed or in some cases where the body is buried after the execution. In Japan and Taiwan, for example, the administration of the death penalty is clouded in secrecy. In particular, the execution date is not made known to the condemned or to his or her family; the condemned is only informed an hour or so before the execution, which leaves the inmates in a constant state of anxiety, not knowing if each day is their last, while family members are only informed of the execution after it has taken place (Johnson 2006; FIDH 2003; Ryden 2001).

Similarly, in Uzbekistan, the implementation of the death penalty prior to abolition[21] was widely condemned by the international community. Family members of those on death row were not informed of the date or place of execution nor where the body had been buried. Then UN Special Rapporteur on Torture, Theo van Boven, stated that:

---

21   Uzbekistan abolished the death penalty in January 2008.

The complete secrecy surrounding the date of execution, the absence of any formal notification prior to and after the execution and the refusal to hand over the body for burial are believed to be intentional acts, fully mindful of causing family members turmoil, fear and anguish over the fate of their loved one(s). The practice of maintaining families in a state of uncertainty with a view to punishing or intimidating them and others must be considered malicious and amounting to cruel and inhuman treatment. (2003: para. 65)

These kinds of criminal justice practices can only add to the suffering of offenders' families, not least by taking away the possibility of saying goodbye. The counter argument offered by the family members of a murder victim is that they do not get an opportunity to say goodbye either; however, this poses the question of whether the family members of the offender, who are also not party to the crime, should be subjected to the same suffering. The intention in these jurisdictions seems to be to add to the retributive element of the offender's punishment by the means described above. The problem, however, is that this applies the 'rebalancing' aim of desert theory to secondary victims, rather than the primary victim and offender.

Furthermore, the stigma of capital offences more often than not filters through to the treatment of offenders' families in the wider community. In many cases, they are attributed blame for the offenders' family environment or upbringing and are therefore also perceived as guilty by association. In the press, for example, the effect the crime has had on the offenders' family members is frequently overlooked. In one study, Beck and colleagues (2002: 400) reported that, of nineteen families of capital defendants interviewed, all felt that the media was 'problematic and hostile' towards them. They note that the manner of reporting, for example the media's portrayal of the offender as some kind of 'monster', can further exacerbate the suffering of offenders' families.

Within any discussion of the effects of the death penalty on offenders' families, it should not be forgotten that family members include not only parents, partners and siblings, but in some cases, young children. The effect of having a parent placed on death row and executed can have a tremendous impact on a child's life, though little formal research has been conducted on the issue.[22] King (2006: 296), noting a case in which a son became extremely distressed after the execution of his father who then within a year was also facing a capital charge, argues that:

---

22 There have, however, been some studies on the criminality of children of incarcerated parents. See Beck et al (2007) for a more detailed discussion on this issue.

...society failed Little Hameen. He was a victim, just as much as the young man who Abdullah killed, yet society did not acknowledge him as such. We offered him no support or understanding, no counseling or services, not even any condolences. We killed his father and left him to figure out how to live with his rage and pain.

A key point in this case is that Little Hameen's father, Abdullah, had undergone an extraordinary rehabilitation, and was expected to receive clemency. Little Hameen testified on his father's behalf; however testimony from another secondary victim advocating the execution resulted in the Delaware Board of Pardons refusing him clemency. This case illustrates the problems of allowing victim evidence to influence capital procedures, and in particular, the ways in which the capital punishment system constructs victims' families' concerns as more 'worthy' of attention than those of offenders' families, despite the similarities of their victimisation.

There are few resources for families of the condemned. The majority of victims' groups tend to focus on the needs and concerns of the primary victim or in the case of homicide, their family members. For the families of the offender, what little support and attention there is comes mainly from religious groups, researchers or sympathetic members of the community who may also have lost someone to murder. In the USA, a few organisations recognise the suffering of the condemned's family. These include Murder Victims' Families for Reconciliation (MVFR), Murder Victims' Families for Human Rights (MVFHR), and the Journey of Hope. These organisations share similar beliefs, include members of both sets of families, and are firmly opposed to the death penalty. MVFR's opposition is that:

> ...endless trials re-open emotional wounds and put off the time when real healing can begin, the vast resources and attention spent on the death penalty is better spent supporting victims and preventing crime in the first place...executions create more families who have lost a loved one to killing, and many of us think it is just plain wrong for the state to kill. (MVFR, n. d.)

Similarly, MVFHR (n. d.) recognise that 'Family members of the executed have been made orphans, widows, and childless. Family members of the victims have been re-victimized over and over by mandatory appeals and overwhelming media attention on the offender.' This highlights once more the unintended consequences of capital punishment and its further victimisation of the families of both victims and offenders.

Restorative justice initiatives

The majority of discussions on the value of the death penalty have focused

76

extensively on its retributive and deterrent elements. As discussed throughout this chapter, however, the application of the death penalty causes unintended harm, certainly to the family members of the condemned, and possibly to the family members of the victim. This further victimisation of the families of those involved in capital trials has not yet been fully recognised by the criminal justice system, and where it has is accepted as an unavoidable casualty of the process. However, partly in recognition of this, a practice that is gaining more popularity, particularly in the USA, is victim–offender mediation based on restorative justice principles, where the offender is viewed as an integral part of the healing process for victims. Restorative justice recognises the harm caused to individuals, their families and the community, rather than a more abstract conception of harm to society. Restorative justice thus attempts to engage all stakeholders, including the offender, in dealing with the aftermath of a crime in a way that encompasses accountability and healing (Umbreit et al. 2002).

Although restorative justice measures are widely used for non-violent crimes, little research has been conducted into the value of restorative justice measures for victims of serious violent crimes, particularly families of homicide victims. Whilst its value comparatively may be limited in capital cases there is, we argue, significant scope for its application to both sets of secondary victims. Some studies have found significant benefits to adopting restorative justice measures as a supplementary approach to the criminal justice process in capital cases (Eschholz et al. 2003; Umbreit and Vos 2000).

In the context of homicide, victim–offender mediation (also referred to as victim–offender conferencing, victim–offender dialogue, victim–offender reconciliation) brings together the family members of the homicide victim and the offender (and the offender's family where appropriate) in the presence of a trained mediator. The process gives victims and/or their families a chance to tell the offender of their pain, fear and the extent to which the crime has impacted upon them. It also gives them the chance to ask questions that only the offender can answer, for example, what happened in the final moments, what were the victim's final words and so forth. For the offender, taking part in the mediation allows him or her to understand the effects of their crime, to take responsibility and to express remorse. The process also enables offenders' families to reach out to the victims' families and apologise or share their grief (Eschholz et al. 2003; Umbreit et al. 2002).

Although victim–offender mediation may not be appropriate in all cases, it seems that in some, it has more a positive and longer-lasting impact on victims' (and offenders') families than the traditional criminal justice responses of execution or witnessing the execution. One study assessing the impact of victim–offender dialogue programmes involving crimes of severe violence found that of the 78 participants (victims, family members and offenders) that took part in victim–offender mediation, all but one was satisfied with the outcome, with 71 participants expressing that they were 'very satisfied' (Umbreit et al. 2002: 15). With this in mind, restorative justice arguably produces better results for victims and secondary victims in terms of their recovery from trauma from the homicide and constitutes a more constructive approach to dealing with the aftermath of homicide for all those affected. It fully acknowledges the needs of both sets of families and views them both as an equal and integral part of the healing process, rather than constructing a hostile opposition between them, as the capital punishment process invariably does.

Conclusion

The experience that the families of homicide victims have of the capital punishment system is in a state of continuous appraisal. In this chapter, we have argued for the importance of developing protocols through which the experiences of all other actors could be examined. However, by widening the participation of those whom we would describe generically as secondary victims, we must acknowledge that inadvertently and paradoxically in the case of the families of homicide victims, this has brought with it a number of negative unintended consequences, which could have been avoided and should now be corrected to avoid them in future. This includes, in particular, the much-lauded policy to permit the families of the victim to witness the execution as the defining vehicle through which 'closure' could be most effectively achieved. The strong anecdotal evidence from the narrative of such families is that, far from achieving 'closure', the experience of watching someone being put to death adds another dimension of distress, thus compounding the suffering. Typically, at this point the state absolves itself of any further responsibility to these particular constituents.

Increased participation of the victim's family in the trial and all subsequent appeals and clemency hearings causes further arbitrariness and inconsistency in a system which already suffers from these deficiencies of the rule of law.[23] Although increased participation in the death penalty process may benefit those victims' families supportive of capital punishment, it prejudices those who oppose it. This chapter has attempted to bring to the forefront of the phenomenon of secondary victimisation, the circumstances of offenders' families, which whilst analogous in many ways to those of the victims' families, are more often than not neglected in the discussion about capital punishment. Our contention is that this group should be distinguished alongside the victims' family as two groups equally deserving of improved service rights.

---

23 See Hoffmann (2002–3) for more detailed discussion of this point.

We believe too that more effort should be made to apply the principles of restorative justice so as to provide some solutions to the problems faced by both sets of families.

The death penalty not only affects the families of the victims and the condemned but many others too. Studies have shown that individuals involved in the operation and administration of the death penalty such as lawyers, judges, jurors, law enforcement and prison staff, wardens, chaplains, medical professionals and execution teams are affected to various degrees by their involvement in death sentences (Owens and Owens 2003). Capital jurors, for example, experience secondary victimisation as illustrated in numerous studies of their roles and experiences. These attest to the trauma experienced by sizeable percentages of respondents, especially those referred to as 'holdouts' who persist, in the face of immense pressure from the rest of the jury, against voting in favour of death (Fleury-Steiner 2004; Bowers et al. 1998; Eisenberg et al. 1996; Sundby 2005). Surprisingly, very few empirical clinical studies have been conducted to evaluate whether any pathological changes have been experienced by those who witness executions (Freinkel et al. 1994). However, one can draw conclusions from the narrative descriptions of media witnesses to executions, and the chaplains and prison wardens who are required to attend executions, whose accounts are replete with examples of a continuum of adverse affects experienced by those who are present at the execution (Pickett 2002; Willett & Rozelle 2004; Reid & Gurwell 2001).

These accounts demonstrate further the ways in which capital punishment re-creates and creates further victimisation in its purported quest to address the needs of those victimised by homicide. The use of capital punishment as a response to homicide creates ripples of suffering extending far beyond the primary victim and offender, or indeed, the current class of secondary victims. Thus the issues explored in this chapter, if taken together with other analyses of the negative effects of the death penalty, fuel the argument that capital punishment creates more problems than it solves.

References

Albanian Human Rights Group (2000—2001) 'The Kanun Bastardised, Dossier: The Blood Feud', *Albanian Human Rights Group Periodical Magazine for Human Rights* 2.

Ashworth, A. (2005) *Sentencing and Criminal Justice*, 4th Ed. Cambridge: Cambridge University Press.

Ashworth, A. (2002) 'Responsibilities, Rights and Restorative Justice.' *British Journal of Criminology* 42, 578–95.

Bassiouni, C. (2004) 'Death as a Penalty in the Shari'ā' in P. Hodgkinson and W.A. Schabas, eds., *Capital Punishment: Strategies for Abolition.* Cambridge: Cambridge University Press.

BBC News (2005) 'Families "to Have Voice in Court".' 1 September 2005, at http://news.bbc.co.uk/1/hi/uk/4202618.stm.

Beck, E., Britto, S. and Andrews, A. (2007) *In the Shadow of Death. Restorative Justice and Death Row Families.* New York: Oxford University Press.

Beck, E., Blackwell, B. S., Leonard, P. B. and Mears, M. (2002) 'Seeking Sanctuary: Interviews with Family Members of Capital Defendants.' *Cornell Law Review* 88, 382–418.

Booth v. Maryland 482 US 496 (1987).

Bowers, W.J., Sandys, M. and Steiner, B.D. (1998) 'Foreclosed Impartiality in Capital Sentencing: Jurors' Predispositions, Guilt-Trial Experience, and Premature Decision Making.' *Cornell Law Review* 83(6) 1476–1556.

Clarkson, C.V., Keating, H.M. and Cunningham, S.R. (2007) *Criminal Law: Texts and Materials*, 6th Ed. London: Sweet and Maxwell.

CNN.com (2001a) 'Some Oklahoma City bombing families fight for McVeigh's life.' 4 May 2001, http://edition.cnn.com/2001/US/05/04/mcveigh.families/index.html.

CNN.com (2001b) 'McVeigh execution: A 'completion of justice'.' 11 June 2001. http://edition.cnn.com/2001/LAW/06/11/mcveigh.02/index.html.

Crown Prosecution Service, Code for Prosecutors, http://www.cps.gov.uk/victims_witnesses/codetest.html.

Department for Constitutional Affairs, 'Hearing the relatives of murder and manslaughter victims: The Government's plans to give the bereaved relatives of murder and manslaughter victims a say in criminal proceedings, available at http://www.dca.gov.uk/consult/manslaughter/manslaughter.htm.

Domino, M. L. and Boccaccini, M. T. (2000) 'Doubting Thomas: Should Family Members of Victims Watch Executions?' *Law and Psychology Review* 24, 59.

Edwards, I., (2004) 'An Ambiguous Participant: The Crime Victim and Criminal Justice Decision-Making.' *British Journal of Criminology* 44, 967–82.

Eisenberg, T., Garvey, S.P. and Wells, M.T., (1996) 'Jury Responsibility in Capital Sentencing: An Empirical Study.' *Buffalo Law Review* 44, 339–380.

Erez, E. (1999) 'Who's Afraid of the Big Bad Victim? Victim Impact Statements as Victim Empowerment and Enhancement of Justice' *Criminal Law Review* 545–56.

Eschholz, S., Reed, M. D., Beck, E., and Leonard, P. B. (2003) 'Offenders' Family Members' Responses to Capital Crimes. The Need for Restorative Justice Initiatives.' *Homicide Studies* 7(2), 154–181.

Fleury-Steiner, B., (2004) *Jurors' Stories of Death – How America's Death Penalty Invests in Inequality.* Ann Arbor: University of Michigan Press.

Frienkel, A., Koopman, C., and Spiegel, D. (1994) *Dissociative symptoms in media eyewitnesses of an execution.* American Journal of Psychiatry 151: 9.

Garland, D. (2001) *The Culture of Control: Crime and Social Order in Contemporary Society.* Oxford: Oxford University Press.

Goodey, J. (2005) *Victims and Victimology – Research, Policy and Practice.* Longman Criminology Series. London: Pearson Education Ltd.

Hodgkinson, P. and Schabas, W.A. (2004) *Capital Punishment: Strategies for Abolition.* Cambridge: Cambridge University Press).

Hoffmann, J. (2002–3) 'Revenge of Mercy? Some Thoughts About Survivor Opinion Evidence in Death Penalty Cases.' *Cornell Law Review* 88, 530–42.

Hood, R. (1996) *Capital Punishment, Deterrence and Crime Rates*, Seminar on the Abolition of the Death Penalty, Kiev, 28–9 September 1996, Council of Europe Parliamentary Assembly, Doc. AS/Jur (1996) 70.

International Federation for Human Rights (FIDH) (2003) *The Death Penalty in Japan: A Practice Unworthy of a Democracy International Federation for Human Rights*, International Mission of investigation. Report No. 359/2, May 2003.

Jamaica Government Victim Charter http://www.jis.gov.jm/victims_charter.pdf.

Johnson, D. T. (2006) 'Japan's Secretive Death Penalty Policy: Contours, Origins, Justifications, and

Meanings.' *Asian-Pacific Law & Policy Journal* 7(2), 62–124.

Kadare, I. (1991) *Broken April*. London: The Harvill Press.

Kanwar, V. (2001) 'Capital Punishment as 'Closure': The Limits of Victim-Centred Jurisprudence.' *Review of Law and Social Change* 27, 215–55.

King, R. (2006) 'The Impact of Capital Punishment on Families of Defendants and Murder Victims Family Members.' *Judicature* 89(5), 292–6.

King, R. (2005) *Capital Consequences: Families of the Condemned Tell Their Stories*. New Brunswick, New Jersey and London: Rutgers University Press.

King, K. (2004) 'It Hurts So Bad: Comparing Grieving Patterns of the Families of Murder Victims With Those of Families of Death Row Inmates.' *Criminal Justice Policy Review* 15(2), 193–211.

Lacey, N. (1988) *State Punishment: Political Principles and Community Values*. London: Routledge.

Langer, G. (2001) 'Death Penalty Ambivalence', 10 May 2001, ABC News, available at http://abcnews.go.com/sections/us/DailyNews/poll010504_deathpenalty.html.

Lithwick, D. (2006) 'Does Killing Really Give Closure?' *Washington Post* 26 March 2006, available at http://www.washingtonpost.com/wp-dyn/content/article/2006/03/24/AR2006032402340.html.

Mosteller, R. P. (2002-3) 'Victim Impact Evidence: Hard to Find the Real Rules' *Cornell Law Review* 88, 543–54.

Murder Victims' Families for Reconciliation. http://www.mvfr.org/ (accessed 27 March 2008).

Murder Victims' Families for Human Rights. http://www.murdervictimsfamilies.org/ (accessed 27 March 2008).

Nadler, J. and Rose, M. R. (2002–3) 'Victim Impact Testimony and the Psychology of Punishment.' *Cornell Law Review* 88, 419–56.

Owens, V.S. and Owens, D.C. (2003) *Living Next Door to the Death House*. Cambridge: William B. Eerdmans Publishing Company.

Payne v. Tennessee 501 US 808 (1991).

Pickett, C. with Carlton S. (2002) *Within these Walls: Memoirs of a Death House Chaplain*. New York: St. Martins Press.

Reid, D. with Gurwell, J. (2001) *Have a seat, please*. Huntsville, Texas: Texas Review Press.

Ryden, E., ed. (2001) *Taiwan Opposes the Death Penalty: Proceedings of the Fujen University International Conference on the Abolition of the Death Penalty*, 24-16 June 2001, Department of Law & John Paul II Peace Institute, Fujen Catholic University.

Sanders, A. and Young, R. (2007) *Criminal Justice*, 3rd Ed. Oxford: Oxford University Press.

Sharp, S. F. (2005) *Hidden Victims: The Effects of the Death Penalty on Families of the Accused*. New Brunswick, New Jersey and London: Rutgers University Press.

Sheffer, S and Cushing, R. (2006) *Creating More Victims: How Executions Hurt the Families Left Behind*. Cambridge, Massachusetts: Murder Victims' Families for Human Rights.

Smykla, J. O. (1987) 'The Human Impact of Capital Punishment: Interviews with Families of Persons on Death Row.' *Journal of Criminal Justice*, 15, 331–47.

Sundby, S. (2005) 'A life and death decision: a jury weighs the death penalty.' Basingstoke: Palgrave Macmillan.

Sweeting, A., Owen, R.,Turley, C., Rock, P., Garcia-Sanche, M.,Wilson L. and Khan, U. (2008) *Evaluation of the Victims' Advocate Scheme Pilots*. Ministry of Justice Research Series 17/08, October 2008.

Umbreit, M. S., Coates, R. B., Vos, B. and Brown, K. (2002) *Executive Summary: Victim Offender Dialogue in Crimes of Severe Violence. A Multi-Site Study of Programs in Texas and Ohio*, Centre for Restorative Justice & Peacemaking in collaboration with National Organization for Victim Assistance, 1 December 2002.

Umbreit, M. S. and Vos, B. (2000) 'Homicide survivors meet the offender prior to execution: Restorative justice through dialogue.' *Homicide Studies* 4(1), 63–87.

Van Boven, T. (2003) *Mission to Uzbekistan.* Report of the Special Rapporteur on the question of torture, Theo Van Boven, submitted in accordance with Commission resolution 2002/38, Economic and Social Council/Commission on Human Rights, Fifty-ninth session, E/CN.4/2003/68/Add.2, 3 February 2003.

Vandiver, M. (1989) 'Coping with Death. Families of the Terminally Ill, Homicide Victims, and Condemned Prisoners' in Radelet, M. L. (ed) *Facing the Death Penalty. Essays on a Cruel and Unusual Punishment* (Philadelphia, Temple University Press).

Victim Support http://www.victimsupport.org.uk/vs_england_wales/index.php.

Von Hirsch, A. (1976) *Doing Justice – The Choice of Punishments.* New York: Hill and Lang.

Warraich, S. A. (2005) "Honour killings' and the law in Pakistan.' In L. Welchman and S. Hossain, eds., *'Honour': Crimes, Paradigms and Violence Against Women.* London: Zed Books.

Willett, J. and Rozelle, R. (2004) Warden. Albany, Texas: Bright Sky Press.

PROLOGUE: **ABORTION**

Like capital punishment, the controversy surrounding abortion remains high even in countries that have legally allowed abortion for many years. With the controversy comes contradiction, such as the behaviour of people who oppose abortion but lodge protests through the murder of doctors, staff, and patients at abortion clinics.

A Christian group called the Army of God is an example of such contradictory perspectives on killing. Kimball (2002) explains that, to those who would promote such views, 'The absolute truth claims uniting members of this loose-knit organization are unambiguous: abortion is legalized murder; abortion is an abomination to God; true Christians must engage in direct action to stop what they see as a slaughter of innocents' (p. 45). Kimball notes that nothing in the Bible specifically addresses the issue of abortion; the Commandment 'Thou shalt not kill' can be used to condemn it, but this again highlights the obvious irony behind the act of murder to condemn those who murder:

> ...among the millions who strongly oppose abortion on religious grounds, only a small, extremist fringe embraces fully the absolute truth claims... Most vocal opponents of abortion accept the practice in cases of rape, incest, or a threat to the life of the mother. Not the extremists. It is sadly ironic that soldiers in the Army of God intentionally break the commandment not to murder in order to stop people they consider guilty of murder. (*ibid.*: 46)

Lawrence Hinman has written extensively on abortion and highlights the main distinctions between the pro-life and pro-choice perspectives. His chapters on abortion and euthanasia take our discussion of killing into even less comfortable realms as we continue to question the consistency of our own beliefs.

Chapter 4

Abortion: Understanding the Moral Issues [24]

Lawrence M. Hinman

Abortion: the two principal moral concerns

The ongoing discussion of abortion is often framed as a debate between two sides, usually called *pro-life* and *pro-choice*. The labels themselves are instructive. Whereas one label (pro-life) points our attention toward the foetus, the other (pro-choice) emphasises the pregnant woman. Each position highlights a different aspect of the situation as the principal focus of moral concern. These two moral concerns are not immediately mutually exclusive in the same way that, for example, the pro- and anti-capital punishment positions are (though they may, of course, be secondarily exclusive insofar as the consequences of one exclude the other). This results in a certain murkiness in debates about abortion, since the opposing sides are often talking primarily about quite different things, either the moral status of the foetus or the rights of the pregnant woman. Let us examine each of these issues.

The moral status of the foetus

Initially, much of the debate about abortion centered around the moral status of the foetus − in particular, if and when the foetus is a person. Most participants in the discussion took for granted that if the foetus can be shown to be a person, then abortion is morally wrong, hence the focus primarily on whether the foetus could be shown to be a person. In order to answer this question, it was necessary to specify what we meant by a person.

Criteria of personhood

In attempting to define personhood, philosophers have looked for the criteria by means of which we determine whether a being is a person or not. This is a search for *necessary and sufficient conditions*, that is, conditions which if present

---

24 An earlier version of this chapter was published in Hinman, L. M. (2005) *Contemporary Moral Issues: Diversity and Consensus*. Third Edition. Upper Saddle River, NJ: Prentice-Hall.

would guarantee personhood and, if missing, would invalidate it. The argument moves thus: a criterion is seen as conferring personhood, and personhood is seen as conferring certain rights, including the right to life. Thus the overall structure of the argument looks like this:

criterion ⟶ personhood ⟶ right to life

We can see the two critical junctures in the argument just by looking at this diagram. The first is in the transition from the criterion to personhood. What justification exists for claiming that this criterion (or criteria) justifies the claim that a being is a person? The second transition has sometimes been less problematic, but it may have more difficulties than are initially apparent. The issue in this transition is whether personhood always justifies the right to life. A number of criteria have been advanced for personhood. Some of these result in conferring personhood quite early in foetal development, sometimes from the moment of conception.

The *conceived by humans* criterion is, at least on the surface, the most straightforward: 'if you are conceived by human parents, you are human' (Noonan 1970). But this straightforwardness turns out to be misleading. We obviously acknowledge that anyone born of human parents is human in some nominal sense. However, we do find cases of tragically damaged foetuses that may not count as 'human' in the stronger, more relevant sense. Anacephalic infants, for instance, are human in the nominal sense, but are they – with only a lower brain stem – human in the stronger sense? We do not obviously and necessarily acknowledge the personhood of everything 'conceived by humans' in the strict sense. Moreover, in an age of rapid advances in assisted reproductive technologies, we must even clarify the word 'conceived.' Is egg and sperm combined in a Petri dish 'conceived by human parents'? If a being is a clone of a single parent, will this count as conceived by human parents? We can see the ways in which this terrain will rapidly expand in the coming decades. This criterion either equivocates or begs the question.

The *genetic structure* argument maintains that a human genetic code is a sufficient condition for personhood. All the genetic information for the fully formed human being is present in the foetus at the time of conception; therefore, it has the rights of a person. Nothing more needs to be added, and if nothing interferes with the development of the foetus, it will emerge as a full-fledged human baby.

The *physical resemblance* criterion claims that something that looks human is human. Advocates of this criterion then claim that the foetus is a person because of its physical resemblance to a full-term baby. Movies such as *The*

Silent Scream (1980) which graphically depicts the contortions of a foetus during an abortion depend strongly on such a criterion. This criterion seems rhetorically more powerful than the appeal to DNA (since DNA lacks the same visual and emotive impact), but less rigorous, since resemblance can be more strongly in the eye of the beholder than DNA structures.

The *presence of a soul* criterion is often invoked by religious thinkers. The criterion is then used in an argument maintaining that God gives an immortal soul to the foetus at a particular moment, at which time the foetus becomes a person. Although contemporary versions of this argument usually maintain that the implantation of a soul takes place at the time of conception, St. Thomas Aquinas – one of the most influential of theologians – claimed that implantation usually occurs at quickening, around the third month.[25] The principal difficulty with this argument is that it attempts to clarify the opaque by an appeal to the utterly obscure: God's will, at least in matters such as the implantation of a soul, is even more difficult to discern than the personhood of the foetus.

The *viability* criterion sees personhood as inextricably tied to the ability to exist independently of the mother's womb. A foetus is thus seen as a person and having a right to life when it could survive (even with artificial means) outside the body of the mother. This criterion is clearly dependent on developments in medical technology which make it possible to keep increasingly young premature babies alive. If artificial wombs are eventually developed, then viability might be pushed back to a much earlier stage.

Finally, the *future like ours* criterion maintains that foetuses have a future, just as adult human beings have a future. Just as killing of adults is wrong because it deprives them of everything that comprises their future, so too does the killing of a foetus deprive it of its future. Don Marquis develops this argument in his article, 'Why Abortion Is Immoral' (1989).

Some philosophers have argued that other criteria are necessary conditions of personhood and that foetuses usually lack these characteristics. These are criteria we usually associate with adult human beings: reasoning, a concept of self, use of language, etc.[26] Several dangers emerge with appeals to such criteria. Most notably, these criteria may set the standard of personhood too high and

---

25 Aquinas also thought this event occurred later for females than it did for males.

26 These criteria are often particularly relevant in discussions of the end of life: at what point, if any, does a breathing human being cease to be a person?

justify not only abortion, but also infanticide, the killing of brain-damaged adults, and involuntary euthanasia.

A number of possible responses to this lack of consensus exist with regard to the conditions of personhood. Two arguments have been advanced which see this lack of consensus as supporting a conservative position on the morality of abortion. The 'let's play it safe' argument states that we cannot be absolutely sure when the foetus becomes a person, so let's be careful to err on the safe side. This is often coupled with the 'let's not be arbitrary' argument, which states that, since we do not know precisely the moment at which a foetus assumes personhood, we should assume that it becomes a person at the moment of conception and act accordingly. The moment of conception provides, according to this argument, the only non-arbitrary point of demarcation.

Other philosophers have taken quite a different tack in the face of this disagreement about the conditions of personhood. They have argued that defining the concept of a person with the necessary precision is impossible. Instead, we should turn to other moral considerations to determine whether and when abortion is morally justified.

Relevance of personhood

A widespread assumption has existed that if the foetus is a person, then abortion is morally wrong. The first major article to challenge this assumption was Judith Jarvis Thomson's 'A Defense of Abortion' (1971), which presented an intriguing example. Imagine that, without your prior knowledge or consent, you are sedated in your sleep and surgically connected to a famous violinist, who must share the use of your kidneys for nine months until he is able to survive on his own. Even granting that the violinist is obviously a full-fledged person, Thomson argues that you are morally justified in disconnecting yourself from the violinist, even if it results in his death. Going back to our diagram of the two main stages of the abortion argument, we can see that Thomson's strategy is to question the transition from 'personhood' to 'right to life.' Even granting that the dependent entity is a full person (whether foetus or violinist), we may still be morally justified in cutting off support and thereby killing that person. Thus, Thomson argues, the morality of abortion does not depend on our answer to the question of whether the foetus is a person. A more developed version of Thomson's example is Jane English's article, 'Abortion and the Concept of a Person' (1975).

Thomson's article has been criticised on many fronts, but despite these criticisms, the major impact of her piece has been to raise the possibility that the question of abortion does not depend solely on the moral status of the foetus. This opened the door to a more extensive consideration of the other principal moral consideration in this situation: the rights of the pregnant woman.

The moral status of the late-term foetus has become an even more contentious issue in the United States due to a successful movement to ban what are called 'partial-birth abortions'. Late-term abortions (which, in fact, are a very small percentage of all abortions performed) have always attracted strong criticism, but the controversy in the United States focused on a technique known medically as 'intact dilation and extraction' (IDX). Abortion critics introduced the political term 'partial-birth abortion' to describe late-term procedures that roughly overlap with IDX. In state and federal statutes, partial-birth abortion refers to a technique in which the foetus is partially extracted in an intact state before its life is terminated. In such procedures, advocates of the ban maintain, the foetus clearly experiences pain. Federal law, upheld by the Supreme Court in 2007 in *Gonzales v. Carhart*, does not make an exception to protect the health of the mother.

The rights of the pregnant woman

The second principal focus of moral concern is on the rights of the pregnant woman. Yet what precisely are these rights? At least four main candidates have been advanced: the right to privacy; the right to ownership and control over one's own body; the right to equal treatment; and the right to self-determination.

The right to privacy

In *Roe v. Wade* (1973), the United States Supreme Court based its support for a woman's right to abortion in part on the claim that the woman has a right to privacy. In US constitutional law, the right to privacy seems to have two distinct senses. First, certain behaviours, such as sexual intercourse, are usually thought to be private; the government may not infringe upon these behaviours without some particularly compelling reason (such as preventing the sexual abuse of children) for doing so. Second, some decisions in an individual's life, such as the choice of a mate or a career, are seen as matters of individual autonomy or self-determination; these are private in the sense that the government has no right to tell an individual what to do in such areas. This second sense of privacy will be discussed below in the section on the right to self-determination. In this section, we will confine our attention to the first sense of privacy.

This appeal to the right of privacy as the basis for a woman's right to choose has proved to be a peculiar justification for two reasons. First, privacy claims are difficult to justify constitutionally, since in fact the US Constitution and Bill of Rights make no explicit mention of a right to privacy. Second, the abortion procedure is certainly not private in the way in which, for example, sexual intercourse is private. It usually takes place outside the home (at a clinic or hospital) and involves a second party (a physician and staff). To be sure, the *decision* may be made in private, but what is at issue is the procedure for implementing that decision. Interestingly, this will change significantly as the French-developed abortion pill, RU-486, is more widely used. Under new protocols developed for the drug, the pregnant woman may only have to make a single visit to a physician to obtain a prescription.

The right to ownership of one's own body

Some have argued that the right to abortion is based on a woman's right to control her own body, and in some instances this is seen as a property right. This approach also seems wide of the mark. To be sure, no one else owns our bodies, and in this sense we appear to have the right to control our own bodies. However, it is doubtful whether the relationship we have with our own bodies is best understood in terms of ownership and whether the presence of the foetus is most perspicuously grasped as the intrusion onto private property.

The right to equal treatment

Some jurists, most notably Ruth Bader Ginsburg (1993), have suggested that a woman's right to abortion may be best justified constitutionally through an appeal to the right to equal protection under the law. Pregnancy results from the combined actions of two people, yet the woman typically bears a disproportionate amount of the responsibility and burden. This line of reasoning seems highly relevant to striking down laws and regulations that discriminate against women because of pregnancy, but it is unclear whether this alone is sufficient to support a right to abortion. In fact, it would seem that some other, more fundamental right must be at stake here.

The right to self-determination

When we consider the actual conflict that many women experience in making the decision about abortion, it would seem that it centres primarily around the effects that an unwanted pregnancy and child would have on their lives. The most fundamental right at issue for the pregnant woman in this context appears to be the right to determine the course of her own life. In this context, it is relevant to ask *how much* the pregnancy would interfere with the woman's life. As John Martin Fisher (1991) has pointed out, one of the misleading aspects of Thomson's violinist example is that it suggests that pregnancy would virtually eliminate one's choices for nine months. In actuality, the violinist case would be comparable only to the most difficult of pregnancies, such as those which require months of strict bed rest. However in most cases, pregnancy does not involve such an extreme restriction on the woman's everyday life; the restrictions on self-determination are much less.

In what ways do pregnancy and childbirth potentially conflict with self-determination? Consider first of all the extremes on the spectrum. On the one hand, imagine a most grave threat to self-determination: a rape that resulted in an extremely difficult pregnancy that required constant bed rest, childbirth that contained a high risk of the mother's death, and the likelihood that the child would require years of constant medical attention. Conception, pregnancy, delivery, and the child would all severely limit (if not destroy) many of the mother's choices in life. These carry enormous moral weight. On the other hand, an easy pregnancy and birth of a perfectly healthy baby are potentially much less restrictive to a woman's power of self-determination. Raising a child, of course, is potentially quite restrictive to self-determination, but in those cases where adoption is a reasonable option, raising the child is not necessary.

There is a further perplexity about self-determination. It is reasonable, as Fisher and others have done, to distinguish between what is central to one's self-determination and what is peripheral to it. We intuitively recognise this when we hear, for example, of a pianist whose hands have been crushed. Although such an accident would be terrible for anyone, it is especially terrible for a person whose life is devoted to making music with his or her hands. If the pianist were to become colour-blind, this would be much less serious since it would not strike as centrally at the pianist's sense of self. We would have a quite different assessment of colour-blindness in a painter, however. Yet the perplexity centres on those cases in which people make something central to their sense of identity that we, as outsiders, would consider peripheral at best. For example, the couple who want an abortion because bearing a child would force them to postpone a holiday for two months seem to be giving undue weight to the timing of their holiday. What if, to take an even more extreme case, a female bank robber decided on an abortion because pregnancy would interfere with robbing banks? Are there any limits to what can legitimately be taken as central to self-determination?

In the politically highly charged context of the United States, opposing sides in the debate recognize that women often make decisions about terminating a pregnancy under conditions that are far from ideal. The so-called pro-life side urges counselling, information sessions, and a built-in delay to allow women to reflect on their choice, presumably in the hope that they will not go ahead with the abortion. The so-called pro-choice advocates oppose such measures, seeing them as coercive. Young women in these circumstances often find themselves faced with other pressures as well from the biological father (either to have the child or to have an abortion), her parents and other family members (again, this may go in either direction), her faith community (usually not to terminate the pregnancy), and financial factors (usually pointing toward terminating the pregnancy).

Other moral considerations

Feminist concerns about abortion

For many thinkers, especially feminists, the issue of abortion must be understood within the context of the oppression of women. Indeed, this gives a special importance to the right of self-determination as one which must be defended all the more vigilantly in a context of oppression. Rape provides the most extreme example of this oppression within the realm of sexuality, but the oppression of women is not confined to this sphere. For some women, rape has become a metaphor for understanding many of the sexual relations between men and women. Whether we choose to use the word 'rape' or not, most of us can agree that many areas exist outside paradigmatic rape cases in which sexual intercourse is less than fully consensual. There is a growing recognition that rape often occurs between acquaintances, friends, and even spouses. Moreover, it is increasingly clear that many situations exist in which women feel pressured (although the threat of physical force is not present) into sexual intercourse without their full consent. In addition to this, we live in a society in which men value highly the feeling that they are the ones in control of sexuality. Given all of this, feminists argue that it is imperative that women have the right to determine whether to bring a pregnancy to term.

Abortion and racism

Among some African-Americans and other minority groups in the United States, there is a concern that the emphasis on abortion rights has racist overtones. In particular, their concern is that abortion and forced sterilisation might be used as a means of controlling minority populations. This concern issue is not limited to the United States: in many countries, members of oppressed minority populations fear that the majority government may be using abortion and enforced sterilisation as means of reducing the minority population. The history of such compulsory sterilisation programs in the early twentieth century in the United States is often seen as providing support for this concern. Moreover, the history of the relationship between the medical establishment in the United States and African-Americans makes such fears understandable. The Tuskegee syphilis experiment, in which African-American men were allowed to die from syphilis without treatment until the early 1970s in order to further research in this area, typifies the type of cases to which African-Americans point in order to make their concerns more understandable to those who have not suffered such discrimination. Similarly, as pressure grows to reduce or eliminate support for welfare programmes to support families in poverty, some see a growing pressure on women, and perhaps especially on minority women, to choose abortion. Ironically, this has resulted in some very conservative, anti-abortion Christian groups being on the same side as outspoken opponents of white racism who are at the opposite end of the political spectrum.

The rights of the father

The past twenty-five years have shown increasing interest in our understanding of fatherhood. This raises important issues in regard to the proper role of the father in making decisions regarding abortion. What rights, if any, does a biological father have when he disagrees with the woman's choice regarding abortion? Do any circumstances exist in which the man's choice should take precedence over the woman's? Two types of cases are imaginable. On the one hand, the man may wish to have the foetus brought to term, but the woman may want to abort it; on the other hand, these roles may be reversed. Under what conditions, if any, do the father's preferences count? Do those conditions have to do with the initial circumstances of conception? With the present state of their relationship? With the assumption of future responsibilities for the child?

Some feminist concerns seem to conflict directly with concerns about the rights of the father in the decision-making process. The issue, of course, is that women's oppression has been primarily at the hands of men, and any attempts at recognising the rights of the father may seem to be an act of returning power to the oppressors. Moreover, it seems to ignore the asymmetry between men and women with regard to child-bearing. Although the act of conception requires both a male and female contribution, it is the woman who carries the foetus to term and undergoes childbirth. A man can be a father and never know it, but the same is not true for a woman. A woman bears the direct weight of pregnancy and childbirth in a way that men do not and cannot. The strongest argument against giving the father a decisive voice is precisely the fact that women bear the responsibilities of pregnancy and childbirth so much more directly, strongly, and unavoidably than men.

Given these reservations, two additional points need to be made about the rights of fathers. First, rights entail responsibilities. To the extent that a father has a voice in the decision, he presumably also has correlative responsibilities toward the baby (and indirectly toward the mother). Second, this situation is perhaps not best understood in terms of rights; rather, especially within the context of long-term committed relationships, the appeal to rights may occur only when the situation has disintegrated.

The principle of double effect

Centuries of Christian theology and philosophy have finely honed what is known at the 'principle of the double effect', which allows us to perform certain actions that would otherwise be immoral. Typically, four conditions have to be met for an action to be morally permissible: 1) the action itself must be either morally good or at least morally neutral; 2) the bad consequences must not be intended; 3) the good consequences cannot be the direct causal result of the bad consequences; and 4) the good consequences must be proportionate to the bad consequences. For example, the principle of the double effect allows a physician to remove a life-threatening cancerous uterus from a pregnant woman, even if the foetus is thereby killed. Removal of the uterus is in itself morally neutral; it is not done in order to abort the foetus; the elimination of the cancer does not result from the killing of the foetus; and the saving of the woman's life is proportionate to the termination of the pregnancy.

A consequentialist concern

Some philosophers have expressed concern about the possible consequences of widespread abortion if it is used to select the sex of a child. The argument is a simple enough one, even if it is not easy to judge the factual claims on which it is based. If abortion is widely used as a means of choosing to bring primarily male babies to term, it may well create a gender imbalance in society with undesirable long-term consequences. This concern does not centre on abortion *per se* and would be equally applicable to pre-conception sex-selection methods, if such methods became widely available. In some Asian countries, we currently see a significant imbalance between newborn males and females. In China, the current ratio is over 120 males to 100 females. India has outlawed the practice of abortion for sex selection.

Abortion and compromise: seeking a common ground

Initially, no room for compromise may seem apparent in matters of abortion. If it is the intentional killing of an innocent human being, then it cannot be countenanced. If it does not involve killing a human being, then it should not be prohibited. It is either wrong or right, and there seems to be little middle ground. Yet as we begin to reflect on the issue, we see that areas of potential cooperation do indeed exist. Let us briefly consider several such areas here.

Reducing unwanted pregnancies

One of the striking aspects of the abortion issue is its potential avoidability. Abortions occur with unwanted pregnancies. To the extent that we can reduce unwanted pregnancies, we can reduce abortions. Certainly there are cases of unwanted pregnancy due to rape or incest, and there are certainly other cases due to the failure of contraceptive devices. Unfortunately, despite our best efforts, none of these types of cases is likely to be completely eliminated in the future. However they comprise only a small percentage of the cases of unwanted pregnancies; moreover, there is already agreement that these should be further reduced.

The single most common cause of unwanted pregnancies is sexual intercourse without contraception. To the extent that this can be reduced, the number of abortions can be reduced. Conservatives and liberals can agree on this goal, although they may emphasise quite different ways of achieving it. Conservatives will stress the virtue of chastity and the value of abstinence. Liberals will stress the importance of contraceptives and family planning. Along with this, many feminists will urge social and political changes that will ensure that women have at least an equal voice in decisions about sexual intercourse. Some will respond to the conservative call, others to the liberal program, still others to the feminist concerns. Yet the common result may be the reduction of unwanted pregnancies and, with that, the reduction of abortions. In addition to this, an increase in responsibility in the area of sexuality may help to reduce the spread of AIDS and other sexually communicated diseases.

Ensuring genuinely free and informed choice

There is widespread agreement amongst almost all parties that a choice made freely is better than one made under pressure or duress. There are several ways of increasing the likelihood of genuinely free and informed choice. First, *the earlier the choice, the better*. Many people maintain that the more the foetus is developed, the more morally serious is the decision to abort. Although conservatives would maintain that all abortions are equally wrong, encouraging an early decision would not contradict their beliefs. Second, *women should have the opportunity to make the choice without undue outside pressure*. Undue outside pressure can be reduced in a number of ways, most notably through providing genuinely impartial counselling in an atmosphere devoid of coercion (demonstrations, etc.). Third, *alternatives to abortion should be available*. These include adoption (for those who wish to give their baby up), aid to dependent children (for those who wish to raise their own babies), child care (for those who work full time and raise children), and adequate maternity leave.

Abortion and sorrow

Naomi Wolf (1995) refers to a Japanese practice that honours the memory of departed foetuses. This is called *Mizuko Kuyo*. A number of resources relating to this practice are available on the web page on abortion at http://ethics.sandiego.edu/applied/abortion/. Philosophically, one of the most interesting aspects of this practice is that it unites two elements that are rarely brought together in the American philosophical discussion of abortion. In the practice of *Mizuko Kuyo*, couples who have had an abortion dedicate a doll at a temple to the memory of the departed foetus. To some extent, this is analogous to the practice of lighting a candle in Christian churches. What is noteworthy is that Japanese society both permits abortion and at the same time recognises that it is a sorrowful occasion. In most instances, American philosophical literature chooses one or the other of these elements, but not both simultaneously.

Living together with moral differences

Abortion is a particularly interesting and important moral issue, for it poses most clearly to us as a society the question of how we can live together with deep moral differences. There are intelligent people of good will on all sides of the abortion controversy, genuinely trying to do what they believe is right. The challenge for all of us in such situations is to view one another in this light and seek to create a community that embraces and respects our differences while at the same time preserving our moral integrity.

References

Aquinas, St. Thomas (1266–73) *Summa Theologica*.

English, J. (1975) 'Abortion and the Concept of a Person'. *Canadian Journal of Philosophy* 5(2), 235.

Fisher, J. M. (1991) 'Abortion and Self-Determination'. *Journal of Social Philosophy* 22, 5–13.

Ginsburg, R. B. (1993) US Senate Nomination Hearing. Excerpts in *New York Times*, 22 July 1993.

Marquis, D. (1989) 'Why Abortion is Immoral'. *Journal of Philosophy* 86 (4).

Noonan, J. T. (1970) 'An Almost Absolute Value in History.' In J. T. Noonan, ed., *The Morality of Abortion*. Cambridge, MA: Harvard University Press.

Roe v. Wade (1973), 410 US 113.

The Silent Scream (1980) Brunswick, Ohio: American Portrait Films.

Thomson, J. J. (1971) 'A Defense of Abortion'. *Philosophy and Public Affairs*, autumn 1971.

Wolf, N. (1995) 'Our Bodies, Our Souls'. *The New Republic*, 16 October 1995.

PROLOGUE: **EUTHANASIA**

Many of the issues raised in the debates about passive or active euthanasia, even in countries where some forms are legalised, bear striking similarities to those in the abortion debate. While most countries prohibit euthanasia, it remains the subject of legal battles in many jurisdictions and has become legally acceptable in a minority (e.g. the Netherlands). The 2005 case of Terri Schiavo in the United States brought the debate to prominence once again. Supporters of the 'right to life' campaign argued that only God had the right to decide when Schiavo's life should have ended. The obvious irony, of course, is that without human intervention, Schiavo would have died years ago. This was the basis of the opposing view and was ultimately the court's view as well. Professor Hinman's examples again highlight this sliding scale of ethical and moral responsibility.

Chapter 5

Euthanasia: an Introduction to the Moral Issues[27]

Lawrence M. Hinman

Introduction

Birth and death, the two most human of events, have become increasingly medicalised in the last half century in many industrialised countries. This has transformed our way of dying, creating unintended consequences that have changed – and at times distorted – the contours of our end-of-life experiences. Because medical technology is increasingly effective at keeping people alive, even when the quality of their lives is minimal, death has become a decision in a way that it has never been before. Ever greater numbers of people must decide to die – or more precisely, to decide to stop fighting to live and to forego life-sustaining treatment in favour of palliative care. Increasingly, people die in a medical context – often a hospital – that is unfamiliar to them and populated primarily by strangers, filled with bright lights and the noises of machines. Currently, 85% of Americans die in some kind of healthcare facility (not only hospitals, but nursing homes, hospices, etc.). Of this group, 70% (equivalent to almost 60% of the population as a whole) choose to withhold some kind of life-sustaining treatment (Miles and Gomez 1988). It is highly likely that many of us will eventually face that same decision about ourselves; it is even more likely that we will be indirectly involved in that decision as family members and loved ones face death.

Dying in a hospital is particularly difficult, for little within medicine itself helps physicians to 'let go', to allow an individual to die peacefully. As Callahan (1995) has pointed out, medicine is often tenaciously committed to winning every possible battle with death, even without hope of ever winning the war. Many physicians show great wisdom in dealing with this, but their wisdom flows primarily from their personal character rather than from their medical knowledge. Medical knowledge alone rarely tells us when to let go, and

---

27 An earlier version of this chapter was published in Hinman, L. M. (2005) *Contemporary Moral Issues: Diversity and Consensus.* Third Edition. Upper Saddle River, NJ: Prentice-Hall.

medical practice – perhaps quite rightly – is often committed to fighting on and on, no matter what the odds. The concept of medical futility, brought to prominence by Larry Schneiderman and others, provides one of the more systematic attempts to articulate quantitative and qualitative guidelines to specify when no legitimate medical purpose exists in prolonging treatment. Such judgements remain both difficult and contentious, despite efforts to make them. Yet this means that each of us as patients and as relatives and loved ones must face this question squarely.

In the United States, the case of Terri Schiavo created the medical equivalent of a 'perfect storm' in which contending and conflicting parties (motivated by personal, political, and legal concerns) vied for control over her fate while she languished in what was diagnosed as a persistent vegetative state for fifteen years. After several years, in which a number of treatments were tried to no avail, Terri Schiavo's husband wanted to have her feeding tube removed. Her parents disagreed. The parties involved made many conflicting claims, as did many who were not directly involved. Political and religious groups became involved, and issues about abortion rights and disability rights hovered in the background. The Florida courts, legislature, and governor became involved in the fray, and eventually the President, the Supreme Court, and Congress of the United States. She died on 31 March, 2005, approximately two weeks after her feeding tube was removed for the final time. Autopsy results were consistent with the diagnosis of a persistent vegetative state, and her brain damage, including to the visual cortex, was judged to be irreversible.

Whatever constitutes a 'good death', this was not it. As the author Joan Didion (2005) subsequently pointed out, the public outrage, charges and counter-charges, name-calling and political posturing served to obscure the most difficult questions about what constitutes a life worth living and about when society is willing to limit an individual's access to advanced health care and indefinite care. Let us now consider some of these questions.

What is our goal?

Before we begin to consider some of the intricate conceptual issues euthanasia poses, we need to ask ourselves what our goal is in this area. In discussions of abortion (see Chapter 4 of this text), most people would agree that the ultimate goal is to have a society with no unwanted pregnancies; at that point, abortion would disappear as a moral issue. In the case of euthanasia the situation is very different. Clearly we are not striving for a society in which there are no unwanted deaths; that would not only be impossible, but also – at least from a population point of view – undesirable. We cannot do away with death or avoid it.

Given this basic fact, our goal in this area presumably centres around *how* we die, not whether we die. The word 'euthanasia' comes from the Greek, *eu*, which means 'good' or 'well', and the Greek word for death, *thanatos*. In its broadest sense, euthanasia is about dying well. How do we do this?

The first and most obvious point is that dying well is intimately linked to living well. It is highly unlikely that we will die well if we have not been able to live well. Those who die surrounded by loved ones and at peace with themselves are likely to be those who have lived lives filled with love and who have come to peace with their lives; their lives are, in a certain fundamental sense, complete and not marred by unresolved fundamental regrets. It is likely to be very different for those who have not found love or peace in their lives, whose deaths are often characterised by loneliness and a sense of incompleteness, a grasping for what could have been. Much of what needs to be said about euthanasia is not about death, but about life. A good life is the best preparation for a good death. Unfortunately, even a good life is no guarantee of a good death; chance can always intervene to make one's death untimely, unbearably painful, or uncharacteristically lonely.

There is a second and much narrower sense of euthanasia, namely a (relatively) painless death free from the distress and the intrusion of medical attempts to sustain life. Most of the philosophical discussion has centred on this second sense of euthanasia, but some of the difficulties that arise in this can be reduced if it is placed within the context of the wider sense of euthanasia. All too often, we try through medical means to help an individual to die well, when in actuality all that is within reach medically is to help the person die painlessly and quickly. A quick and painless death is not the same thing as a good death, but sometimes it is the best we can do.

Some initial distinctions

Several important distinctions have dominated recent discussions of euthanasia, as has disagreement over exactly how the distinctions are drawn and what significance they should have. The three most important of these are the distinction between active and passive euthanasia, voluntary and involuntary euthanasia, and assisted and unassisted euthanasia. The next sections consider each of these in turn.

Active v. passive euthanasia

The distinction between active and passive euthanasia seems, on the surface, easy enough. Active euthanasia occurs in those instances in which someone takes active means, such as a lethal injection, to bring about someone's death; passive euthanasia occurs in those instances in which someone simply refuses to intervene in order to prevent someone's death. In a hospital setting, a DNR (Do Not Resuscitate) order is one of the most common means of passive euthanasia. The American Medical Association condemns active euthanasia but permits passive euthanasia. Beginning with the work of James Rachels, both the conceptual clarity and the moral significance of this distinction came into question.

Conceptual clarity

This distinction has been attacked in at least two ways. First, some have attacked the conceptual clarity of the distinction, arguing that the line between active and passive is much more blurred than one might initially think. One reason this distinction becomes conceptually slippery, especially in regard to the notion of passive euthanasia, is that it is embedded in a set of assumptions about what constitutes normal care and what constitutes the normal duties of care-givers. Typical hospital settings distinguish between ordinary and extraordinary care. At one end of the spectrum, giving someone food and water is clearly ordinary care; at the other, giving someone an emergency heart and lung transplant to save that person's life is clearly extraordinary care. Refusing to give food and water seems to be different to refusing to perform a transplant. Both are passive, but one involves falling below the expectations of normal care while the other does not. Typically, DNRs would fall somewhere in the middle of this scale. The source of this conceptual slipperiness comes from the need to distinguish between two levels of passive euthanasia: a) refusing to provide extraordinary care, and b) refusing to provide any life-sustaining care at all. Just as in daily life we would distinguish between the person who refuses to jump into a turbulent sea to save a drowning child and the person who refuses to reach into a bathtub to save a baby drowning, so too in medical contexts we must distinguish between refusing to take extraordinary means to prevent death and refusing to provide normal care (such as nutrition and hydration) to sustain life.

There is at least a second reason why this distinction is conceptually slippery, especially with regard to the notion of active euthanasia. In Chapter 4 of this text on abortion, philosophers distinguish between the intended consequences of an action and the unintended (but foreseeable) consequences. This distinction is crucial to the principle of the 'double effect', which under certain specifiable conditions morally permits an individual to perform an action that would otherwise not be allowed. Many Catholic ethicists, for example, would argue that a physician may be morally permitted to perform a surgical procedure such as a hysterectomy to remove a cancerous uterus even if this results in the death of a foetus, as long as the intention was not to kill the foetus, the cause was serious, and no other means to that end was evident. Similarly, physicians might give certain terminal patients painkillers in large dosages, realising that such dosages might cause death but having no other way of alleviating the patient's extreme pain.

Moral significance

In addition to attacking the conceptual clarity of the active/passive distinction, some ethicists have attacked the moral significance of this distinction. The standard view is that active euthanasia is morally much more questionable than passive euthanasia since it involves actively choosing to bring about the death of a human being. Critics of the moral significance of this distinction have argued that active euthanasia is often more compassionate than passive euthanasia and thus morally preferable. The typical type of case they adduce is one in which a) there is no doubt that the patient will die soon; b) the option of passive euthanasia causes significantly more pain for the patient (and often the family as well) than active euthanasia and does nothing to enhance the remaining life of the patient; and c) passive measures will not bring about the death of the patient. Certain types of cancers are not only extremely painful, but also very resistant to pain-killing medications in dosages that still permit patients to be aware of themselves and those around them. It is not uncommon for situations to occur in which patients will undoubtedly die (within several days, if not hours) and in which their remaining time will be filled either with extreme pain or unconsciousness resulting from pain medication. Removal of life-support may not bring about the death of such patients if their heart and respiratory systems have not been seriously compromised. In such situations, passive euthanasia seems to be more cruel than active euthanasia and therefore morally less preferable.

Voluntary, non-voluntary, and involuntary euthanasia

The second crucial distinction in discussion of euthanasia is among voluntary, non-voluntary, and involuntary euthanasia. Voluntary euthanasia occurs when the individual chooses to die; non-voluntary euthanasia occurs when death is brought about (either actively or passively) without the individual's choosing to die; and involuntary euthanasia occurs when the death is brought about against the individual's wishes. Several points need to be made about this distinction.

The distinction between non-voluntary and involuntary

Involuntary euthanasia covers those cases in which an individual does not want to be euthanased; non-voluntary euthanasia refers to those in which the individual cannot make an expressed choice at all. The former class of cases is clearly troubling: the individual wishes to live and someone else intentionally terminates that individual's life. Most would say that this is simply murder. The latter class of cases is more common and morally more ambiguous. How do we treat those individuals, usually terminally ill and unable to choose (due to coma or some other medical condition), who may be in great pain and who have never clearly expressed their wishes about euthanasia in the past?

103

Similarly, infants are unable to express their wishes about this (or any other) matter. If euthanasia is employed in such cases, it is involuntary, but not in the same sense as it is involuntary when the patient has expressed a clear wish not to be euthanased.

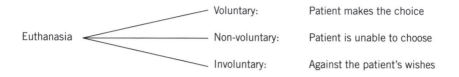

Euthanasia
- Voluntary: Patient makes the choice
- Non-voluntary: Patient is unable to choose
- Involuntary: Against the patient's wishes

Cases of involuntary euthanasia in which the patient is unable to choose are arguably the most morally troubling.

Assisted v. unassisted euthanasia

The final important distinction in the discussion of euthanasia centres on the fact that many instances of euthanasia occur when an individual is no longer physically able to carry out the act. Assistance becomes necessary either to perform the action at all or at least to die in a relatively painless and non-violent way. Situations in which assistance is needed are common: someone may not be able even to reach for a bottle of pills; swallowing functions may be compromised due to stroke or other debility, and so on. Several important points need to be noted about this distinction.

The following chart helps us to see the ways in which these basic distinctions relate to one another, the types of acts they designate and, in the United States at least, their current legal status.

Euthanasia: Some fundamental distinctions in the US

	Passive	Active: not assisted	Active: assisted
Voluntary	Currently legal; often contained in living wills	Equivalent to suicide for the patient	Equivalent to suicide for the patient; possibly equivalent to murder for the assistant
Non-voluntary Patient not able to choose	Sometimes legal, but only with court permission	Not possible	Equivalent either to suicide or being murdered for the patient; legally equivalent to murder for the assistant
Involuntary Against patient's wishes	Not legal	Not possible	Equivalent to being murdered for the patient; equivalent to murder for assistant

Equipped with these distinctions, the next section turns to a consideration of the fundamental moral issues euthanasia raises, looking first at justifications for and against euthanasia, then considering the three most typical types of cases: defective newborns, adults with profoundly diminished lives, and those in the final and painful phase of a terminal illness.

Euthanasia as the compassionate response to suffering

One of the principal moral motives for euthanasia is compassion: we see needless suffering, whether in ourselves or others, we want to alleviate or end it, and euthanasia is the only available means. The paradigmatic situation here is that of a patient who is near death, who is in great pain that is not responsive to medication, and who has made an informed choice to die. At that juncture, those who care about the patient simply want the patient's suffering to end – there seems to be no point in further suffering, for there is no hope of recovery – and euthanasia becomes the way of ending it.

It is important to understand the *intention* contained in this kind of response. The direct intention is not to kill the patient; neither does its utilitarian intention concern the reduction of the overall amount of suffering; nor is it an egoistic intention that simply seeks to be rid of an annoying relative. Rather, the direct intention is simply to stop the patient's pointless suffering. In passive euthanasia, this means withholding or withdrawing life-sustaining treatment; in active euthanasia, this requires some action, such as a lethal injection, that brings about the death of the patient. There are certainly situations in which passive euthanasia would not quickly end the suffering; patients may continue to live, sometimes for days, in great agony once life support has been removed. In such cases, active euthanasia offers the only avenue for ending the pain. It is precisely this type of response that has come to be known as 'mercy killing'. If any situation justifies active euthanasia, this would seem to be the epitome.

Some cases of compassionate euthanasia can be viewed as an instance of the principle of double effect: if a physician were administering increasingly large doses of pain medication which eventually and foreseeably resulted in the patient's death, this could be covered under the principle of double effect, as long as the intention throughout was to relieve the patient's pain. It is not clear, however, whether this is really euthanasia; it seems better described as a last-ditch, high risk attempt to alleviate the patient's suffering.

In one sense the motivation and justification of compassionate euthanasia may appear to be utilitarian, or at least consequentialist, in character: the concern is with eliminating pointless suffering. It asks what good comes from the suffering and what bad comes from the termination of the suffering. However two ways exist in which the motivation for this response is not utilitarian in the standard sense. First, it is concerned principally, perhaps even

105

exclusively, with the welfare of the patient, not with the *overall* welfare. Second, it is not a *calculated* response in the way in which classical utilitarianism is; rather, it is a response from the heart, a compassionate response that seeks to eliminate the pointless suffering of someone we care about. It arises not out of calculation, but out of care.

The adjective 'pointless' is crucial here for two reasons. First, it indicates that euthanasia is not a proper response to *all* suffering – only to that suffering which serves no purpose. Generally, suffering that results in the patient's getting better (or at least improving to some minimally acceptable level) is not seen as pointless. Second, it helps explain part of the disagreement in our own society about the morality of euthanasia. Our views on euthanasia will depend in part on our background assumptions about the nature and purpose of suffering. Once again, we see that at least two distinct traditions exist here. On the one hand, many in our society hold that suffering always has a purpose – usually a purpose that God can discern, even if we mere mortals cannot. It may build character, purify an individual, provide an example to others, provide retribution, or serve some part in a larger plan beyond our grasp. On this view, even the suffering in the final stage of a terminal illness serves some purpose, although we may not be able to say what it is. On the other hand, many others in our society believe that suffering is simply an unqualified evil that should be eradicated whenever possible. Suffering, in this view, is pointless in itself, even if it is sometimes unavoidable for the sake of some other goal such as recovering from an illness. These two views on suffering will be discussed in more detail in the next section.

This compassionate response may not be limited just to cases of extreme pain in terminally ill patients; it may extend, at least in respect to passive euthanasia, to cases of extreme physical debility or to cases of Alzheimer's where the individual's personal identity has long been lost. The principal criterion here would seem to be the individual's wish no longer to be alive under such conditions – whether that wish is currently expressed or had been expressed clearly at an earlier point in life. Again, the focus here is on what the person wants and what is in the person's best interest.

The sanctity of life and the right to die

Very few villains exist in the debate over euthanasia, but disagreements are evident about the interpretation and relative place of certain fundamental values and rights. One of the most prominent areas of conflict centres around the relationship between the sanctity of life and the right to die.

The sanctity of life

At one end of the spectrum is the belief that human life is sacred. In its original form, this belief is a religious one; the sanctity of life is an indication that life is a gift from God and therefore cannot be ended by human hand without violating God's law or rejecting God's love. Moreover, in its original form – one sees this most clearly in Buddhism, but also in other religious traditions – this belief encompasses *all* life, not just human life. In this form, it is not only a tradition that encompasses pacifism and opposes capital punishment, abortion, and euthanasia, but also one that respects the lives of animals and the living environment as a whole. Life is a sacred gift from God, and it is not the proper role of human beings to take it away from anyone. Respect for life, in the words of one Catholic bishop, is a 'seamless garment' which covers the entire fabric of living creation (Bernardin 2000). No distinction is drawn about the quality of life. All life is to be respected, loved, and cared for. It is this tradition which leads to the compassion of the Buddha and of Mother Theresa.

Followers of this tradition do not support either active or passive euthanasia in the senses discussed here. However, they certainly are committed to the broader sense of 'dying well' discussed above, and spiritual discipline is often part of that commitment. So, too, is ministering to the sick and dying. Their alternative to active or passive euthanasia in the Western sense is not neglect, but compassion and love and ministering to the sick, the infirm, and the dying.

The right to die

Those who argue that human beings have a right to die usually differ from those who stress the sanctity of life on two principal points. First, and more importantly, those at this end of the spectrum do not see life as a gift from God which cannot be disposed of at will; instead, they often see life ontologically as an accident and almost always morally as the possession of an individual. The dominant metaphor here is of life as property rather than gift. In this tradition, each person is seen as *owning* his or her own life, and owners are allowed to do whatever they want with their property. Second, respect for life in this tradition entails allowing the proper owner – that is, the individual – to decide for him or herself whether to continue living. This tradition does not deny respect for life; rather, it has a different view of the source of life and of who holds proper dominion over life.

Those in this tradition respond quite differently to illnesses that profoundly reduce the quality of an individual's life or produce great and needless pain. Their focus is on reducing suffering, maintaining a minimal threshold of quality for the individual's life, and encouraging individuals to make their own decisions about the termination of their own lives. The focus is thus on the quality of life and individual autonomy. The types of cases that those in this tradition point to are usually cases in which individuals want to die in order to end their suffering but are kept alive against their own wishes because a family member, the court, or in some cases the administrators of health care facilities, ever fearful of legal action and investigations, are unwilling to let them die.

However an irony is also evident in this tradition, for its emphasis on technology and control helps to create the very problem which it then seeks to solve through euthanasia. Just as it prolongs life through technology, it then must figure out how to end life technologically. Active euthanasia for the chronically ill and slowly dying rarely arises as an issue in non-technological societies because, prior to the introduction of modern, high-tech medicine, people either died or got better.

The conflict of traditions

Understanding the nature of this disagreement is important − and it is especially important to avoid certain foreseeable domains of misunderstanding. This is not a conflict between those who respect life and those who do not, nor is it a conflict between those who are indifferent to suffering and those who seek to eliminate it. Rather, it is a conflict between two traditions, both of which respect life, and both of which encourage compassion and the reduction of suffering. The differences between them centre around how they understand life, how they place suffering within that larger understanding of life, and what they accept as legitimate ways of reducing suffering.

How do we respond to such a conflict? Certainly one common response is to look for a winner, marshalling arguments in support of one tradition and against the other. My own inclination, however, is quite different. I argue that we are better off as a society precisely because both of these traditions are present and vital. Each keeps the other in check, as it were. The sanctity of life tradition continually reminds us of our own frailty, of the fact that we are not masters of the universe; it checks our inclination toward *hubris*. The 'right to die' tradition, on the other hand, stresses the importance of reducing suffering in the world and increasing individual autonomy. Our moral world would arguably be impoverished if we had only one of these traditions. The next section examines how this works in practice.

The value of life and the cost of caring

In *Groundwork of the Metaphysic of Morals*, Immanuel Kant drew a crucial moral distinction between rational beings and mere objects. Everything, Kant maintains, has either a *price* or a *dignity*. Mere objects always have a price, that is, an equivalent value of some kind (usually a monetary one); they can be exchanged one for the other. Rational beings, however, have dignity, for the value of a human being is such that it is beyond all calculations of price; they cannot be exchanged. In drawing this distinction, Kant articulated a moral insight which remains powerful today: the belief that human life is priceless and that we therefore ought not to attach a price tag. Human life is to be preserved at all costs, for the value of human life is beyond that of any costs. Indeed, this may well be one of the motivations in critical care situations when the full arsenal of medicine's skill and technology is brought to bear on a frail, old, dying person in order to prolong his or her life for a few days, weeks, or even months. We cannot put a price tag on human life, the Kantian inside us says. There is something morally odious about thinking that a human life can be traded for something else.

Many of us find that Kant's insight strikes a resonant chord in our moral lives, but that another, potentially dissonant note is present in all of this. Costs *do* matter, as utilitarians such as Richard Brandt (1992) make clear, although much disagreement exists about the kinds of costs and how much they matter. We can see this on both the personal level and on the level of social policy. On the personal level, individuals and families struggle with this issue. Imagine a family with a member who requires costly and continual medical care that goes well beyond insurance or state provision; family resources – emotional as well as financial – may be drained in the attempt to continue care. Here costs are not simply monetary, but also emotional and spiritual. Financial costs are not limited simply to restrictions on the family holiday, but may extend into areas such as education that directly affect the welfare and futures of any children in the family. Similarly, emotional, social, and spiritual costs to the family may be quite high, although these costs may be more evenly distributed over the range of options.

On the social policy level, we recognise that an amazingly large percentage of our taxes for health care are spent on people during the final weeks of their lives, and ethicists such as Daniel Callahan (1995 and 1999) have maintained that we ought not to spend our resources in this way. Although firmly opposing active euthanasia, Callahan maintains that we should respect the natural life span and that we should not use intrusive means such as respirators and feeding tubes to keep the elderly alive. Here we have some degree of passive involuntary euthanasia, at least for those who lack the private financial resources to pay for continued extraordinary care in countries without socialised medicine. This raises the spectre of involuntary passive euthanasia for all but the rich. Of course, this is only an inequity if we believe that a longer life under such conditions is better than a shorter one.

Slippery slopes

Even among those who are not opposed to euthanasia in principle, serious reservations arise about the possibility that legalisation of euthanasia could lead to abuses. Once the door opens even a little, the danger is that more will be permitted – either through further legalisation or because of objectionable but common abuses which, while not permitted by the new proposal, could not be curbed effectively – than we originally wanted. History makes us cautious. Euthanasia of the physically and mentally handicapped was part of Hitler's plan, and by some estimates as many as 200,000 handicapped people were killed as part of the Nazi extermination programme. Not surprisingly, many are watching the Netherlands very carefully now, where active euthanasia has been tolerated for a number of years and was legalised in 1994.[28]

Undervalued groups

The 'slippery slope' argument has an added dimension when placed within a social context of discrimination. In a society in which the lives of certain classes of people are typically undervalued, legalised euthanasia could become a further instrument of discrimination. The classes discriminated against may vary from society to society, and the classes may be based on race, ethnicity, gender, social orientation, religious beliefs, social class, age, or some other characteristic. However the classes are determined, the point remains the same: legalised euthanasia may be more likely to encourage the early deaths of members of those classes that are discriminated against in society. For this argument to work, it must either presuppose that euthanasia is bad in itself or else that it would encourage certain morally unjustified kinds of euthanasia such as involuntary euthanasia. The latter line of argument seems to be plausible, namely, that the legalisation of voluntary euthanasia would result in undue pressure on certain segments of society to 'choose' euthanasia when the choice has clearly not been theirs.

The United States certainly has no shortage of undervalued groups. Some groups are racially constituted: some Native Americans and some African Americans feel that their people have been treated in ways that have genocidal overtones (see for example Stannard 1983; Churchill 1998; Davis 1983). For them, it is extremely important that they have especially strong guarantees that they will not be the objects of euthanasia disproportionately. Similar issues exist for the poor and the homeless, but they are often less able to advance their own interests in public fora. Finally, and perhaps most pervasively, the elderly in the United States (and elsewhere as well) form a group that is highly undervalued. Several factors contribute to this. First, our (Western) society tends to value youth rather than age, aggressive problem–solving intelligence and new ideas rather than the wisdom of long experience. Second, our society tends to value work, and the elderly are often retired and no longer deemed to be productive. Third, our society tends to be highly mobile, and as a result elderly parents often live in a different location from their children; extended, loving families are hard to find. Fourth, as the percentage of the entire population that is over the age of sixty–five grows, this will put increasing pressure on social welfare resources; the possibility of increasing resentment toward the aged by younger generations in Western societies is certainly great.

---

28   For further discussion on this issue, see for example Pool (2000) and Griffiths et al. (2008).

Moral pluralism

Any satisfactory proposal for liberalising the euthanasia laws must contain adequate provisions to prevent a slide down the slope to unacceptable practices. In this way a pluralistic approach has much to recommend itself, for by encouraging both traditions it provides a check on each. Just as pro-choice forces will try to minimise cases in which people are kept alive and suffering against their will, so too pro-life forces will try to ensure that euthanasia is used only in cases where everyone wants it. It is precisely the tension between traditions that helps to reduce the likelihood that one will slide down the slope.

References

Bernardin, J. L. (2000) 'Selected Works of Joseph Cardinal Bernardin.' In A. P. Spilly, ed., *Church and Society* 2, 81–142.

Brandt, R. B. (1992) *Morality, Utilitarianism, and Rights*. Cambridge: Cambridge University Press.

Callahan, D. (1995) *Setting Limits: Medical Goals in an Aging Society*, with 'A Response to My Critics'. Washington DC: Georgetown University Press.

Callahan, D, and Callahan, D, (1999) *False Hopes: Overcoming the Obstacles to a Sustainable, Affordable Medicine*. Piscataway NJ: Rutgers University Press.

Caplan, A., McCartney, J., and Sisti, D., eds. (2006) *The Case of Terri Schiavo: Ethics at the End of Life*. Amherst, New York: Prometheus Books.

Churchill, W. (1998) *A Little Matter of Genocide: Holocaust and Denial in the Americas 1492 to the Present*. San Francisco: City Lights Publishers.

Davis, A. (1983) *Women, Race, & Class*. New York: Vintage Press.

Didion, J. (2005) 'The Case of Theresa Schiavo.' In *The New York Review of Books* 52: 10.

Griffiths, J., Weyers, H., and Adams, M. (2008) *Euthanasia and Law in Europe: With Special Reference to the Netherlands and Belgium*. Oxford: Hart Publishing, 2nd ed.

Kant, I. (1969) *The Moral Law. Kant's Groundwork of the Metaphysic of Morals*, translated and analysed by H. J. Paton. London: Hutchinson University Library, 96–7.

Miles, S. and Gomez, C. (1988) *Protocols for Elective Use of Life-sustaining treatment*. New York: Springer-Verlag. Cited in Margaret Battin, 'Euthanasia: The Way We Do It, the Way They Do It,' *Journal of Pain and Symptom Management* 6(5), 298–305.

Pool, R. (2000) *Negotiating a Good Death: Euthanasia in the Netherlands*. Philadelphia: Haworth Press Inc.

Rachels, J. (1975) 'Active and Passive Euthanasia.' *New England Journal of Medicine* 292.

Schneiderman, L. J., Jecker, N. S., and Jonsen, A. R. (1990) 'Medical futility: its meaning and ethical implications.' *Annals of Internal Medicine* 112: 949–54.

Schneiderman, L. J., Jecker, N. S., and Jonsen, A. R. (1996) 'Medical Futility: Response to Critiques.' *Annals of Intern Medicine* 125: 669–74.

Stannard, D. E. (1993) *American Holocaust: The Conquest of the New World*. New York: Oxford University Press.

PROLOGUE: **SUICIDE**

As with euthanasia and abortion, suicide has been treated as a criminal offence in some countries and many religions view it as an abomination. Alternatively, it may be viewed as a final cry for help, the 'right to die' in cases of terminal illness, or even as a noble and honourable act (e.g. harakiri amongst warriors in Japan). Kay Nooney's chapter discusses motivations and inhibitors for suicide, primarily based on her experience of prison-based suicide research.

This chapter on suicide and Rohan Gunaratna's later chapter on terrorism potentially overlap regarding acts such as suicide bombings. The motivations for these acts are entirely different, however, with suicide bombings falling firmly into the realm of terrorism, and the perpetrators defining the acts as martyrdom rather than suicide. This in itself raises further questions about our explanations for behaviour: why do we justify these acts in such different ways when ultimately the individuals are, in both cases, taking their own lives?

Chapter 6

Suicide

Kay Nooney

When life is so burdensome death has become for man a sought after refuge...

Herodotus 485–425 BC

Introduction

Anyone who has spent time with a suicidal person, professionally or personally, will remember the intensity and stress of the experience and recognise the range of associated emotions, from compassion and empathy to frustration, impatience and even anger. It follows that interested parties, and society as a whole, are engaged in a search for suicidal motive, with the aim of both preventing individual suicides and lessening in general the possibility of self-harm as an option for all of us.

The act of suicide or self-murder is a complex one; it is an individual response, linked to an environmental aversion. This chapter attempts to disentangle these two factors by examining first, the vulnerable person responding to what he or she perceives as overwhelming individual circumstances and second, the group processes that might lead to such a response. It will examine the definitions of suicide, the individual pathology and societal trends. Many of the resources and examples used are based on people in prison custody, as this is the context in which I have worked.

Legal definitions[29]

Suicide is defined as self-killing in which the declaration of intent is unambiguous; however, suicide falls within a broader range of self-inflicted death, overlapping into accidental death, drug overdose, reckless behaviour, and other explicitly self-destructive activity. On the occasion of a self-inflicted death, an inquest will be held. This process is non adversarial – that is, it does not seek blame. The inquest requires a public airing of the circumstances and precursors of the death; often, this serves as a protection for society against death through negligence. In cases of self-inflicted death, however, it can mean

---

29 Unless otherwise stated, all procedural and medical practices discussed here refer to England and Wales.

an exacerbation of distress for those close to the deceased, as personal details and difficulties are examined.

Legally, the term 'suicide' applies only to a self-inflicted death when proof is beyond reasonable doubt of the intent to kill oneself. Self-inflicted deaths, where this level of proof has not been met, may be assigned to the accidental, misadventure or open category. No legal distinction exists between accident and misadventure as inquest verdicts.

The level of proof required by a coroner's court is rigorous, even when intent to kill oneself is apparent. The coroner may decide, for example, that other factors undermine the stated intent, such as 'when the balance of the mind is disturbed'. We are immensely reluctant to let go of our fellow members of society in the name of suicide. Suicide was an illegal act in the UK until 1961, and people were still being sent to prison for attempting suicide in the 1950s. The current legislation on suicide makes a pathway for the 'right to die' (see Chapter 5).

The inquest procedure is undoubtedly geared in part towards the protection of vulnerable individuals and, indeed, society as a whole. Strong emotions are elicited in those close to the deceased when a suicide verdict is passed. These often centre on anger and blame – emotions common to many bereavements – but are intensified immeasurably by the problematic psychological components of self-killing. It remains illegal in the UK to assist

Table 1: Death rates per 100,000 for males in England and Wales, 1997 (Sattar 2001)

Type of Death	Community Offenders	Prisoners	General population
15–44 years			
Natural causes	86.5	71.0	61.7
Suicide/Self-inflicted injury	109.6	87.3	13.4
Accident/Misadventure	152.1	29.1	24.0
Homicide	30.1	3.4	1.1
Other violence	4.6	0	7.3
Other: drug-/alcohol-related	81.1	0	0
Overall mortality	464.0	191.7	107.5

someone to kill him or herself; consequently, we prefer to limit the possibility or naming of deaths as suicide.

That said, a class of deaths within suicides is associated with the socially excluded or less integrated members of society. This accounts for a significant proportion of all suicides. Taking the criminal population as a microcosm, offenders outside prison custody, perhaps surprisingly, have a higher risk of unnatural death than those inside.

Prison populations cannot be seen as society in miniature; looking at the large disparity between the number of suicides and other deaths among the offender population and that among the general population of a similar age, offenders are at higher risk on many levels. This, in turn, has a bearing on the way we can interpret the figures for accidental/misadventure verdicts. While many of the deaths are the result of road traffic accidents, figures as a whole indicate a huge recklessness. One can speculate that normal hazards play only a small part in the risk as a whole, with the more significant danger being posed by the individual's self-destructive impulse.

Such findings are not confined to England and Wales: earlier studies in Australia revealed a similar pattern. Table 2 gives an approximate guide to the pattern of deaths that is remarkably similar; adult offenders who are not in prison manifestly pursue activities that put them in a high death risk category. While these premature deaths may or may not be recorded as suicide, they are nevertheless the result of lack of self-protection or disregard for harmful consequences which are difficult to disentangle from deliberate intent to self-harm. This is further evidenced in studies on the mortality rates of released offenders (Graham 2003; Shaw et al. 2006).

Table 2: Deaths per 1,000 Prisoners, Community Offenders, and General Population (1996) per year, Australia (Biles, Harding and Walker 1999)

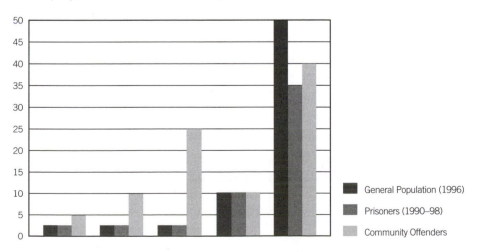

117

A state of denial exists, both academically and politically, about the occurrence and scale of this self-destruction, as well as its implications. Nevertheless, as concern grows about the rising rates of actual or 'completed' suicides, the 'self-destructive' category of self-harm is naturally getting more attention. Interestingly, cases of suicide and attempted suicide in the general population show a similar socio-economic profile to offenders: they are young, male and unskilled.

The remainder of this chapter discusses suicide at the level of the individual act and at a further level as a response to societal influence.

Where self-inflicted death cannot be ignored: investigative reports into prison suicides

The professional response to a suicide, from those in a position of care over the deceased, is often to deny that suicidal intent was possible to perceive. This is not just an organisational defence, but rather a genuine psychological self-defence or denial. Relatives, who may have background knowledge indicating the person's damaged psychological history, will often seek to blame those in immediate proximity of the death. Both sets of reality can be correct. Analysis of deaths in custody shows that the majority of suicide and self-harm occurs during the days and weeks immediately following reception into prison. This is a volatile and uncertain time for individuals; assaults are also most prevalent after reception. An initial assessment takes place on reception into custody for all prisoners, which includes risk of suicide. Investigative reports following a death in custody often emphasise that no suicidal intent was perceived at the reception stage. So, there are two possible interpretations: the first is that, if no suicidal intent was perceived at the time of the assessment, the individual became suicidal rapidly as a response to incarceration. The second is that the assessment was inadequate. There can be no definitive adjudication between these two perspectives.

In the process of self-destruction, there is a combination of individual vulnerability and external stimulus. The next section describes some of the thinking that characterises suicide as an act of individual pathology. The chapter then examines the environmental aspects that influence suicide numbers, as well as the unexplained 'protective' factors and the way in which we see them.

The individual response: suicide as a pathological act

The desire to kill oneself is generally regarded as a temporary state or an impulse that should be resisted. It is the ultimate act of both taking control and losing all other options. The reasons for this act are often cited under psychiatric and psychological dysfunction.

Depression

Depression is often quoted as the major determinant of suicide. There is a degree of tautology here, since thoughts about suicide are an important element in the diagnosis of depression. We all experience difficulty and disappointment in our dealings with the environment. Suicide can be described in cognitive behavioural terms as the ultimate escape from feelings of hopelessness, regarding both present circumstances and future anticipation.

Beck describes a cognitive behavioural perspective of everyday functioning as follows:

> Common sense psychology includes the psychological operations, reflections, observations and introspection by which someone attempts to determine why he is upset, what is bothering him and what he can do to relieve his distress. Through introspection he can determine the main subject of his ideation and relate this to his unpleasant feelings (tension, sadness, irritation) … in the area of strictly psychological problems a person acquires a host of techniques and generalisations which enable him to judge whether he is reacting realistically to situations, to resolve conflicts regarding alternative courses of actions, to deal with rejection, disappointment and danger. (1989: 14)

But, also based on behavioural principles, any individual's ability to negotiate the environment will vary, having been shaped by early learning experiences.

The perspective of cognitive behavioural therapy sees depressive thoughts or suicidal intent as the consequence of cognitive distortions. Experiences are appraised in a negative way; they are over interpreted in terms of defeat or deprivation. Depressed people foresee a life of unremitting hardship, frustration and deprivation, which they attribute to their own defects. They blame themselves and become increasingly self critical. Apathy can follow, in which the depressed person becomes less able; hopelessness leads to a loss of motivation, and the expectation of a negative outcome diminishes the probability of any action and chance of the negative expectations being confounded.

In cognitive behavioural therapy, the sequence and interpretation of events is examined, and people are taught to reinterpret events. Their cataclysmic interior narrative[30] is challenged, and they are asked to examine questions such as 'Does this happen all the time?' 'Does that mean it happens to quite a lot of people?' 'Yes, it is not pleasant but what sort of a problem is it?' 'How do you

---

30 Where people expand minor incidents into statements of future and present hopelessness: a parking ticket can be transcended into 'this always happens to me, nothing goes right, I can't cope with things like this happening all the time'.

solve it?' Thus, the cycle of pessimism and inaction starts to be interrupted.

The importance of a cognitive behavioural approach is evident when linking depression and suicide. The physical act of suicide does not appear to be related to the depth of the depression; indeed, suicidal acts are more likely to occur when a person is coming out of a depressive episode. Cognitive therapy, unlike medicinal intervention, examines negative thoughts rather than subduing physical symptoms; it halts the downward spiral of these thoughts, and patients slough off apathy and rediscover a sense of personal agency. So, they may regain control, without yet conquering their negative patterns, which is one of the classic risk zones for suicidal action (as opposed to ideation).

Other psychiatric disorder

The risk of suicide is elevated at around 10–15% amongst people diagnosed with schizophrenia. However, apart from the occasional suicide during a psychotic episode, the greatest risk for suicide occurs during non-psychotic, depressed phases of the illness.

Other correlates of suicide or suicidal thinking such as anger and remorse may be considered under the individual pathology perspective. These are unlikely to be independent of each other and are discussed below.

Anger

Suicide can be seen as an act of anger. Studies using violence and anger in the investigation of suicidal behaviour have predominantly been German (for example Ille et al. 2001). The North American and British studies have approached the link between violence and suicide more obliquely (i.e. American Psychiatric Association 1974). Many of the studies of aggression cite suicidal intent and self-harm as important diagnostic predictors of violence in the psychiatric population, but few examine anger as a causal factor in suicide. Impulsive aggression and suicide have also been linked in psycho-pharmacological research (see for example Rujescu et al. 2002).

In the prison population, violent offenders are over represented among the self-inflicted deaths (Nooney 2000; Adeniji 2007). Research using psychometric measures of anger (State Trait Anger Expression Inventory, or STAXI) has shown elevated rates of anger among self-harming prisoners compared with other prisoners (Pollard et al. 2000). These were adult males, but there have been similar findings for adolescent offenders.

It is not difficult to see the link between acts of suicide and acts of anger or violence. Frequently, people who have been the victims of violence find their anger takes its natural expression in self-harm. This is especially true when considering the history of self-harming and suicidal women who have frequently been subject to physical and sexual abuse. In terms of cognitive psychology, their behavioural options have been distorted and limited, not only by the memory of actual abuse but also by the corresponding helplessness and lack of control. This can result in feelings of depression but also of deep anger. The expression of anger has been limited and lacks an appropriate target.

Among the female prison population, many women have previously attempted suicide or self-harm. Suicides of female prisoners tend to occur later in custody rather than as a response to the immediate impact of imprisonment, possibly as their problems inside and outside prison do not diminish but remain without solution, particularly domestic problems including responsibilities for children. It is also possible to see anger as a motive for suicidal behaviour among the young when the act is a means of articulating to others how hurt or how deeply they are feeling. They seek vengeance against those who care about them via a threat to their own wellbeing.

Remorse

The act of suicide to demonstrate deep feelings is also traditionally associated with remorse. Prisoners convicted of murder or manslaughter are considered to be at risk of suicide and are placed under special observation. There is a good statistical basis for this proactive strategy.

Only a minority of suicides will include a written account of the emotion and motives of the person. In the case of violent and sexual offenders, they may contain elements of not being able to live with the consequences of the act. These would include the destruction of their self-image and social standing, and the prison sentence itself, with its enforced separation from loved ones. That said, it is not rare for prison-based suicide notes to contain a protestation of innocence. Suicide in both these instances is used as a demonstration to others of the sincerity of the individual.

Communication

Deficits in self-disclosure and communication are believed to make people vulnerable to suicidal intent. This corresponds to findings on incarcerated young offenders (Leibling 1992), while a more recent prison study (Marzano 2001) found that male prisoners who self-harm are less willing to communicate their emotions and have fewer social contacts. They are generally less able to assert any control in the social environment.

This is mirrored in the community outside. The Samaritans[31] have sought a solution for those who find personal contact and communication difficult. Among other initiatives, the organisation has set up an email 'helpline' service. This has a successful uptake among those young men who are vulnerable and who find interpersonal communication difficult.

---

31 The Samaritans is a charitable organisation which provides an emergency contact service for the distressed and suicidal.

Higher rates of suicide and attempted suicide have been apparent among gay men and lesbians (Gibson 1989; Trenchard and Warren 1984). Open communication is a continuing difficulty for this group where same-sex relationships are not legally recognised and discrimination or stigma still exists. Sources of expertise and support exist within this group, but this may still leave some individuals more isolated if they do not wish to be associated with or integrated in the gay community (*ibid.*).

Destruction

So far, the terms suicide, suicidal behaviour and self-harm have been used as aspects of the same destructive behaviour. Self-harm and suicide attempts are not necessarily at the lower end of a continuum to suicide. It is possible to experiment repeatedly with self-harm without ever graduating to or even intending completed suicide. It is impossible to be exact in the prediction of an individual's suicide risk, but the existence of self-destructive behaviour certainly changes the risk group or probability of suicide for an individual. A wide variety of behaviour can be described as self-destructive. In the group of prisoners who kill themselves, the offences of arson and criminal damage are highly over represented. The actual numbers are small, as these crimes are relatively infrequently given custodial sentences, but the existence of these offences in a person's history constitutes a significant risk factor. It is difficult to differentiate the behaviour as being exclusively violent, angry or disturbed, but it is destructive.

Substance abuse

Substance misuse may also be described as self-destructive behaviour, though the subject of addiction is too wide a topic to be discussed in depth here. Substance abuse in itself is another facet of individual pathology which is a known risk factor for suicide. This includes both drug and alcohol misuse.

A history of alcohol abuse and heavy drinking is present in an estimated 10–54 % of suicides (Ramstedt 1998). This represents a wide margin but is nevertheless instructive. Three major mechanisms are said to be involved: the pharmacological effect of alcohol in inducing depression; the way in which the state of intoxication may allow or disinhibit feelings of hopelessness and low self esteem; and, finally, the indirect effect of loss of family, employment and friends, resulting in extreme social isolation. It has been estimated that among the homeless, the risk of suicide is thirty-five times that of the general population (Stuart 2001).

Drug misuse can lead to similar isolation from reliable support. It also provides the means of suicide. Suicide statistics are always slightly skewed by the difficulties of interpreting drug overdose: it is not always clear whether the act is suicide, accident or deliberate recklessness.

The preceding sections have examined suicide as a response of vulnerable individuals. In prisoners at least, this vulnerability is often the result of impaired early learning, which leaves individuals unable to adapt; this, in turn, makes them doubt that they will ever have any influence over their circumstances, which leads to a strongly negative interpretation of the present and a lack of hope for the future. Individual pathology may lead to combinations of anger, violence and drug and alcohol misuse. These behaviours are risk factors for suicide.

The people who have made the decision to kill themselves are more heterogeneous than these descriptions suggest. The prison population is a specialised group; it has been estimated that they have a rate of suicide which is six or seven times higher than that of the general population (Samaritans 2002). Nevertheless, even within this specific group there are significant variations in motive: the intent to kill oneself will be different for a prisoner undergoing enforced drug withdrawal as a part of imprisonment, to that of a long-term prisoner who decides after several years that suicide is the only choice. Similarly, a 16-year-old boy who kills himself in custody will have experienced yet other pressures and feelings.

Decisions to attempt suicide are influenced by greater feelings of instability and change associated not only with the immediate impact of imprisonment but also of release. Both these times produce an elevated risk of suicide.

The decision to kill oneself seems to involve a combination of factors very personal to the individual. In practice it is very difficult to discern the suicidal from others sharing the same risk factors. In the analysis of suicides in England and Wales (Dept. of Health 1999), only 24% of those committing suicide had been known to psychiatric services, but even amongst this in-group under specialist care it has been difficult to assess suicide risk. Most (85%) of these patients had been seen by professional psychiatric staff within the previous seven days of their suicide and had not been perceived to be at risk. This is not as improbable as it may seem: people who have displayed great distress may seem calm and more content, having made their decision to kill themselves. This is a known risk factor with the suicidal but may be not easy to distinguish from actual recovery. It is not known how many of the remaining 76% had sought primary healthcare and similarly not been assessed as a suicide risk.

Suicide as a group process

As previously stated, killing oneself seems to be a very personal choice made under circumstances which are overwhelming to the individual. However, we are also responsive to the influences of the larger community or society. The obvious influence of social trends forces the question: why is this deeply personal decision taken by so many people within a specific group? Why, in other words, is it so *impersonal*?

Durkheim, more than one hundred years ago, brought the very private tragedy of suicide into the arena of sociological study. He provided a sociological explanation for a phenomenon traditionally regarded as exclusively psychological and individualistic.

Durkheim defined suicide as follows: 'The term suicide is applied to all cases of death resulting directly or indirectly from a positive or negative act of the victim himself, which he knows will produce this result' (1897: 44). He used this definition to separate true suicides from accidental deaths. He then collected statistics on suicide rates from several European nations, which proved to be relatively constant among those nations and among smaller demographics within those nations. Using this method, a collective tendency towards suicide was discovered.

Durkheim drew theoretical conclusions on the social causes of suicide, proposing four types based on the degrees of imbalance of two social forces: social integration and moral regulation. One of the four types proposed is *egoistic suicide*, which results from too little social integration. Individuals who are not sufficiently bound to social groups (and therefore to well-defined values, traditions, norms, and goals) are left with little social support or guidance and therefore tend to commit suicide. An example Durkheim discovered was that of unmarried people, particularly males who, with less to bind and connect them to stable social norms and goals, committed suicide at a higher rate. Current statistics recognise this group, even if the underlying sociological process remains unknown.

In current studies, comparing and hypothesising suicides in different cultures and nations is made more difficult by the fact that nations apply different definitions of inclusion (Hawton 2008). This usually depends on who is responsible for determining whether a death is suicide. For example, Commonwealth countries are likely to use the coroner system, but in others this may be a decision of the police or based on a medical report. Attitudes to suicide and, especially, religious and legal factors may also influence the recording of suicide verdicts. A study in India showed that official suicide rates in rural areas of India were about ten times lower than rates based on semi-structured interviews with family members (*ibid.*).

Regardless, it is clear that instructive differences exist, even if the scale of those differences cannot be quantified precisely. Most studies refer to World Health Organisation (WHO) figures, of which Table 3 opposite is one example. It contains the rates per 100,000 population in 2004:

Table 3: Suicides per 100,000 population

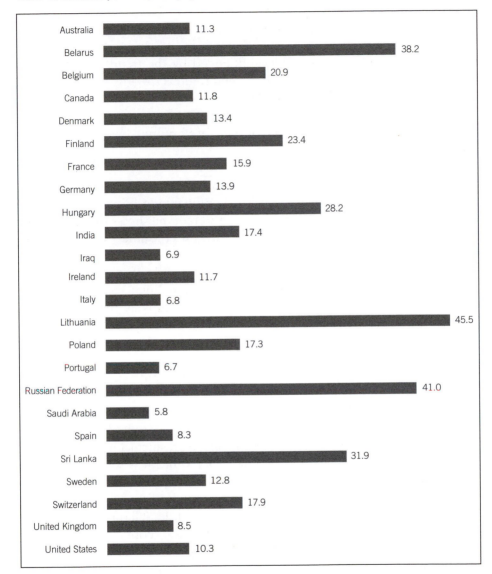

Australia	11.3
Belarus	38.2
Belgium	20.9
Canada	11.8
Denmark	13.4
Finland	23.4
France	15.9
Germany	13.9
Hungary	28.2
India	17.4
Iraq	6.9
Ireland	11.7
Italy	6.8
Lithuania	45.5
Poland	17.3
Portugal	6.7
Russian Federation	41.0
Saudi Arabia	5.8
Spain	8.3
Sri Lanka	31.9
Sweden	12.8
Switzerland	17.9
United Kingdom	8.5
United States	10.3

The differences invite theory and hypothesis. It is difficult to regard suicide as an individual act, even with the flaws of international statistical comparison. However, we are aware of other aspects of apparently personal choice that our membership of society governs. At a superficial level, we all experience pressure from the vacillations of fashion in clothing, music and lifestyle, which appear genuinely important but are in fact temporary. We are aware that people are open to deliberate manipulation through media and propaganda; this manipulation sometimes extends to engendering serious hostility towards specific groups, which in turn undermines core values and can be so extreme as to become genocidal (Cohen 2001).

Other influences are less discernible. The decision to have children offers an example: there are no marketing campaigns to influence individuals either way, and yet people are powerfully influenced by the trends that surround them. In Western Europe, the strong societal trend is towards smaller families, and people generally follow this trend.

Many attempts have been made to identify the triggers within society which influence suicide rates. Some of these are outlined below.

Alcohol

A familiar stereotype is of high suicide rates associated with Scandinavian countries, a vision of economic wealth accompanying heavy drinking and long hours of darkness. Examination of the stereotype shows that, per capita, Scandinavian countries feature among the lowest consumers of alcohol, and the suicide rate is not uniform across the separate countries; only Finland could be regarded as having an elevated rate of suicide. It is still tempting to apply the high alcohol consumption and suicide rate link to Russia. However research has not shown consistent links, and it is unlikely that the possible cultural influences could be merged into a single variable.

Religion

The relatively lower rates of suicide in the Mediterranean countries have been attributed to religious influence, particularly that of the Catholic Church. The dogma of the Catholic Church places suicide as one of two sins that cannot be forgiven; presumption and despair supersede even 'mortal sin'. This may act as a deterrent or inhibitor for some people with suicidal impulses.

However, Biblical prohibition of self-inflicted death is somewhat vague. There are seven early Biblical references to suicide and one reference to attempted suicide, all of which are presented neutrally or as appropriate under the circumstances: for example Saul, defeated in battle, 'fell on his own sword' (1 Samuel 31). The New Testament, likewise, contains no specific condemnation of self-killing (ASBS 2001). It is generally held that the denunciation of suicide occurred much later, in the fourth century, to oppose heretics who courted death in order to ensure martyrdom and a place in Heaven. Donatism — one aspect of which included this form of heresy — originated and was strongest in North Africa and persisted until the region was conquered by Islam. The argument against suicide was incorporated into Christian dogma by the joint efforts of Augustine in the 5th century and medieval theologian Thomas Aquinas. They both supported the view that life was God–given and therefore that only God should decide on the duration of life. Suicide was eventually outlawed in England in the 10th century. Then the condemnation was complete, to the extent of not allowing burial in hallowed ground to those who had killed themselves.

The role of Christianity in preventing suicide is more substantial than a simple prohibition; like all religions, it has protective and communal aspects that may militate against suicidal thoughts. Catholicism in particular condemns suicide. The declining influence of Catholicism may therefore be implicated in the increase in suicides, but this is not a uniform finding. In the Republic of Ireland, suicide is increasing alongside diminishing religious practice; however in Mediterranean countries, suicide rates have remained roughly static (Birt et al. 2003; Cassidy 2002). Furthermore, the decline of religious practice must be assessed as part of a more widespread change in values and adherence to tradition (Tovey et al. 2003).

Comparing commands regarding suicide in other religious traditions offers additional insights. Some elements of Hindusim encouraged suicide for widows (see Chapter 1), though this is not generally acceptable in contemporary society. The Koran contains unequivocal condemnation of suicide, and the reportage of suicide in Islamic countries is correspondingly low. The order and way of life embodied in the religion of Islam offers an unambiguous set of rules for what is expected and therefore may reduce anxiety. This may be a key cultural influence in lower suicide rates, in conjunction with the more explicit religious injunction against suicide.

The concept of martyrdom has a different basis: it is an action designed not to bring an end to unbearable personal circumstances but to gain a positive advantage in an afterlife. Chapter 7 discusses this in more depth.

Nationality

It is methodologically problematic to take elements of cultures and make valid conclusions in relation to cause and effect on suicide rates. Comparisons within the same culture are more revealing since they offer a less problematic potential for interpreting the societal influences in suicide. For example, statistics in the UK and Republic of Ireland from 1995–2005 (Office of National Statistics, cited in Samaritans 2007) show the following trends:[32]

- 9.5 % decrease in the United Kingdom overall
- 11 % decrease in England
- 15 % decrease in Wales
- 0 % change in Northern Ireland
- 1 % increase in Scotland
- 13 % increase in the Republic of Ireland

---

32 These figures include undetermined death by injury.

The uncertainty for the future, combined with the arguably violent environment, may influence individuals in Northern Ireland, but across Northern Ireland and the Republic of Ireland, the decline of the Catholic Church and increased prosperity may be more relevant. Although figures limited to one country are easier to interpret, they still allow for a great deal of discretion and supposition.

Analysis of suicide numbers within Australia, the United States, the United Kingdom, and the Republic of Ireland all show changes within those cultures that would spark public concern. Even in countries where the numbers of suicides have decreased, there have been worrying increases among specific demographics (usually young men).

United States

The following statistics were produced in the United States for the American Association of Suicidology (2004):

- In 2004 there were 32,439 suicides in the US (89 suicides per day; 1 suicide every 16 minutes). This translates to an annual suicide rate of 11.5 per 100,000.
- Suicide is the eleventh leading cause of death.
- Suicide rates in the US can best be characterised as mostly stable over time. Since 1990, rates have ranged between 12.4 and 10.7 per 100,000.
- Males complete suicide at a rate four times that of females. However, females attempt suicide three times more often.
- Rates of completed suicide are highest among the elderly (age 80 and over).
- Youth (ages 15–24) suicide rates increased more than 200% from the 1950s to the late 1970s. From the late 1970s to the mid 1990s, suicide rates for youth remained stable and, since then, have slightly decreased.
- Suicide ranks third as a cause of death among young Americans (age 15–24); only accidents and homicides occur more frequently.
- Firearms remain the most commonly utilised method of completing suicide by essentially all groups. More than half (52%) of the individuals who took their own lives in 2004 used this method. Males (58% firearms; 42% other method) used firearms more often than females (33% firearms; 67% other method).
- The most common method of suicide for females was poisoning. In fact, poisoning has surpassed firearms for female suicides since 2001.
- Caucasians (12.3 per 100,000) have higher rates of completed suicides than African Americans (5.2 per 100,000).

Genedrally speaking, Australia and the United Kingdom focus on similar factors in their analyses, but the trends differ. For example, in contrast to the American findings, the rate of suicide in these countries in older males has decreased.

Australia, the United Kingdom and the Republic of Ireland [33]

Age

Suicide rates in Australia peaked in 1997, followed by a steady decline. The age dynamics have also changed: the rates for men aged over 60 have gradually declined. An upsurge in suicides among males aged 15 to 19 years has since stabilised. Suicide accounted for approximately 22% of all deaths for those aged 20 to 34 years in 2004 and 27% of deaths for men aged 25 to 29.

Similarly, throughout the 1980s in the UK and Republic of Ireland, the suicide rate amongst young men aged 15 to 34 increased; however, between 1993 and 2005 it fell by 32%. The number of suicides amongst all 15 to 24-year-olds in the UK and Republic of Ireland continued to decrease in 2005. The rate per 100,000 for 25 to 34-year-old men remained at 20 per 100,000, compared with an increase to 31 per 100,000 in the 55 to 64 age group. There is no obvious explanation for this shift.

Gender

Females continue to be at greater risk of self-harm, but they are proportionately under-represented in suicide numbers. In the UK between 1971 and 1996, the suicide rate for women almost halved, whereas the suicide rate for men during this period almost doubled. We can seek explanation in gender politics and the lack of identity for the young men; certainly it has been shown that young men with suicidal intent significantly lack positive relationships with older men (Katz 1999). Regardless, this shift in suicide rates suggests an extraordinary societal influence on personal distress. The increased availability of better anti-depressant medication can only partly account for such changes.

Ethnic group

A consistent finding in American population and British prison studies has been that white males and females are over represented in suicides. This finding has no explanation; the apparently protective factors of race are not understood. Similarly the elevated rates among Native Americans and the indigenous native populations of Australia and Canada indicate strong societal influence. Some females in the UK do not share this unknown protective factor: the suicide rate of young Asian women is three times higher than that of white British women.

---

33   Sources include ABS figures (2006); Samaritans (2007).

Method of suicide
Other facets of self-killing show change within cultures over time. For example, the availability of firearms in the US and Northern Ireland influences their prominence as method of choice (Killas 1999). It is less obvious why hanging should now predominate in Australia: there, the use of firearms has decreased, but the rate for males of suicide by hanging tripled between 1979 and 1998. Similarly, there has been a sharp increase in the number of hangings for males in England and Wales.

Prison staff in England have speculated that the use of hanging is linked to drug misuse and the familiarity of applying tourniquets. Substance misuse is thought to be a highly significant factor in youth suicides. Differences between choice of method have been consistently gender based; hanging possibly has a macabre 'macho' image.

Occupation
Another aspect of suicide analysis is categorisation by occupation. This provides further insight on the effect of interaction between society and the individual. The figures in Table 4 are based on a fairly complex statistical process: the proportional mortality ratio (PMR) is calculated by comparing the number of suicides in a particular group to the average for the total population. It gives an indication of suicide risk: the average figure is 100, therefore a PMR of 200 and 50 represent twice and half the average risk respectively.

These figures offer a different insight into suicide as an act of a pathological individual. A high proportion of the occupations shown entail easy access to the means of death – witness the prevalence of vets, doctors, dentists, and pharmacists. The most worrying implication of this is that many more suicides may occur if more people had the wherewithal (i.e. ready access to powerful medications).

Individual factors

This does not, however, explain the feelings and motivations which propel the individual; for this we need to return to the consideration of suicide as an individual act. These individuals are likely to be high achievers and in caring professions. One of the greatest producers of anxiety and depression is the perceived gap between ideals and actual achievement. This perceived gap between what is set as a self-goal and what is attained can be a great source of unhappiness to many people in many different circumstances.

In many Western societies there is the additional pressure of media presentation through advertising of successful happy lifestyles (buy the image, buy the product), which is designed to feed the imagination of how life should or could be (see Ellis and Dryden 1986; Beck 1989). The feelings of inadequacy of the individual against the image portrayed can be assuaged or

Table 4: Proportional mortality ratio for males and females by profession in the UK 1991–96

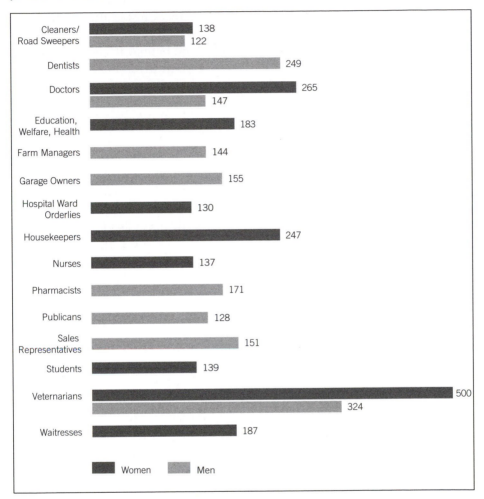

'bought off' through purchase of the product, but this is not always possible; young men and women are bombarded with glamorised images of idealised bodies and unaffordable lifestyles. This produces a schism with reality, the psychological gap of dissonance between what the person feels they need or should be, against what they currently experience. This void can be the starting point of harmful rumination, fermenting self-doubt and hopelessness for the future.

Conclusion

The statistics indicate that strong societal influences have a bearing on suicides, but quantification of the effects and ascribing direct cause is more difficult.

So, paradoxically, an examination of the social and career accoutrements of suicide force us back to the individual pathology behind it: these are not all deaths as a result of hardship or social exclusion. In psychological terms, the underlying mechanisms which cause a person to feel that both the present and future are too unbearable to endure can be found in early learning. In psychological learning experiments, rats were given electric shocks (Badia et al. 1973). The rats that showed the most trauma were not the ones most extensively shocked, but those in the 'no win' situation which, no matter what they did, were given random electric shocks. Animals can cope with extreme pain, but they cannot cope with being unable to predict. Uncertainty disables the ability to develop a coping strategy and therefore can only beget more anxious uncertainty. So, suicide does not necessarily occur as a result of terrible circumstances. It is more about ongoing hopelessness than immediate psychological pain.

At least two interlocking mechanisms are in operation. Firstly, the personal rating system which forms part of the interior narrative, in which people rate themselves according to their own scoring system and target setting ('How am I doing? Am I succeeding? Could it be better?'). If their cognitive strategies to manage life have not developed adequately, they will have no feeling of mastering problems or of success, and the answers and consequent personal rating will always be negative. Secondly, people in this state of negative affect will feel they are not able to predict, adapt and act accordingly. This will engender not only the perception that circumstances are outside a person's control, but also they can never be improved – the person has placed themselves in the 'no win' situation of the unfortunate rats.

Cultural and community influences will have an important role in the internal judgement of success and the setting of attainable goals. However, society will continue to measure its own success based on the assumption that life is basically valuable and good and that its members should find it humane and bearable and want to live within it. Despite any evidence to the contrary, we will continue to want to see suicidal impulses as a temporary and probable psychiatric event and ignore the extent of self-destructive behaviour in the non-psychiatric population.

References

Adeniji, T. (2007) *Safer Custody Group Self-Inflicted Deaths Annual Report: 2005/06.* London: HM Prison Service. Unpublished report.

American Association of Suicidology (2004) 'Suicide facts and Statistics (U.S)'. www.suicidology.org/displaycommon.cfm?an=1&subarticlenbr=185.

American Psychiatric Association (1974) *Clinical Aspects of the Violent Individual.* Arlington, VA: APA.

Australian Bureau of Statistics (ABS) (2006) 'Suicides' ABS catalogue no. 3309.0. http://www.ausstats.abs.gov.au/Ausstats/subscriber.nsf/0/FF573FA817DC3C84CA25713000705C19/$File/33090_1994%20to%202004.pdf.

ASBS (2001) *The Bible, Christianity and Suicide.* http://ashbusstop.org/Biblesuicide.html.

Badia, P., Culbertson, S. and Harsh, J. (1973) 'Choice of Longer or stronger Signalled Shock over Shorter or Weaker Unsignalled Shock'. *Journal of the Experimental Analysis of Behavior* 19, 25–33.

Beck, A. (1989) *Cognitive Therapy and Emotional Disorders.* London: Pelican.

Biles, D., Harding, R., and Walker, J. (1999) 'The Deaths of Offenders Serving Community Corrections Orders.' Canberra: Australian Institute of Criminology.

Birt, C., Bille-Brahe, U., Cabecadas, M., Chishti, P., Corcoran, P., Elgie, R., van Heeringen, K., Horte, L-G., Marchi, A. G., Ostamo, A., Petridou, E., Renberg, E. S., Stone, D. H., Wiik, J., and Williamson, E. (2003) 'Suicide mortality in the European Union.' *European Journal of Public Health* 13(2), 108–114.

Cassidy, E. (2002) 'Religious Belief and Practice in Ireland and a European Context: 1980–2000.' In E. Cassidy, ed., *Measuring Ireland: Discerning Values and Beliefs.* Dublin: Veritas Publications.

Charlton, J. Kelly, S. and Bunting, J. (1992) 'Trends in Suicide in England and Wales'. *Population Trends* 69. Office of National Statistics. London: HMSO.

Cohen, S. (2001) *States of Denial: Knowing About Atrocities and Suffering.* Cambridge: Polity Press.

Department of Health (1999) *National Confidential Inquiry into Suicide and Homicide by people with mental illness.* London: Department of Health.

Douglas, K., Webster, C. D., Hart, S., Eaves, D., and Ogloff, J. R. P. (2001) *HCR-20 Violence Risk Management Companion Guide.* Mental Health, Law and Policy Unit. Simon Fraser University.

Durkheim, E. (1897) *Suicide: a study in sociology.* Reprinted (1993), London: Routledge.

Ellis, A. and Dryden, W. (1986) *The Practice of Rational Emotive Therapy (RET).* New York: Springer Publishing Company.

Gibson, P. (1989) 'Gay Male and Lesbian Youth Suicide'. *Report of the Secretary's Task Force on Youth Suicide* 3, *Prevention and Intervention in Youth Suicide* (Alcohol, Drug Abuse and Mental Health Administration), US Government Print Office, Washington DC.

Graham A. (2003) *Post-prison mortality: unnatural death among those released from Victorian prisons between January 1990 and December 1990.* Aust N Z J Criminol ; 36: 94–108.

Hawton, K. (2008) Personal communication on 1 February 2008 from Professor Keith Hawton, Director of the Centre for Suicide Research, Oxford.

Hawton, K. , Salkovskis, P., Kirk, J. and Clark, D. (1990) *Cognitive Behaviour Therapy for Emotional Disorders.* Oxford: Oxford University Press.

Ille, R., Huber, H. P. and Zapotoczky, H. G. (2001) 'Aggressive and suicidal behaviour. A cluster analysis study of suicidal and non-clinical subjects' *Psychiatry Prax.* 28 (1), 24–8.

Katz, A. Buchanan, A., and McCoy, A. (1999) ' Young men speak out'. Stirling: The Samaritans.

Killas, M. (1999) 'Gun Ownership, Suicide and Homicide: an International Perspective.' School of Forensic Science and Criminology, University of Lausanne, Switzerland.

Leibling, A. (1992) *Suicides in Prison.* London: Routledge.

Marzano, L. (2001) *The Relationship Between Styles of Communication and Self-Expression and Self-Harm amongst Adult Male Prisoners.* Unpublished dissertation, Middlesex University.

Meyer, V. and Chesser, E. (1971) *Behaviour Therapy in Clinical Psychiatry.* Penguin Modern sychology.

Nooney, K. (2000) *'Self- Inflicted Deaths in Prisons 1988–1999'* London: HM Prison Service Safer Custody, unpublished report.

Pollard, J., Rowlands, K., Sorbello, L., and Morison, M. (2000) *A preliminary study of suicide risk factors and coping skills in a prison population.* Victoria, Australia: Caraniche Pty Ltd.

Pratt, D., Piper, M., Appleby, L., Webb, R., and Shaw, J. (2006) *Suicide in recently released prisoners: a population-based cohort study. The Lancet* 368: 119–123.

Rujescu, D., Geigling, I., Bondy, B., Gietl, A., Zill, P., and Moller, H. J. (2002) 'Association of anger related traits with SNPs in the TPH gene'. *Molecular Psychiatry* 7(9), 1023–9.

Ramstedt, M. (1998) 'Alcohol and suicide in fourteen countries – a time series analysis'. Stockholm: Centre for Social Research on Alcohol and Drugs, Stockholm University.

Samaritans (2002) & (2007) *Samaritan's Resource Pack – 2007.* London: Samaritans Organisation.

Sattar, G. (2001) *Rates And Causes of Deaths Among Prisoners And Offenders Under Community Supervision.* HO Research Study 231. London: Home Office.

Speilberger, C. D. (1988) 'State Trait Anger Expression Inventory' (STAXI Professional Manual). Psychological Assessment Resources.

Steenkamp, M. and Harrison, J. (2000) 'Suicide and Hospitalised Self Harm in Australia.' Australian Institute of Health and Welfare.

Stewert, G. (2001) *Suicide fact sheets.* London: MIND Organisation.

Tovey, H., Share, P., and Corcoran, M. P., eds. (2003) *A Sociology of Ireland*, 3rd Edition. Dublin: Gill Macmillan.

Trenchard, L. and Warren, H. (1984) *Something to tell you.* London Gay Teenage Group.

World Health Organisation (2004) *World Health Statistics Annual 2002.* Geneva: WHO.

PROLOGUE: **TERRORISM**

Terrorism has been particularly prominent in the news in recent years. At the time of writing, British and American newspapers often focus on acts carried out by Muslims. Previously, it would have been extreme right wing nationalist groups. Yet, despite their continued prevalence across Europe and fatal resurgence in some parts, we currently hear very little of the latter groups' actions. As this book has discussed, factionalism exists across the globe in different forms, and with appalling consequences.

Terrorist suicide bombings offer a clear example of cases in which religious texts are used to justify extreme action. The terrorist attack on the World Trade Center and the Pentagon on 11 September, 2001 is the most obvious example of an act that divided the Muslim world. Many Muslim leaders publicly denounced the attacks as un-Islamic.[34] Kimball notes that:

> The term *Islam* literally means 'submission to God' and 'peace'. The ideas are linked in the notion that submission to the will of God brings peace…. The requirement for Muslims to seek 'peace' in their communities and beyond involved both avoiding conflict when possible and the even more challenging task of establishing a stable social order characterized by peace and justice. (2002: 171)

Terrorist acts entirely overlook the main moral principles that provide the foundation behind religions such as Islam. Similar to Christianity and Judaism, Islamic belief is based on guidance of God through religious scripture and belief in ultimate judgment based on one's faith in God and one's actions based on that faith while on earth. Also like Christianity and Judaism, Islam is divided into varying branches of belief. Like most religious scriptures, Islamic texts can be interpreted in a number of ways. Verse 2:154 of the Qur'an – 'Say not of those who die in the path of God that they are dead. Nay rather they live' – has been interpreted as a promise for martyrs.

What is particularly unclear is what constitutes martyrdom. More extremist leaders such as the late Ayatollah Khomeini have made calls to action based on such scriptures with a promise of paradise for martyrs. The call to martyrdom is not something devotees take lightly. Two young Palestinian men interviewed for a television programme in the UK called 'Inside the Mind of the Suicide Bomber' (Channel 4, 2003) described it this way:

> Martyrdom leads us to God; I want to become a martyr. I don't want this life. I want to be with God to enjoy the Second Life. I want to go to Paradise where there is happiness and joy, where there are no problems. There, I get all I want. I get to be with the 70 virgins. Here, our life is full of problems. We Palestinians prefer to die, just kill ourselves, rather than live

---

34   Though such pronouncements received little coverage in the media (Kimball 2002: 179).

in this worthless life. My life is worthless. We are hollow bodies leading a pointless life. Israelis enjoy their life. They go out at night, they have cafés and night clubs. They travel all over the world; they go to America and Britain. We can't even leave Palestine. (17-year-old Palestinian Mohammed Abu Tayun; en route to a suicide bombing; he changed his mind at the last minute and returned home.)

The martyr knows that his house might be destroyed, his family left homeless. But Allah promised us that every martyr atones for 70 members of his family to enter paradise. So they've lost nothing. They might lose a house, or money, but that can all be replaced. It's worth destroying all the houses to achieve freedom for Palestine. (23-year-old graduate student who recruited the Haifa bomber)

French filmmaker Pierre Rehov found similar views amongst people he interviewed for his film, *Suicide Killers*: 'These aren't kids who want to do evil. These are kids who want to do good.... The result of this brainwashing was kids who were very good people inside (were) believing so much that they were doing something great' (in Curiel 2006: E6). Equally Silke (2003), an expert on the subject, noted that 'The most terrifying thing about suicide bombers is their sheer normality.'

A third interviewee for the television programme, 18-year-old Amir, absolved himself of responsibility for the deaths following terrorist attacks through his own interpretation of the scriptures:

The Qur'an says, you didn't kill them; it's Allah who killed them. So it's God who kills. I carry out the operation, and the rest is up to God. He might kill them all, or kill none of them. He might leave some mutilated. It's God's decision how many die.

Cohen discusses this type of neutralising response to horrific acts in his extensive exploration of denial: people do not attempt to deny the facts of their behaviour so much as 'find convenient rationalizations to explain themselves' (2001: x).

Notably, the majority of the Muslim population does not accept 'martyrdom' in such extreme forms as a legitimate act:

Only a highly selective reading of the Qur'an can produce this kind of narrow interpretation. Such a stance ignores completely the multiple and unambiguous admonitions in the *hadith* against any form of suicide. It also overlooks strict Islamic prohibitions against killing women, children, and non-combatants, even during times of war. (Kimball 2002: 56)

In the UK, the Muslim Council's denunciation of the bombings in London on 7 July 2005 emphasised that mainstream religious views do not support terrorist acts.

What is also clear is that 'While nothing justifies indiscriminate violence, it is also true that terrorism doesn't occur in a vacuum' (Kimball 2002: 180). People do not commit acts of terrorism simply because they are 'evil' or because they enjoy violence: they are done out of religious and/or political convictions which have driven the terrorist to believe violence is the only (or at least the most effective) means of making an impact. Mistrust of the powerful, largely Christian nations of the West, for example, is deeply embedded in other cultures (*ibid.*). Similarly, 'Inside the Mind of the Suicide Bomber' noted that scenes of violent oppression of Palestinians by the Israelis are repeatedly broadcast on Palestinian TV and are part of pop culture (e.g. music videos). In this context, the programme argued that it is not possible for a young man to grow up leading a normal life.

A clear pattern is that such extreme action by a small number of individuals can be effective in drawing attention to a cause or, very unusually, to achieving particular political or religious aims. Hezbollah fighters and suicide bombers eventually succeeded in driving Israeli forces out of Lebanon. The then Prime Minister of Israel, Yitzhak Rabin, commented that 'These terrorists are willing to kill themselves to strike our soldiers. They believe they are going directly to heaven' (BBC 1987). The attack on the US marine barracks in Beirut in 1983, in which 239 Americans died, was another example: 'Whether or not people agreed with the action directed at the marines, one message came through clearly: the suicide truck bomber succeeded in striking the Achilles' heel of the United States; terrorism worked' (Kimball 2002: 131). It is important to emphasise here that one of the reasons people resort to terrorism is precisely because such low numbers of extremists are involved; if such extreme beliefs were held more widely, one could argue that more 'conventional' methods of warfare may be employed.

Rohan Gunaratna's chapter explains how terrorist acts stem from political and/or religious beliefs and can either be viewed as evil or alternatively as laying claim to a higher cause. Terrorist acts often derive from deep-seated conflicts between warring parties, even when punctuated by 'Golden Ages' of apparent peace and reconciliation. Dr Gunaratna explains that, far from being random acts of treachery, most terrorist attacks are highly organised events, preceded by careful targeting, indoctrination, and training of recruits and supported through well-developed funding and infrastructure. In other words, he helps us answer questions not only about what terrorism is, but also about why people commit such acts.

References
British Broadcasting Corporation (1987) *The Sword of Islam*.

Channel 4 (2003) 'Inside the Mind of the Suicide Bomber.' UK.

Cohen, S. (2001) *States of Denial: Knowing About Atrocities and Suffering*. Cambridge: Polity Press.

Curiel, J. (2006) 'The Mind of a Suicide Bomber'. *San Francisco Chronicle*, 22 October 2006.

Kimball, C. (2002) *When Religion Becomes Evil*. New York: HarperCollins Publishers Inc.

Silke, A. (2003) 'Analysis: Ultimate Outrage.' *The Times*. London, 5 May 2003.

Chapter 7

Terrorism: a Unique Form of Political Violence

Rohan Gunaratna

Terrorism is a political campaign backed by threats and acts of violence. It must be systematic, deliberate and must seek to influence a wide audience by generating fear. It primarily targets civilians with the intention of competing for and controlling political power over the public. Other forms of political violence include attacks against infrastructure (sabotage), political leaders (assassination), military (guerrilla warfare), and ethnic groups (genocide). While attacks against civilians, or 'soft targets', are the most common in the initial wave of terrorist operations, terrorist groups subsequently develop the capability to attack security forces ('hard targets'). The tactical repertoire of contemporary terrorist groups includes forms of political violence other than terrorism. For instance, the National Liberation Army (ELN) has sabotaged gas and oil pipelines in Colombia; Basque Fatherland and Liberty (ETA) have assassinated moderate politicians in Spain; the Tareek-e-Taliban Pakistan (TTP) conducts guerrilla warfare against Pakistani security forces, and the Liberation Tigers of the Tamil Tigers (LTTE) have 'cleansed' Sri Lanka's northern province of Muslims.

Terrorist groups are extremely complex and well organised. They often have elaborate infrastructures of leadership and highly developed methods of funding their work. Weaponry ranges from crude homemade devices to extremely advanced high technology; equally the training terrorists receive can be equal to, or arguably even exceed, that of the most advanced government specialists. This chapter focuses less on how terrorist groups operate, however, and more on why people become terrorists. Why do people choose to engage in behaviour that leads to the severe injury and death of sometimes thousands of civilians – men, women, and children alike?

The context

Terrorism differs from common crime: crime is often driven by economic motive, while terrorism is driven by political motive. However, with the decline of state sponsorship, terrorist groups increasingly resort to crime to build their capacities and capabilities. For instance, the Revolutionary Armed forces of Colombia (FARC) extorts money from foreign companies in Colombia, the Abu Sayyaf Group (ASG) kidnaps foreigners, the Islamic Movement of Uzbekistan traffic narcotics, the Revolutionary United Force of Sierra Leone (RUF) smuggles diamonds, the Armed Islamic Group of Algeria (GIA) steals cars, and Al Qaeda engages in credit card fraud. Therefore, contemporary terrorist groups traverse along the political violence–criminality nexus. Overall, terrorist groups are armed political parties. Strategically their goal is always political. Operationally, it is to build support and operational infrastructure; tactically, the goal is to build military power, accumulate economic wealth, and gain political strength.

Over 100 definitions of terrorism exist. While no one definition has gained universal acceptance, there is agreement that terrorism is the threat or the act of politically motivated violence directed primarily against civilians. Some supporting the Palestinian, Kashmiri, and Kurdish struggles have argued that they are legitimate campaigns and therefore that these actions against civilians are not terrorism. They have also argued that, when a campaign is legitimate, the fighters are 'freedom fighters' and not terrorists. Killing unarmed combatants, including women and children, is not an act worthy of a freedom fighter. Whether a campaign is legitimate or not, deliberate attacks against civilians to achieve a political goal is terrorism. Irrespective of legitimacy, perpetrator, location and time of the attack, terrorism is a means to an end.

Often terrorism is a by-product of protracted armed conflicts. Conflict conditions create the milieu for the spawning and growth of terrorist groups. With the increase in the number and intensity of terrorist and guerrilla conflicts during the last decade, political violence affects two-thirds of the countries of the world. Recently, Iraq has emerged as the epicentre of global terrorism. Of the 14,499 reported attacks in 2007, resulting in over 22,000 deaths, almost 43% – about 6,200 – occurred in Iraq. The killings in Iraq constituted 13,600 fatalities, or 60% of the worldwide total.

Terrorist aims and objectives

Terrorist groups develop secular and religious ideologies or belief systems to politicise, radicalise and mobilise their actual and potential followers. By conducting a terrorist campaign within an ideological framework, a terrorist group seeks to advance its aims and objectives. Although the aims differ according to the ideological orientations of the groups, the objectives range from gaining recognition at local, national and international levels, and intimidating and coercing both the target population and the government, to provoking the government to overreact for the purpose of generating greater public support. Three principal ideological strands have generated the ideological fuel required to spawn and sustain terrorist campaigns around the world, namely ideological terrorism, ethno-nationalist terrorism, and politico-religious terrorism. The next sections discuss each of these in turn.

Ideological terrorism

Ideological terrorism is driven by both left-wing and right-wing ideologies. Marxism, Leninism and Maoism provide the ideological fuel to left-wing terrorist groups to advance their aims and objectives. They seek to overthrow existing regimes and establish communist and socialist states. Most of the groups driven by left-wing ideologies – Communist Combatant Cells (CCC) of Belgium, Red Army Faction (RAF) of Germany, Red Brigades (RB) of Italy, Action Direct (AD) of France – disintegrated with the end of the Cold War. Although the ideological justification for these groups to continue ended with the death of the Soviet Empire, a few groups driven by left-wing ideologies survive in the poorer regions of the world. They include FARC in Colombia, Tupac Amaru Revolutionary Movement (MRTA), Sendero Luminoso (Shining Path), New Peoples Army (NPA) in the Philippines, and People's War Group (PWG) in Andhara Pradesh in India. Of these groups, FARC, Nepal Maoists and NPA pose a severe national security threat to Colombia, Nepal and the Philippines. Among the left-wing groups still active in Europe are the Revolutionary Organisation 17 November and Revolutionary Nuclei, both of Greece, and the Revolutionary People's Liberation Party (DHKP-C) in Turkey.

Groups driven by right-wing ideologies include the Ku Klux Klan, Aryan Nations (Church of Christian Aryan Nations, Church of Jesus Christ Christian), Aryan Liberation Front, Aryan Brotherhood, Arizona Patriots, the American Nazi Party (National Socialist Party, United Racist Front) and the United Self-Defence Forces of Colombia (AUC). A group driven by a right-wing ideology conducted the bombing of the Alfred P. Murrah Federal Building in Oklahoma City on April 19, 1995. Overall, groups driven by right-wing ideologies pose a low threat compared to other categories of terrorism. In contrast to the left-wing groups, the bulk of the right-wing groups are located in North America and in Western Europe. Most right-wing groups are neo-Nazi, neo-fascist, anti-Semitic and racist groups. These groups, dominated by 'skinheads', attack immigrants and refugees, mostly of Asian and Middle Eastern origin. After the 9/11 terrorist attacks in the United States in 2001, the pace of these attacks increased.

Ethno-nationalist terrorism

The first wave of ethno-nationalist campaigns was by national liberation movements directed against the Colonial rulers. They included the Irgun and Lehi opposing the British rule in Palestine in the 1940s and French rule in

141

Algeria in the 1950s. Contemporary groups driven by ethno-nationalism can be divided into three sub-categories. These groups fight for autonomy, unification, or reunification (irredentism). For instance, Al Aqsa Martyrs Brigade, Jammu and Kashmiri Liberation Front (JKLF), and the Liberation Tigers of Tamil Eelam are fighting for independence from Israel, India, and Sri Lanka respectively. The members of these groups are motivated by Palestinian, Kashmiri and Tamil nationalism. Similarly, Continuity and Real IRA are fighting for reunification with the Republic of Ireland. Likewise, the PKK is fighting for linguistic and cultural autonomy for the Kurds in South-eastern Turkey. In comparison to other types of terrorism, ethno-nationalist conflicts produce the largest number of fatalities and casualties, the largest number of displaced persons and refugees, and the biggest human rights violations. Groups that have adopted virulent ethno-nationalist ideologies pose a significant threat to their opposing ethnic communities and governments.

Politico-religious terrorism

Groups driven by religiosity include those from the Christian, Jewish, Sikh, Hindu, Buddhist and Islamic faiths. They include Army of God in the US, Kach and Kahne Chai of Israel, Babbar Khalsa International of Punjab, India, Aum Shinrikyo (recently renamed Aleph) of Japan, Islamic Resistance Movement (Hamas), Palestinian Islamic Jihad (PIJ), and Armed Islamic Group of Algeria. Aum, an apocalyptic group, aimed at taking over Japan and then the world. In contrast to other Islamist groups campaigning within their territories, Al Qaeda and (to a lesser extent) Lebanese Hezbollah have a global or a universalistic Islamic agenda. To justify violence, politically motivated religious leaders propagate corrupt versions of religious texts, often misinterpreting and misrepresenting the larger religions.

Of the religious category of groups, Islamists or groups motivated by radical Islamic ideology have been the most violent. Two pivotal events in 1979 – the Islamic Revolution in Iran and the Soviet intervention in Afghanistan – led to the increase in the number of groups driven by Islamism. By holding on to US hostages for 444 days, the Islamic Republic of Iran defied the US, and the anti-Soviet multi-national Afghan mujahidin defeated the largest land force, the Soviet Army. After successfully defeating one superpower, the Islamists turned their energies towards building a capability to defeat the remaining superpower – the United States of America, its allies, and its friends in the Muslim world. With martyrdom becoming widespread and popular among Islamist groups throughout the 1980s and 1990s, the scale of violence these groups unleashed surpassed that from secular ethno-nationalist, left-wing, and right-wing groups. For instance, the Palestinian Liberation Organisation, the Popular Front for the Liberation of Palestine, and the Abu Nidal Organisation killed far fewer people than their Islamist counterparts, Hamas and PIJ. In the evolution of politico-religious groups, Al Qaeda and its family of groups are new actors, operating globally and willing to kill in large numbers.

Other categories

Terrorist campaigns are also driven by ideologies that lack mass appeal and are therefore less common, for example state-sponsored, anarchist, and single-issue terrorism. As terrorism is a low-cost, high-impact form of violence, states wishing to advance their foreign policy goals have supported terrorist groups to attack their inimical states. Due to sanctions imposed by the international community against states that sponsor terrorist groups, this clandestine surrogate form of warfare has declined throughout the 1990s into the 21st century. Although the US government accuses a range of countries for supporting terrorism, little evidence exists that North Korea, Sudan, or Cuba currently sponsor terrorism. Throughout the 1990s, Sudan and Libya were active sponsors of terrorism. Although the scale of sponsorship has declined, governments in Iran, Syria and, to a lesser extent, Lebanon continue to support terrorism. For instance, 'Iran has arranged a number of shipments of small arms and associated ammunition, rocket-propelled grenades, mortar rounds, 107-millimeter rockets, and plastic explosives, possibly including man-portable air defense systems, MANPADs to the Taliban since 2006.'[36] The politically coloured US list does not include another dozen countries that support foreign terrorist groups clandestinely.

Single-issue terrorist groups include violent animal rights activists and anti-abortion groups that seek to change a specific policy or practice rather than the political system. Anarchist terrorists seek to overthrow established governments by waves of bombings and assassinations. The recent wave of protests against globalisation parallels anarchist violence from 1870–1920. However, the trajectory of anti-globalisation movements is yet to be seen. State response to anti-globalisation movements will determine whether we are likely to witness the emergence of terrorist groups espousing the cause of anti-globalisation.

Some groups have overlapping ideologies. Although PKK is ethno-nationalist, it has a strong Marxist–Leninist orientation. Similarly, the original ideological disposition of the LTTE was Marxist–Leninist. Likewise Hamas and PIJ are religious, but they have a strong nationalist dimension. Although Al Aqsa Martyrs Brigade is ethno-nationalist, it has a strong religious dimension. Ideologies of groups tend to shift with the changes in the political environment. Groups in North America and Western Europe driven by left

---

36   US Government source and interviews with Afghanistan government officials including National Security Advisor, Kabul, March 2008.

wing ideologies declined in strength and size at the end of the Cold War. Conversely, the post-Cold War period witnessed a resurgence of groups driven by ethnicity and religiosity. As a result, groups driven by ethnicity and religion account for about 70–80% of all terrorist groups. Furthermore, the ethno-nationalist and religious groups have the greatest staying power: unlike left- or right-wing conflicts, ethno-nationalist and religious conflicts are protracted.

Why do people join or support terrorist groups?

By the cunning use of propaganda, terrorist groups have a high capacity to indoctrinate and motivate their ethnic and religious brethren to join them as full-time and part-time members, collaborators, supporters, and sympathisers. Protracted socio-economic and political conflicts create the conditions to spawn and sustain virulent ideologies. Terrorist ideologues indoctrinate members, supporters, sympathisers and potential recruits through propaganda disseminated by word of mouth, sermons and lectures, leaflets and booklets, printed media, radio, television, and the internet. Theorists have long argued that poverty, lack of education, and unemployment produce terrorist recruits and supporters. However, Osama bin Laden comes from the richest non-royal Saudi family, and his principal strategist, Dr Ayman Al Zawahiri, is from one of the most educated families in Egypt. Although those who live in poverty or are underemployed are most vulnerable to ideological indoctrination, it is this ideological indoctrination rather than deprivation or relative deprivation that generates recruits and supporters for terrorism. However, as the socio-economic and political conditions in the Global South (Asia, Africa, Middle East, Latin America, and the former USSR) are conducive for the inculcation of terrorist ideologies, the bulk of the terrorist groups are located in the poorer regions of the world. Both territorial and migrant communities harbouring actual and perceived grievances and aspirations provide significant political, economic and military support for terrorist groups.

Often the most committed members of terrorist groups are those directly affected by political violence, often by a state or a state-sponsored group. Those who have suffered the loss of their families, friends, and other loved ones or their homes and schools become the most committed. The victims join or support a terrorist group as a vehicle to seek revenge or as an alternative form of government. By its own political and military actions, it is hard for a terrorist group to grow in strength and size. Often to generate widespread public support, terrorist groups provoke security forces to overreact. A restrained response from law enforcement officials is therefore critical to prevent terrorist groups from expanding the support bases essential for their recruitment and sustenance. On the factors that escalate and de-escalate support for political violence, especially terrorism, formal and informal education and re-education of government is essential.

As the end goal of a terrorist group is always political, terrorist groups are armed political organisations. Therefore, the motivation for a person to join a terrorist group is similar to that of joining a political party. The difference is that a terrorist group uses violence, while a political party uses non-violent means to influence its audience. Many join terrorist groups because they have failed to achieve their political goal by political means. The terrorist justifies the use of violence because they see no other path available. However, unlike most political parties that are democratic and tolerate dissent, almost all the terrorist groups are totalitarian movements led by dictators. The internal and external political environments of members are controlled with limited or no access to the outside world. Like members of a cult, members of a terrorist group share certain values and beliefs. Singularly and collectively, its members believe they can accomplish the aims, objectives, and goals of the terrorist group.

While ideology is the key factor, other motivations exist for a person to join or support a terrorist group. These may include the belief that the political process has failed and that the only way to achieve the end goal is to support or use terrorism, or the belief that by employing terrorism – as opposed to democratic means – the end goal is feasible. A person may feel driven to support or join a terrorist group by leftist or rightist indoctrination, ethnic affinity or common religious belief. Terrorist ideologues can also raise the awareness or impression that a community has been wronged or deprived. More than deprivation itself, relative deprivation makes people rebel (Gurr 1970). Furthermore, people may believe that joining or lending support to the terrorist group will correct the situation.

Sustained terrorist indoctrination can construct new grievances (feelings of insecurity) or exacerbate existing grievances (lack of education and employment opportunities; linguistic and cultural rights; land settlement and colonisation; regional autonomy). Similarly, by heightened propaganda the aspirations of an affected community – for instance, to statehood – can be elevated. Young people are particularly vulnerable to indoctrination. Some recruits are driven by altruistic reasons: genuine desire to sacrifice his or her life for the people, the land, or for any other ideal could drive a recruit or a serving member to commit an act of terrorism. Terrorist propaganda inculcates a belief in sacrificing one's life to create a better future for the community, religion, etc., attracts fresh recruits, and increases the commitment of existing ones. Inculcating the belief that death is inevitable and that (opposing) government troops would harm a potential recruit because of differences in ethnicity, religion or ideology can drive people to join a terrorist group and to contribute to the cause before dying.

Revenge is another powerful motivation. A wild form of justice, revenge is often triggered when security forces harm an individual, his or her loved ones, or property. Joining or supporting a terrorist group may be perceived as the only avenue of exacting revenge. Although conscription is not widespread and is often highlighted by governments for propaganda purposes, terrorist groups may also coerce some recruits to join or support them. In an atmosphere of fear and uncertainty, a potential recruit can be threatened by a terrorist group to join or support them. Such recruits harbour the belief that joining or supporting a terrorist group protects family members from the terrorist threat. Based on interviews with detainees, some are drawn to terrorist and guerrilla groups by the membership of a secret organisation, attracted by the weapons, shining boots and uniform. They feel a sense of excitement or being different from the rest of society. Some join or support a terrorist group for social recognition or social acceptance – a romantic notion of being a key figure or a special person, even a sort of a crusader. As opposed to the 'ordinary public', being a terrorist means one can command power and strength.

As contemporary terrorist groups engage in organised crime – from trading in diamonds to trafficking in narcotics and human smuggling and credit card fraud – to fund their existence and operations, a few people perceive joining a terrorist group as lucrative. A person can join a terrorist group for reasons driven by personal gain and greed. Often in conflict zones, the opportunities for livelihood are limited. Instead of starving, a potential recruit prefers to join a group in order to survive and reduce the burden on the family and at times even to feed the family.

Overreaction by governments enhances support for extremism and its by-product, terrorism. Over the years I have personally observed how terrorist groups draw strength from government overreaction. A terrorist group by its own action cannot be successful. Often government overreaction or underreaction generates overwhelming support and recruits for terrorism. This perceived inappropriateness of government actions can drive individuals to become terrorists or to support terrorism. Mass arrests by the security forces – including arrests on mistaken identity or on false information from a personal enemy – can humiliate and turn a non-terrorist sympathiser into a terrorist sympathiser. Similarly, collateral damage by the security forces which results in the death of a person's mother, father, brother or sister can motivate that person to join a terrorist group. Intelligence is therefore paramount to identify and target accurately the terrorist and terrorist infrastructure. If for every terrorist killed or captured, the terrorist group can recruit five, the battle against the group is lost.

The policy of collective punishment meted out in Israel and in some other theatres of conflict has proved to be counterproductive. Often when a colleague is killed, the security forces tend to enforce collective punishment. To prevent such counter-productive actions and especially overreaction, accountability and oversight must exist at all levels in the counter-terrorist organisation. By investing in counter-propaganda such as criminalising support meant for terrorist groups and eroding the legitimacy of the group, governments can reduce the motivation for people to join or support a terrorist group. Targeting the terrorist 'rank and file' with counter-propaganda and offering irresistible incentives for desertions and surrenders can weaken a group from within. Non-military methods are equally or more important than military methods. Political and economic measures are enduring and can have a lasting impact on a terrorist group as well as a terrorist support base.

Terrorist training

Terrorist groups pose a significant threat to domestic, regional, and international security because of the access they have to professional training and weaponry. Today, terrorist groups have access to the same level of training available to personnel in the security forces. Dependent on the need, resources, and opportunities, terrorist groups impart both ideological and physical training to their recruits. Although physical training may appear to be the more important component of the two, ideological training is absolutely critical. To inculcate commitment of fresh recruits to the aims and the objectives of a group, ideological indoctrination is considered paramount. Terrorist groups therefore emphasise ideological training, which is usually imparted by ideologues.

After the initial training of a recruit, ideological training does not cease but continues as long as a recruit retains membership of the group. Often, both the motivation and endurance of a terrorist, especially to survive in a hostile zone, depends more on his or her commitment to ideology. More than the physical training, ideological training ensures the staying power of a terrorist. For instance, most of the 9/11 suicide hijackers lived in the US for over a year without changing their mind because of the high level of indoctrination they had received over the years. Even after Zacarias Moussaoui was captured three weeks before 9/11, it was his belief in Al Qaeda's aims and objectives that precluded him from divulging the organisation's elaborate plans and preparations as well as the identity and location of Al Qaeda members and leaders in the US.

Ideological training differs between organisations. If ethno-nationalist ideology drives a group, its members will be indoctrinated about the suffering of their ethnic brethren and the need to sacrifice their lives so that future generations will be able to live in safety. The opposing ethnic community will be portrayed as subhuman, evil, and destructive. Furthermore, the member will be indoctrinated to the point that he or she will believe that only through a sustained terrorist campaign will they be able to recover their homeland.

Members of an Islamist group will be made to believe that it is a Muslim's duty to wage jihad (holy war). Almost all the Islamist terrorist groups waging jihad in Palestine, Algeria, Kashmir, Bosnia, Chechnya, Afghanistan, Eritrea,

Somalia and the Philippines are driven by the Salafi school. Members of this branch are indoctrinated to worship and love Allah above all else. They do not even believe or follow the Imams and the Sheikhs; they only pledge their allegiance to Allah and to his Messenger. Contemporary ideologues draw from the writings of Sayed Abdul A'la Maududi, the founder leader of the Pakistani political party Jamat-I-Islami, and Sayed Qutb, the ideologue of the Egyptian Muslim Brotherhood who sanctioned the use of violence for the establishment of Islam. They also appealed for the return of the Koran and Sunnah, with the principles of Islam applied to modern society by the use of rational judgment in religious matters. Maududi and Qutb reaffirmed the function of Islam in politics and civilised societies under the control of secularism and the Western development paradigm of democracy. They both opposed Western political thought, especially the concept of sovereignty, and called for the establishment of a revolutionary 'vanguard' of true believers to organise Islamic states (Azzam 1988). By citing the successes of the Iranian revolution of 1979 and the anti-Soviet Afghan jihad (1979–89), they build confidence to take on their enemies – both Muslim regimes friendly to the West and the West itself.

The curriculum and duration of training for a recruit depends on the environment. If the terrorist has to survive a longer period in the battlefield in a guerrilla role, then he or she is trained for a longer period. This prevents demoralisation and desertion as well as injury and death. A poorly trained terrorist in a guerrilla role is likely to suffer injury and die, demoralising other members, encouraging desertion and restraining recruitment. Training and retraining is the key to success of a terrorist group, whether operating in a terrorist or a guerrilla context. Therefore, most sophisticated groups place emphasis on continuous training to ensure that their members are mentally and physically prepared for battle at all times.

For urban operations, Al Qaeda uses a manual of the Islamic Group of Egypt for its terrorist training. The title is imposed on a drawing of the globe through which a sword pierces through the continent of Africa and a section of the Middle East. In its introduction, the manual is dedicated to the 'young Moslem men who are pure, believing and fighting for the cause of Allah. It is my contribution towards paving the road that leads to majestic Allah and establishes a caliphate according to the prophecy.'

Training for terrorists can be extremely in-depth, lengthy, and highly specialised. What is apparent is that a generation of terrorists now exists with knowledge comparable to regular soldiers in service of governments. Well-funded groups have hired some of the best available Special Forces trainers in the world. Therefore, to fight contemporary terrorism, it is essential to provide highly specialised counter-terrorism training to troops assigned for counter-terrorism functions.

Terrorist tactics and targets

Terrorist ideologies provide the justification and framework for the selection of certain tactics and targets. Each tactic has its own specific motivation and purpose. Hijackings, kidnapping and hostage-taking belong to one sub-category of tactics. Terrorists tend to be 'copycats', so hijackings, hostage-taking and kidnappings become 'fashionable' during certain periods. In addition to these tactics, terrorist groups use threats to advance their aims and objectives. The threat of a violent action (bombing, assassination) to cause fear or to coerce an action or inaction is also an act of terrorism. Terrorist targets are both human and infrastructure in land, air and sea. Human targets include political leaders, administrators, military personnel, business leaders and population centres, while infrastructure targets include aviation, maritime, symbolic, and other national critical infrastructures. Symbolic and high prestige targets are terrorist favourites. Attacking the latter magnifies the terrorist group's power and influence, prompting the respective government to engage in massive retaliation and thereby increasing the group's profile and influence.

Assassination

When a specific person is targeted for a political purpose, retribution or retaliation, it is an assassination. This is not a random killing, but focuses on an individual for perceived grievances. Executions by self-imposed sub-state courts, 'kangaroo' courts, or judges fit into this category. Often, terrorist assassins are motivated through ideological indoctrination to hate the target for his or her action, inaction, nationality, religion, belief system, political position, and so on.

Traditionally, assassination has been used in the case of heads of state or government for the specific purpose of toppling governments. By assassinating strong leaders, especially those who fought terrorism steadfastly, terrorists have been successful in bringing to office leaders willing to compromise or to follow a course of inaction. Therefore, leadership targets are strategic targets, aimed at bringing about change. Terrorists have also targeted moderates to eliminate support for a negotiated political settlement or a voice (including journalists) against a terrorist group. By assassinating important leaders selectively, terrorists demonstrate the vulnerability of a society to terrorism. This drives fear into the enemy quarter, especially if the leader was well protected and the terrorist breached security. By assassination, terrorists seek to break the will of the public. Loss of quality leaders, especially if they enjoyed mass support, has led to mass demoralization. When commanders of militaries are assassinated, it leads to demoralisation of troops, especially frontline troops.

Armed assault

Most armed assaults are direct attacks using bombs, grenades, and guns. Of all weapons, bombs remain the most favoured, used in over 60% of all terrorist attacks. Many groups favour the tactic of bombing because the terrorist is usually far removed from the event. As a long-distance weapon, it preserves the elements of surprise and shock. Depending on the quantity of explosives and the target environment, it is likely to kill several hundred people; if a bomb is positioned strategically, it could kill even more. The plan of Ramzi Ahmed Yousef, who parked a car bomb in the basement of the World Trade Centre in February 1993, was to topple one WTC tower on top of the other and thereby kill up to 250,000 people. Terrorists can also use bombs to target and kill individuals, such as by placing bombs under car bonnets, seats, or chassis.

Ambush

In terms of volume of attacks, terrorist ambushing follows terrorist bombing. Like armed assault, an ambush is a coordinated surprise attack, but unlike assault involves lying in wait for the target. If an ambush is well planned, those coming within the kill zone of an ambush are unlikely to survive. In a guerrilla situation, this can involve the use of mines and mortars. While a mine attack involves an explosion directed against personnel on foot or against a vehicle (i.e. carrying troops or civilians), a mortar attack uses indirect fire against the intended target. An ambush against civilians is categorised as an act of terrorism, while an ambush against military personnel is categorised as a guerrilla attack.

Hostage-taking

International law defines hostage-taking as seizing or detaining and threatening to kill, injure, or retain a person in order to compel particular action or inaction from a third party. Terrorists take hostages either from an aircraft or by barricading a building to negotiate demands or to gain world attention. After taking a hostage or hostages, the terrorist group will make a set of demands, which usually include money and safe passage. The international publicity and attention enables the terrorists to highlight their cause. In a few cases, the families, businesses, insurance companies and even governments yield to the demands made by the hijackers, which increases the threat of terrorism even further. For instance, the Islamic Movement of Uzbekistan kidnapped American tourists after a Japanese businessman paid to seek the release of Japanese geologists kidnapped in Kirygyzstan. After Libya paid ransom money for the release of one batch of hostages, the Abu Sayyaf Group kidnapped even more. Likewise, after India freed Ahmed Saeed Omar Sheikh after Harakat-ul-Mujahidin took hostages of passengers in an Indian airline flight, he was involved in the kidnapping and murder of Daniel Pearl, the first US terrorist casualty since 9/11. The policy of appeasement rarely works with a terrorist group.

Some terrorist groups such as Hezbollah, FARC, ELN, AUC, and Al Ansar Mujahidin are notorious for hostage taking and hostage holding. Although most hostages are eventually freed, a few groups – regardless of whether their demands are met – kill their hostages. As the Afghan Taliban and Al Qaeda in Iraq demonstrated, killing hostages contributed to the objective of many terrorist groups: to drive terror and fear into their enemies. Two terrorist leaders introduced and developed the method of graphic killings of hostages and their publicity on the internet. After Khalid Sheikh Mohamed, alias KSM, alias Mokhtar, the mastermind of 9/11, kidnapped and beheaded Daniel Pearl, a Wall Street journalist, Al Qaeda posted the video of the beheading on the internet. Similarly, the leader of Tawhid wal Jihad (later Al Qaeda in Iraq), Abu Musab al Zarqawi, an associate of KSM, introduced video recording of graphic killings and their postings on the internet.

Hostage-taking for large cash ransoms is the fastest growing form of terrorist activity in Colombia, Chechnya, Mexico, Yemen, the Philippines, Pakistan, Afghanistan and Iraq. Even UN peacekeepers, officials and aid workers have been taken hostage in Bosnia, East Timor, and Sierra Leone. Many of these countries lack either the resources to control the security environment or the elite units to respond to a hostage taking.

Hijacking

A hijacking occurs when a terrorist or a group of terrorists forcibly takes over a vehicle or transportation system. The vehicle or transportation system can be public or private (e.g. car jacking), and it can be for the purpose of inciting fear and/or for murder. In contrast to other tactics, hijackings give mobility, an opportunity to highlight their grievance, and unparalleled media attention. The hijacking of aircraft beginning in the late 1960s has been the single biggest threat throughout history. By the early 1970s, Israelis eliminated the threat of hijackings by introducing sky marshals and a range of other initiatives. The counter-measures displaced the threat and forced the Palestinian hijackers to consider other options.

Kidnapping

A kidnapping occurs when an individual or a group is abducted by force for ransom or coercion. To increase the ransom payment or coercive power, some terrorist groups refrain from publicising immediately that they have abducted a person. Often the person targeted is a prominent political or military figure, wealthy person or businessperson, or an opponent. As kidnapping is a lucrative industry in some countries, terrorist groups such as FARC subcontract kidnappings to other organisations. A few terrorist groups such as Al Qaeda conduct a specialised course on kidnapping both for its members and for members of other groups. In addition to funds, motivations for terrorist kidnappings include publicity, political concessions, release of terrorist detainees and prisoners, and revenge and retaliation.

Suicide terrorism

Suicide terrorism is one of the most difficult terrorist threats to manage. In a suicide bomb attack, bombers intend to kill themselves and to destroy their targets by using improvised explosive or non-explosive devices. In contrast with a non-suicide terrorist, who seeks to survive to fight another day, a suicide terrorist is indoctrinated to kill and to die with the completion of the mission. As suicide terrorists concentrate their maximum attention and effort to destroy targets and not to protect themselves, it becomes difficult to stop a suicide attack once a bomber has been launched. In saying this, by investing in high-grade intelligence, a suicide attack can be detected and disrupted in the planning and preparation stages.

Traditional law enforcement is based on the principle of deterrence by punishing the perpetrator. While destroying his or her target, the suicide terrorist defies punishment by actively seeking his or her death. Suicide terrorism is what enables a terrorist group to inflict severe damage to targets such as the US Marine Barracks, US diplomatic targets in East Africa, the USS Cole, the World Trade Centre and the Pentagon. By being willing to die, a terrorist retains a high potential to destroy targets that cannot be attacked successfully using non-suicide terrorist operations. Furthermore, by integrating suicide terrorism into the chemical, biological, radiological and nuclear realm, the potential for destruction is unprecedented.

Since the beginning of the contemporary wave of suicide terrorism with Hezbollah in Lebanon in the early 1980s, suicide terrorism as a phenomenon has been adopted by a wide range of groups. Although the largest number of groups that conduct suicide attacks is Islamist, secular groups – especially the ethno-nationalist groups – have conducted the largest volume of attacks. Today, a range of terrorist groups have developed the capability to conduct suicide operations. As suicide terrorism is cost-effective and difficult to defeat, the number of terrorist groups using this tactic is steadfastly growing.

In addition to conducting intelligence operations and enacting protective security measures to counter the terrorist threat, governments and non-governmental organisations can develop non-military operations to reduce the threat of terrorism. These measures can include reforming the education system, providing formal and informal education, using the media, and other prophylactic measures such as improving the quality of life of areas affected by the violence. Furthermore, sustained measures using educators, clerics and other prominent figures to counter the misinterpretation, misrepresentation and propagation of corrupt versions of religious and political texts is essential. For example, the Islamic clerics constituting the leadership of terrorist groups intertwine Islam with earthly force, stressing sacrifice with the intention of increasing the appeal of martyrdom for their cause. Suicide is contrary to the teachings in the Koran, but istashaad – self-sacrifice or martyrdom in the service of Allah – is viewed as an admirable death. Terrorists groups may promote the latter definition of their actions in order to encourage recruits.

To contain the spread of terrorist propaganda videos, many with graphic footage reinforcing a demonic impression of the opponents, disseminating terrorist propaganda must be criminalised. Otherwise, suicide terrorism will persist and even grow as a phenomenon. Terrorists have yet to realise the full potential of suicide terrorism, especially in the target-rich countries of the West.

The future

Based on my past research, Al Qaeda, its associated groups, and its home-grown cells is likely to pose the most dominant threat to the US, its allies and its friends in the foreseeable future. The Asian and Middle Eastern Muslim countries will suffer the brunt of terrorism by Al Qaeda and its associated groups. Nonetheless, the US and their European and Australian allies will witness periodic spectacular attacks mounted primarily by home-grown cells. In the spectrum of Muslim and non-Muslim groups, Al Qaeda directed and inspired groups will pose the single biggest threat. The principal ideological and operational threat will stem from two international epicenters of terrorism: Iraq in the Middle East and tribal Pakistan (FATA). Although Al Qaeda has suffered significantly since 9/11, the group has been able to re-establish a presence by working with likeminded groups. For instance, Al Qaeda co-opted Tawhid Wal Jihad, now operating as Al Qaeda in Iraq and the Levant, and Al Qaeda co-opted the Salafist Group for Call and Combat, now operating as Al Qaeda organisation of the Islamic Maghreb in Algeria, North Africa and in Europe. By co-opting, Al Qaeda transferred its operational practice of mass fatality suicide attacks and ideological reference of targeting the US, its allies and friends.

In the Middle East, the Levant, North Africa, and to a lesser extent the Arabian Peninsula will suffer from terrorist attacks in the coming years. Likewise in Asia, South Asia will suffer most from terrorism, followed by Central Asia and Southeast Asia. With the exception of Xinjiang in China, the threat of terrorism to Northeast Asia will be low. Similarly, Sub-Saharan Africa, especially in Eastern and Horn of Africa, governments, private sector and the society will suffer from intermittent terrorist attacks. With suicide being adopted as a popular tactic, more groups will conduct both vehicle-borne and human-borne suicide attacks.

Conclusion

Today, terrorism presents itself as a top threat to national security for most governments. Most governments face a moderate to high threat from group terrorism and home-grown extremism. In the conflict zones in the global South, where most of the threat groups originate, the threat is high. In North America, Europe, Australia and New Zealand, the threat is moderate. In the West, the pre-eminent threat stems from radicalisation of migrant and diaspora enclaves and pockets. Creating a counter-terrorist and counter-extremist environment in Europe requires both tactical and strategic responses.

The spearhead of counter-terrorism has been intelligence. Against terrorism, informants and, increasingly, community sources as well as technical assets have proved effective in the immediate term (1–2 years). Investment in law enforcement and intelligence has prevented and deterred acts of violence. However, the strategy for defeating terrorism and extremism in the mid (2–5 years) and long (5–10 years) term is to develop a robust ideological, educational, media, financial, and developmental response. At the heart of strategic response is de-radicalisation both of the Muslim community (currently viewed by the West as the pre-eminent threat) and detainees.

Before the West became interested in de-radicalisation as a tool, several governments in Asia and the Middle East developed and implemented de-radicalisation programmes. To different degrees of success, Egypt, Uzbekistan, Jordan, Morocco, Yemen, Saudi Arabia, Singapore and Indonesia invested both in community engagement and detainee rehabilitation. Ideologically motivated extremism, and its vicious by-product terrorism, can be defeated only by counter-ideology and operational counter-terrorism. Without over or under-reaction, it is essential for governments to target precisely both the conceptual and operational infrastructures.

References

Azzam, A. (1988) 'Al Qaeda Al Subah.' *Al Jihad* Magazine, Peshawar, Pakistan.

Gurr, T. R. (1970) *Why Men Rebel.* Princeton: Princeton University Press.

PROLOGUE: **COLLECTIVE VIOLENCE AND WAR**

War is probably one of the most universally accepted forms of killing – a 'necessary evil', perhaps. While most people are taught that killing is bad, this chapter talks about the contradiction that 'they are sent to war with the instruction that killing is necessary, honourable, and even heroic'. This dissonance poses serious problems for those who find themselves in such a situation.

Cohen, in his excellent exploration of denial, describes how people learn to justify behaviour they may otherwise define as unacceptable. Cohen defines denial as the 'need to be innocent of a troubling recognition' (2001: 25). A powerful example of this is soldiers who must learn to kill in times of war:

> A soldier kills, but denies that this is immoral: those he killed were enemies who deserved their fate. He is *justifying* his action. Another soldier admits the immorality of his killings, but denies full volition for his action: this was a case of involuntary obedience to orders. He is *excusing* his action. (*ibid.*: 59)

The massacre at My Lai during the Vietnam War is a classic example of such behaviour. Cohen (*ibid.*: 90) commented that in such cases 'Each step becomes a mechanical action, solely means-directed. In [Lieutenant] Calley's chilling words, each My Lai killing was "no big deal".' Cohen goes on to summarise, 'You are not required to deny moral values, but only their application to this particular situation: you are allowed to harm *these* others here (surely a better explanation than "splitting of the ego")' (2001: 89).

Despite later confidence in resorts to war, Christians were pacifists for the first 300 years of Christianity. Early Christians were 'given over to peace, that God prohibits killing even in a just cause, without exception, that the weapons of the Christian were prayer, justice and suffering' (Ferguson 1978: 103). Development of the 'just war' doctrine took place under the Emperor Constantine, when the Roman Empire was under attack, but this continued to develop from the fourth to the seventeenth centuries. Ferguson comments that this original pacifism contrasts tremendously with acts committed in the name of Christianity during the Crusades, 1100 years after Jesus. He also notes that the just war doctrine 'continues to provide a basis for some Christians' response to the legitimacy of war' (*ibid.*: 164).

Former President George W. Bush's rhetoric that a 'pre-emptive war' was somehow necessary and beneficial to the world as a whole won over the hearts of many Americans with the genuine (and comforting) belief that, through war, they were 'doing good'. Indeed, he referred to the war in Iraq as a 'crusade' – a term which has much greater depth of meaning for those in the Middle East. Former Prime Minister Tony Blair also referred to his faith in a number of statements regarding his support for the war in Iraq.

In contrast to these perspectives, the editor of a notable Christian publication in the US argued that:

> George [W.] Bush believes God told him to level a military strike against Iraq. Once such God-on-one directions are accepted, there is no common ground for moral discussion. After all, maybe God is speaking to him in a manner unique to my own mystical experience. That, to me, represents a dangerous theology. (Batstone 2004)

Kimball, too, notes that 'This much is crystal clear: holy war is not holy... Healthy religion speaks not of war but the promise of peace and justice' (2002: 182–3). This again exemplifies the fact that, even within a relatively unified culture, people may be 'two nations under God'. Daya Somasundaram's chapter helpfully examines root causes of aggression in humans, both in terms of how violence originates as well as why it continues. He takes primarily a psychological approach to this, yet acknowledges the wide range of influences that can ultimately result in violence, aggression, and war.

References

Batstone, D. (2004) 'God-talk and moral values.' *Sojourners Magazine* on line, 11 September 2004. www.sojo.net/index.cfm?action=sojomail.display&issue=041109#2.

Cohen, S. (2001) *States of Denial: Knowing About Atrocities and Suffering*. Cambridge: Polity Press.

Ferguson, J. (1978) *War and Peace in the World's Religions*. New York: Oxford University Press.

Kelman, H. C. and Hamilton, V. L. (1989) *Crimes of Obedience*. New Haven: Yale University Press.

Kimball, C. (2002) *When Religion Becomes Evil*. New York: HarperCollins Publishers Inc.

Chapter 8

Collective Violence and War

Daya Somasundaram

Introduction

While most people are taught that killing fellow human beings is wrong, they are sent to war with the instruction that killing is necessary, honourable, and even heroic. In the beginning, this contradiction will therefore be difficult for many people to cope with or to justify in their own minds. Thus in most wars, the soldiers who actually have to carry out the killing of the 'enemy' need to be mobilised mentally through a complex procedure of indoctrination and training. Throughout history, most societies have evolved very similar patterns of behaviour in the context of warfare and the methods of preparing the nation or group to justify the mass killings involved. Most people are then able to carry out the killing of their 'enemy' with minimal inhibition or even with enthusiasm. Once people have 'bloodied their hands', as it were, then killing appears to become easier, even to the point of addiction.

Killing can take place at an individual level, one person killing another (homicide) in self-defence, or due to personal animosity or feud. The killer usually knows the victim, so the act is more personal. Killing can also take place collectively, with members of one group killing members of another. Here, group membership determines the killers and the killed. This kind of collective killing takes place in situations of racial riots or war and can be quite impersonal. Usually social sanction and encouragement for killing are present in these circumstances; people are given a 'license to kill'. Indeed, it may be seen as a social duty or responsibility, mixed with righteous anger and 'militant enthusiasm' (Lorenz 1966). Although the psychological characteristics of individual killing differ from those involved in collective acts, and while it may be misleading merely to extrapolate from the individual to the collective level, there is some degree of overlap.

This chapter will look at aspects of individual killing that may help in understanding collective killing, as well as explore the factors involved in mass killing found during war.[36]

Biological mechanisms

A basic biological mechanism – a 'hardwiring' in the brain – for aggressive behaviour exists in all animals, including humans. This rarely ends in killing. Anatomically, certain areas of the brain that are deeper and older in evolutionary terms, particularly the amygdaloid nucleus, parts of the hypothalamus and other limbic areas, consistently elicit aggression or 'sham rage' when stimulated by disease or implanted electrodes. Removal of these centres (or destruction by pathology such as brain tumours) produces pacificity. This knowledge has been used successfully to treat patients with uncontrolled violence, especially when secondary to brain disease, by implantation of electrodes or other neuro-surgical procedures. Whether these same centres are involved when an organism goes for the kill, or whether other centres are activated while inhibitory centres are overridden, is not clear. In addition, human society has evolved moral, ethical, legal, religious, social and cultural inhibitions to killing, particularly individual killing within a community. Anatomical and biological mechanisms may well underlie these inhibitions. However, these same socio-cultural elements are also called upon to justify and motivate collective killing in the context of war. That is, moral, ethical, religious, social and cultural reasons are given to justify going to war and killing the enemy.

It is often argued that, biologically and historically, humans have an innate propensity towards aggression. According to Freud (1961), a drive or instinct for aggression or destructiveness exists in man called thanatos. Civilised man's attempt to repress his destructive nature does not always succeed, and there are periodic outbreaks of conflicts and war. This kind of tendency in humankind has been called 'bestiality' or referred to as the animal or lower nature. According to the ethnologist Lorenz (1966), humans share with other animals an innate mechanism for aggression, which has served a variety of adaptive functions for the survival of the species during its evolutionary history. However, no real evidence exists of an inherent tendency for killing in the animal kingdom. Man is the only species to kill its own kind in such numbers, with such cruelty and abandon. Inter-species aggression is very rare in the animal kingdom except in a prey–predator relationship, and that is limited to what is needed for food. Intra-species aggression takes place only during natural feeding and breeding, where it is defensive and adaptive (i.e. furthering the survival of the species). The aggression is territorial (serving to space out individuals) and hierarchical (to establish social order for mating, feeding, defending and leading). Such aggression usually falls far short of actual fighting, often expressed in ritualised displays and threats, and rarely ends in killing (Mathews 1964).

---

36 While this can include acts of genocide, genocide is discussed more fully in Chapter 9.

Although aggression has an adaptive function, rarely does such fighting within the species ever lead to dangerous physical contact or death, for that would work against the survival of the species. Through natural selection, nature has evolved a highly complex behaviour pattern, minutely ritualised into display, threat, and submission or appeasement, so that fights are generally no more than trials of strength, followed by disengagement and rapid withdrawal by the weaker. These ritualised appeasement or submission gestures to signal surrender, such as a dog rolling over to expose its (vulnerable) neck, sets off instinctive mechanisms inhibiting the killing and injuring of fellow members of the species. Mathews (1964) comments, 'It is, indeed, very difficult to find any examples of true overt fighting resulting in the death of the loser among mammals under normal conditions in the wild. It occurs only when population numbers have overtaken the resources of the environment so that serious overcrowding is brought about.'

Lorenz (1966) describes the adaptive function of this limited intra-species aggression which humans share with other animals as spacing out of individuals, selection of better genes, and establishment of a social rank order. The establishment of a dominant hierarchy reduces inter-group quarrelling, provides stability and structure, and facilitates efficient decision-making.

Territoriality

The spacing of the individuals within a habitat would ensure an even distribution of resources. In animals that function in social groups, territoriality serves an adaptive function by enhancing differential survival and reproduction (Boelkins 1970) as well as sufficient supply of food and other resources. In *The Territorial Imperative*, Robert Ardrey (1967) attributes most of man's war-making to his drive to conquer and maintain a geographical territory. Mathews, a professor of animal behaviour, puts it explicitly:

> ... the *roots of man's war-making* are not to be sought, as so many have claimed, in the defence of individual or family territories (although this too is done by our species), it is in our tendency to defend a group territory.... War, then, has its origins in group territoriality, a system of indirect massive killing of surplus individuals in the interest of the well-being of the victors. Cultural developments have changed this into highly organized, socially sanctioned, direct mass-murder. Abhorrent though it is, for most of even our recent history, this mass killing was not biologically maladaptive: whatever the victors might have had to sacrifice, they always emerged better off than the losers. (Mathews 1964; emphasis added)

The problems of territoriality and control of resources was at the heart of most wars, past and present. No greater motivation exists for a collective taking up of arms than in defense of one's homeland, however that is perceived. The development of the concept of nation states in Europe in the 19th century and the more recent development of ethnicity in the last century were both based on the perception of home territories. When people are socialised to invest strong emotions and attachments to a particular territory that becomes the basis of their group identity, they can then be easily mobilised to go to war for this territory. Thus, we have seen the plethora of national and ethnic wars. In addition to people going to war to defend their territory, people can also be made to invade others' territories either to prevent a future threat, to enhance their group's control of vital resources, or as mere political or military strategy. The colonial and imperial wars were basically to establish control over resources. As an example, the more recent US-led war in Iraq was constructed as a preventive war to neutralise weapons of mass destruction that could have been a future threat, allowing the leaders of the US- and UK-led coalition to mobilise their armies. However, the war may have actually been for the control of vital oil resources.

Overcrowding

The rapidly growing human population and increasing densities have led to overcrowding and shortage of space, food and other resources. This has made aggression and violence much more likely. High density of population *per se* may not be directly (causally) related to aggression, but rather has its effect in profoundly altering behavioural and physiological regulatory systems. Many experimental studies have shown that growth-limiting factors develop within the population through physiological changes that decrease the birth and survival rate while increasing the death rate (Boelkins 1970). Along with the other Malthusian principles of disease and famine, war and killing of 'surplus' individuals may be one way nature deals with populations that exceed certain limits to re-establish ecological equilibrium.

A positive correlation is evident between population density, mental illness, and crime rates. Also evident is a correlation between inside-density (number of people within a residence) and such indices of social pathology as murder, assault, and rape. It is quite possible that high population densities cause socio-economic deprivation in terms of poverty, unfulfilled aspirations, frustrations and unemployment, which in turn are responsible for aggressive behaviour that may reduce inhibitions to killing. One of the factors that led to the expansion to the sparsely populated 'New World' in the Americas and the subsequent wars of conquest from overcrowded Western Europe from the 15th century was the rapidly increasing population and dwindling resources.

Social mechanisms

Apart from biological and ecological mechanisms that result in war, humans are social animals living in groups and communities. In addition to the collective interest of groups, nations and states, such as the capture of resources, defence or pre-emption of threats, the avenging of old scores or new affronts, leaders can create and use war to further their own interests as a means to power or strategy to hold on to power. It can also result from miscalculation and misperceptions. In present day contexts, wars have become increasingly internal conflicts – civil wars between groups and communities rather than between nation states. War becomes 'politics through other means', and propaganda, rhetoric, media and social institutions can be mobilized to manufacture the 'war fever' necessary for communities to start fighting each other. Society will then give the sanction for soldiers to be recruited and trained to kill on their behalf. Leaders and military authorities still have to stimulate the very same biological mechanisms for aggression while neutralising the natural inhibitions to killing.

Inhibitions to killing

In the animal world, aggression rarely ends in actual death due to some inborn inhibition to killing. It is pertinent to ask why such inhibitions do not operate in humans – virtually the only species with a history replete with genocidal behaviour, the only 'unhinged killer'(Lorenz 1966).

Humans, thanks to their cerebral dominance, have gradually eliminated the pressure of natural selection in reducing death rates and prolonging life for all members of the species. Western medicine has conquered disease, and technology the problem of food, shelter, temperature and other natural forces. Humans are no longer subject to environmental evolution, though they have created potential dangers: over-population, ecological disequilibrium, pollution, and threat of nuclear holocaust. Thus some argue that, though still left with older, instinctual drives and tendencies like aggression, humans have not been able to evolve socio-culturally (civilised ways of solving problems) to keep pace with technological progress. Modern powerful and efficient weapons have made it possible for killing to take place at a distance, or even by remote control, so the killer does not directly experience the consequences of his or her actions. Had the killing been less remote, then one would expect that inhibitory mechanisms would be more likely to have been activated and to have exerted more influence (Lorenz 1966; Andreski 1964). Modern war is fought with modern weaponry that operates at a distance: machine guns; land mines; artillery and gun boat shelling; aeroplane and helicopter bombing; and rockets and missiles. The combatants are rarely in direct sight, and most casualties are civilian. Further, the political leadership and military hierarchy that determine the policies and overall logistics are far removed from the firing line.

However, it is equally true that many instances of direct slaughter of civilian men, women and children by swords and other 'direct' weaponry continue. This kind of 'unhinged killing' appears to take place wherever there is collective violence, usually as a reactive rage. Atrocities through systematic genocide have taken place in Rwanda, Bosnia, Algeria, Cambodia, Sri Lanka, and in armed conflict such as with the US army in Vietnam at My Lai. Lorenz (1966) has argued that humans, like other omnivores which lack any natural weapons, would not have the usual inhibitions to killing, unlike the heavily armed (teeth, claws) carnivores which have reliable inhibitions which prevent the self-destruction of the species. An estimated 2% of combat soldiers belong to a category called 'aggressive psychopaths' who are natural killers with no inhibitions (Grossman 1996). The excessive aggressive drives of anti-social or psychopathic personalities found in society can be well harnessed by recruiting these individuals into a military establishment and having them vent their energy on 'enemies' of the state while society is made safer. It is clear that war provides ample opportunity for sadistic personalities to derive pleasure from acts of violence, cruelty and torture on hapless victims (Somasundaram 1998).

The claim in March 2003 of the US-led coalition forces in Iraq that they would carry out a precise, clinical operation with minimum civilian casualties turned out to be illusory. Yet the casualties were still not as great as would have happened in a conventional war (the low number of casualties during the war itself may have been more due to the lack of stiff resistance and heavy fighting in population centres). However, modern warfare with sophisticated weaponry against precise military targets, avoiding so-called collateral damage, would be a radical development in human history.

Though territorialism and excessive population may explain killing from an ecological standpoint, we have to go deeper into the human psyche to look for explanations of the causes of human aggression, here in the context of war and collective violence.

Aggressive behaviour

As already mentioned, Freud (1961) saw aggression as a basic instinct to destroy and kill that builds up until discharged. Civilisation's attempts to inhibit man's aggressive drive result in outbreaks of collective violence or war from time to time. Later psychoanalysts do not accept aggression as a primary drive but rather see it as only one other way of striving for instinctual aims in response to obstruction or frustration (Solomon 1970).

Aggression can occur as a response to pain and as a response to threat to status (Boelkins 1970). Pain is the most consistently reliable single cause of aggression. Animals with complex brains readily learn when an event is a threat of pain, and they will respond aggressively to the perceived threat. Psychological pain and threat (such as the loss of identity) may represent analogues to physical pain. Similarly, a threat to status is commonly responded

162

to with aggression. However, these kinds of defensive aggression usually do not result in killing.

Neo-Freudian humanist Erich Fromm (1973) distinguished between defensive aggression, which all animals share as a physiologically programmed reaction to threats, and malignant aggression. Defensive, 'benign' aggression serves the survival of the individual and the species, is biologically adaptive, and ceases when the threat no longer exists. 'Malignant' aggression, in contrast (e.g. cruelty and destructiveness), is specific to humans. It is malignant aggression that makes people the only primate to kill and torture members of their own species without any reason, either biological or economic, and who espouse satisfaction in so doing:

> A woman arrived at a refugee camp in Safala Province from an area under attack by RENAMO. She appeared physically unharmed, but she had been forced to watch her son being killed. Her son's murderers then chopped up the corpse, cooked it, and threatened to kill her if she did not eat the portion they served to her... 'I did what they asked. I was scared. I did not know what else to do.' (recounted in Nordstrom 1995: 263)

Fromm (1973) further delineates two character-rooted passions as part of malignant aggression: *sadism* – the passion for unrestricted power over another sentient being, and *necrophilia* – the passion to destroy life and the attraction to all that is dead, decaying and purely mechanical.

Looking at the expression of aggressive behaviour, Tabias and Neziroglu (1981) discuss clinical studies that may have relevance to different types of violence:

> Megargee (1960) has made distinctions between habitually aggressive individuals who are under-controlled, and those who commit crimes of extreme violence but who have no previous history of assaultive behaviour and are over-controlled. The under-controlled type is impulsive and usually responds to frustration through aggression. The over-controlled type rarely responds with aggression because of strong generalised inhibitions. Therefore, he aggresses only when the instigation has built over time.

It is possible that, at a socio-cultural level, in communities that are tightly controlled, aggression may be strongly inhibited. Thus, violent crimes and homicide rates would be characteristically low. However, it may be possible for community leaders to mobilise and direct members to kill collectively in an organised way, as in war against a common target group. On the other hand, under-controlled societies may be characterised by high homicide rates. Leaders may find it easy to unleash communal violence but find it difficult to control. Some examples of tightly controlled societies may be the Tamils and Israelis – societies which are very close-knit and traditional with strong, arguably authoritarian leadership and clearly defined rules and regulations the members follow carefully. Strong conscience and guilt when breaking norms would be characteristic of tightly controlled societies. In contrast, under-controlled examples could be the Sinhalese – societies which are more loosely-knit with a fair amount of freedom for members to act entirely independently from others.

Learning

> Some thrash in agony on the ground, while others lie motionless. The captured and wounded are punched, kicked and dragged through the dust. Some are blindfolded and guns are held to their heads. I am watching this while standing against a crumbling concrete wall near a school in Jabalia Camp [a Palestinian refugee camp in the Gaza Strip]. The people before me are Palestinian children – the youngest perhaps 4, the oldest no more than 17. They are playing a game they call 'Arabs and Jews'. (Semeniuk 1995: 36)

According to Social Learning Theory, aggression is learned through observation or imitation, and the more often it is reinforced, the more likely it is to occur. From a series of laboratory experiments, Bandura (1973) concluded that children will learn from and imitate adult models of physical aggression. Children preferentially imitate models who are of high status, influential and who are rewarded for their aggressive behaviour. From observing the behaviour of others, one can learn general strategies that provide guides for actions which go well beyond the specific modelled examples. Thus an aggressive style of coping with problems can generalise to a large number of situations through observing just one such successful modelling. Exposure to modelled aggression can affect not only observers' actions but also their attitudes and values. Children will adopt the behaviour of a successful aggressor and hold him or her in high regard even though it may initially go against their value system. Children do not necessarily learn only what is overt and consciously taught by adults but can pick up unconscious, covert and subtle messages through non-verbal and other clues.

Finally, learning theory indicates that, as violent behaviour comes into vogue, it is learned by imitation, particularly by growing children, to be relied upon increasingly in subsequent encounters. The most unfortunate repercussion of collective violence is the perpetuation of the violent process itself. One must distinguish the destructive long-term effects of violence – repression, fear, mistrust and brutalisation of the practitioner – from the short-term results of violence, which often appear favourable (Ilfeld 1970).

The passage which opens this section – describing Palestinian boys beating each other as they 'play' 'Arabs and Jews' – is a chilling example of how societal and political pathologies can be reflected, perpetuated, and 'learned' through play. The same types of pathologies may be conveyed in different forms both within and outside classroom walls. The loss of childhood to militarised violence follows a gradual process of socialisation whereby the development of confidence and sense of responsibilities are short-circuited. The hard world of violence violates the protective shell of childhood as the child is thrust into the horrors of war: they are shot at and shelled; they are kidnapped and forced to slave and fight for militarised groups; girls are raped and forced to act as 'wives' in rebel groups; they are forced by militarised groups to inflict atrocities on their own family members and villagers so that they will be ostracised and have nowhere to go but to that group (see Zimbardo 2007).

It is well known that animals can be bred selectively for special attacking and killing abilities (e.g. bulls, dogs, fighting cocks). Certain human societies appear to have special martial abilities – for example, among Indians, the Gurkhas (Grossman 1996), Sikhs and Rajputs are famed for their fighting prowess (Trawick 2007), which may be the result of sub-cultural influence. Amongst Tamils, the very roots of their relatively passive and conformist society (ibid.) have been used to mould their youth into suicidal fighting units. Thus, it is clear that aggression and violence can be learned when the need arises.

One of the most powerful sources for observational learning is the modern mass media, particularly television and video. Mass media presentations are imbibed subliminally as authentic and credible, giving an impression that the world is really the way it appears in these representations – blurring the distinction between reality and fantasy. The media teaches that the world is a violent and untrustworthy place and demonstrates violent techniques for coping with the putatively hostile environment (Ilfeld 1970; Grossman 1995). We can therefore conclude that aggressive behaviour and killing can be learned through observation of real life happenings or media, socialisation, reinforcement, or as a response to need.

Sex differences in aggression

All the villagers are rounded up and warned not to resist in any way. The threat: the leader of the group attempts to rape an eight-year-old girl. Unable to do so because of her small size, he finishes the deed with his knife, leaving the child to bleed to death in front of her family and friends who were forced to look on. (A story of an attack by RENAMO in Mozambique, recounted in Nordstrom 1995: 264)

Historically war has been a male preoccupation. Females have usually played a more peaceful, caring, nurturant and protective role. Males are biologically more aggressive than females. Even as children, boys tend to be more aggressive, indulging in more 'rough and tumble' play, preferring rigorous activity. This may be due to the differential effect of sex hormones, and partly due to the different ways the sexes are brought up, social expectations and the role models they imitate (Vaughan and Hogg 2002). Though males spontaneously perform more imitative aggression than girls, girls are able to perform aggressive acts when given incentives to do so (Bandura 1973). Thus it would appear that social sanction for females to behave aggressively can bring out aggressive acts they had learned, as was seen in quite competent female wings of the Tamil (Tiger) militants.

Collective killing

Although individual aggression and killing behaviour may tell us something about how people can or can not be made to kill other people, the basic processes involved in collective killing as happens in war have different psychosocial dynamics, basically taking place at a collective or social level. Usually the line between collective violence and killing is blurred compared to individual violence and killing. Collectively it would appear that groups readily cross over from violence to killing with less inhibition due to a variety of social factors such as herd mentality, identification with group, group absolution, social sanction, and peer support (Grossman 1996). Thus, collective violence directed against an out-group often ends up in killing of some at least. Under the herd mentality, the momentum appears to push excited groups into going further with less inhibition.

Biologically, the positive aspect of collective violence and killing in group adaptation and coping is enhancing group survival, while group territorial defence promotes group unity and reduces strife among members. Collective violence and killing may be perceived as the most productive tactical option available to a group, be it in self-defence, when the group's interests are threatened, or against oppression. Violence may seem to be the most direct means of getting the job done and the means involving the least danger of compromise. Alternatively, when an outside force is perceived to threaten a group's annihilation, violence may seem to be the only means to achieve an important goal. Violence often appears to promise favourable short-term results, and it readily discharges frustration that may have built up due to political repression. In the absence of sufficient group cohesiveness to sustain other 'slower' options, violence requires much less discipline and is easily understood and adopted. Violence increases group cohesiveness by pushing people into opposing groups, each of whom sees the other as an enemy. The perception, then, of an increasing threat to group survival facilitates inter-group cohesion and solidarity. Similarly killing and other types of repressive violence may be intended to break up group cohesion and solidarity but actually result in more defiance and willingness to fight back.

Collective killing usually takes place in the context of social grievances and inequalities, violation of human rights and socio-economic deprivation. Most modern-day conflicts and civil wars erupt in the context of Complex Political Emergencies (CPE) with socio-political oppression. Killing can be the tool of the oppressor or the oppressed as a form of retaliation or reaction.

Brown (1965) argued that intergroup aggression is due to three universal (psycho)social processes: ethnocentrism, stereotyping, and perceived inequity as a result of unfair distribution of resources. The emotional response to perceived unfair disadvantage – to unjust distribution of resources in comparison to the 'other' group – has been hostility and aggression. Thus labouring under the power of ethnocentrism and perceived inequity or injustice, a group will be prepared to kill the 'other' group members. Basically what makes collective killing possible is the social process of sanction or licence to kill a stereotyped enemy who is perceived to have some unfair advantage, to have done some wrong or simply belong to another group. However, these collective passions of groups and nations that can create the resolve to kill others are often manipulated and fanned by adroit, ambitious leaders.

Collective violence increases hostility and terror, leading to a vicious cycle of defiance and counter-killing. Killing then becomes institutionalised, closing the normal channels of communication and negotiations. This is turn increases violent reactions, confirming the necessity for more counter-killing. More individuals become convinced of the need for violence, and a vicious cycle builds up with a self-fulfilling effect. If unrestrained, collective violence can yield human misery of a magnitude unimaginable with non-violent options.

According to Bush and Saltarelli (2000), the development of a 'kill or be killed' logic requires, and justifies, 'war' against both immediate *and future* threats. When the language of 'future threats' is combined with dehumanisation, demonisation, and zero-sum logic, then children and women become threats to be eliminated – from the gas chambers of Nazi Germany, to the killing fields of Pol Pot's Cambodia, to the ditches and villages of post-1994 Rwanda. Thus, in spurring and directing the anti-Tutsi massacres in Rwanda, *Radio Mille Collines* broadcast such messages as: 'To kill the big rats, you have to kill the little rats.' The result was the murder of as many as 300,000 Rwandan children in 1994 (UNICEF 1996: 14).

Erikson (1968) describes how the need for group identity, to be a 'special kind', can lead to collective killing:

To reinforce the illusion of being chosen, every tribe recognizes a creation of its own, a mythology and later a history; thus was loyalty to a particular ecology and morality secured. Other tribes came to be useful as a screen of projection for the negative identities which were necessary, if most uncomfortable, counterpart of the positive ones. This projection, in conjunction with their territoriality, gave men a reason to slaughter one another in majorem glorious.

Training

Perhaps the most tragic long-term consequence of collective violence and killing is the development of a cult of violence. Violence becomes institutionalised within the state and society itself. It becomes a way of life. Part of this system is the aggression training function used for war.

This is a most remarkable function, as Bandura (1973) points out, for the system can, within a relatively short period, transform people who have been taught to deplore killing as morally reprehensible into skilled combatants who feel very little compunction or even a sense of pride in taking human life:

> The task of converting socialized men into proficient combatants is achieved not by altering personality structure, aggressive drives or traits. Rather willingness and ability to kill in combat are attained by direct training combining several important features. In the first place, the moral value of killing is changed so that people can do it free from restraints of self-condemning consequences. This is accomplished through indoctrination that assigns a high moral purpose to warfare. The force of the moral appeal is strengthened by portraying the enemy as servile fanatics or subhumans driven by ruthless leaders.... People selected as targets are... often dehumanised... by being viewed not as individuals with sensitivities, feelings and hopes, but as stereotyped objects bearing demeaning labels [e.g. terrorists, traitors, subversives, dogs, gook, Kraut etc.]. (Bandura 1973)

Daniels, Marshall and Ochberg (1970) explain that the psychology of sanctioned violence:

> ... depends on attribution of evil motives to the 'outsiders'. Then because 'they' are violent (evil), 'we' have to be violent; or (twisted even further) because 'they' are violent, it is good for us to be violent. Through this process we seem capable of justifying any violence, but perhaps the most invidious justification of violence is the moral application of violence either as 'a last resort' or because 'our cause is the truly right one'.

This is exactly the type of reasoning used to legitimise the war against Iraq by US-led forces in March 2003. The enemy was characterised as belonging to the 'axis of evil', hell-bent on international terrorism and the release of weapons of mass destruction.

The military or militant training is a closely regulated process whereby

new recruits are indoctrinated or 'brainwashed' into accepting a new way of life. All aspects of their lives are brought under control, while their old ties are completely eliminated. They are strongly disciplined and willing to take orders without questioning, to kill without apparent compunction.
Bandura (1973) describes the process of militarisation:

> … self-censuring reactions to brutal acts are repeatedly neutralised by a variety of self-absorbing devices, as well as by ideological justifications. Powerful social sanctions (and economic inducements) are also effectively used to promote acceptance of warfare. Combat heroism is glorified, while opposition to military mission is treated as an unpatriotic social disgrace. The social influence process is greatly facilitated by immersing recruits in a totally new reality. Arrivals are promptly dispossessed of most civilian accoutrements and outfitted with military gear. During the periods of intensive training, rookies are isolated from family, friends and normal community life, thus removing customary social supports for their behaviour and beliefs. Instead, almost every aspect of their daily life is closely regulated in accordance with the new reinforcement structure. Throughout this process they are subject to obedience tests and firmly disciplined for non-compliance. In addition to legitimisation of military killing, recruits receive intense training in the intricate techniques of warfare. A host of coordinated skills must be mastered, such as hand-to-hand fighting, tactical maneuvers, reconnaissance patrols, field fortifications, and artillery and aerial bombardment. Training proceeds by demonstrating how combat activities are executed and by having recruits practice attacks against simulated targets until proficiency is attained. The third feature of military training is concerned with reducing fear of battle. Various methods are used for this purpose. Action extinguishes fear. Inductees are therefore drilled repeatedly in combat performances until they reach the level of automatic action.

Lt. Col. Dave Grossman (1996) describes in his book, *On Killing*, the psychological mechanisms used in the training that have been developed by armies over the centuries to overcome the innate human resistance towards killing one's own species. Pavlovian classical conditioning and Skinnerian operant mechanisms are used to drill an automatic reflexive response by immediate, positive feedback to simulated but lifelike situations, shooting and killing, a system of rewards and punishment. Group absolution, diffusion of responsibility, and social sanction for killing, pre-packaging denial defence mechanisms and obedience to authority, are all systematically developed during the training to programme the recruit for killing. War, after all, is 'the business of killing'. Desensitisation to killing fellow human beings comes from this indoctrination and practical initiation: 'Once a man has killed a couple of times, his reluctance to do so again wanes: he can even become an addictive killer. And this can in addition become infectious' (Tinbergen 1981).

Dostoevsky explored the psychology of murder and conspiracy and the binding effect of collective killing in *Crime and Punishment* and *The Possessed*. In all organisations for murder and homicide, whether military or militant, it is the initial act that is crucial and binding. That is perhaps why so much importance rests on initiation. Excessive violence and killing can brutalise the person to become addicted to violence and killing, a condition referred to as malignant Post-Traumatic Stress Disorder (Rosenbeck 1985). My own clinical observations have shown that children, specifically adolescents, are particularly vulnerable during their impressionable formative period, causing permanent scarring of their developing personality. The psychological consequences for children who had become militants were particularly severe. In those that came for treatment, we found that they had joined the movement when very young and been exposed to massive trauma where they have witnessed gruesome deaths and mutilating injuries to many of their comrades or had themselves been badly injured. They had frequently been involved in atrocities, having been responsible for many cruel deaths and torture. The following case history (Somasundaram 1998) illustrates this:

R., a pleasant looking 15-year old boy, came with complaints of insomnia, irrational talk, abnormal behaviour and aggressive outbursts towards camp mates. R., like any other boy, had a normal upbringing in a farm in Eastern Sri Lanka. He had good relations with his family. He joined the militant group at the age of 11 in 1989. He was given extensive training and taught that those who do not support the struggle are his enemies and should be killed. When starting active combat duty the killings at first affected him, but gradually he became obsessed by the need to see blood and got pleasure from brutally killing people. After one attack where he lost many of his comrades, he was shown videos of killed women and children and told that his enemies had done this.

This group was then taken to attack a village inhabited by another ethnic group. He recounts how he killed the inhabitants. He felt no remorse when he described how he held a child by its legs and bashed the head against the wall until the brain matter came out, of how he enjoyed the mother's screams and how he hacked the mother, among others, to death later. He said that they deserved to die. He partook in four village massacres. When inactive he felt bored and restless. He longed to go into combat and brutally kill people. He was obsessed with the sight of blood. He became easily irritable and broke out in sudden violent outbursts at the slightest thing.

They found it difficult to control him. He felt anger and contempt when he saw people enjoying themselves at temples and wedding festivals.

Another important factor in legitimised killing is obedience to authority. In Nazi Germany from 1933 to 1945, millions of innocent people were systematically put to death in concentration camps. Many investigators found that those who ran the day-to-day operation, who built the ovens and gas chambers, filled them with human beings, counted bodies and did the necessary paperwork, were just ordinary people following orders from superiors. Hannah Arendt (1963), in *A Report on the Banality of Evil*, characterised the Nazi war criminal Lieutenant Colonel Adolf Eichmann, who was hanged for 'causing the killing of millions of Jews', as a dull, uninspired, non-aggressive bureaucrat who saw himself as a little cog in the machine. Half a dozen psychiatrists examined him and found him sane. His sentiments for and actions toward his parents, wife and children were all normal, even ideal. The officials running the extermination system at the Auschwitz concentration camp were otherwise ordinary, average, middle-aged married men. Stephen Smith discusses killing in the context of genocide in more detail in Chapter 9.

Bandura (1973) comments that, during the process of socialisation, people are extensively trained to obey orders by rewarding compliance and punishing defiance. He adds:

Given that people will obey orders, legitimate authorities can successfully command aggression from others, especially if the actions are presented as justified and necessary and the enforcing agents possess strong coercive power. Indeed, as Snow (1961) has perceptively observed, when you think of the long and gloomy history of man, you will find more hideous crimes committed in the name of obedience than have been committed in the name of rebellion.

Stanley Milgram (1974) demonstrated through a series of experiments how orders from authority figures can make ordinary people carry out inhuman aggressive actions against helpless victims. Social psychologist Roger Brown (1986) argues that institutionalised authoritarian systems need not only have rigid, sado-masochistic, ethnocentric and prejudiced individuals but also clever propagandists, clear thinking ministers, sensitive diplomats and courageous military people.

It may be worthwhile describing the authoritarian personality, which refers generally to the majority of ordinary soldiers who are part of an organised military system where they readily accept and carry out orders from above while being autocratic and domineering with those below in the hierarchy. An authoritarian personality is characterised by rigidity in thinking, failure to see all relevant sides of the problem, dogmatism, a narrowing and constriction of the cognitive process, and low self-awareness while showing marked intolerance of other views. Authoritarians think in clear and definite categorical terms, dichotomising the world into good and evil, right and wrong, accentuating the distinction between their group and other groups. They have unrealistically high opinions of themselves and their ethnic group (ethnocentrism), though repressed from consciousness are their own unacceptable impulses of sex, aggression, animosity and other negative characteristics. Authoritarians unconsciously project these repressed, negative qualities onto other groups. They externalise conflict and are extra-punitive. Ever ready to blame others, they hold rigidly moralistic views, and their judgements are often harsh, requiring severe or violent punishment for minor transgression.

A deep insecurity lies at the root of the authoritarian personality, as a result of which he or she is extremely distrustful and paranoid. The authoritarian personality needs order, especially social order, where there is a definite hierarchy and power arrangements are clear (Allport 1958; Brown 1986). Authoritarians like authority, discipline and admire leaders who exercised power and control over others (Napoleon, Bismarck, Hitler), whereas tolerant personalities admire artists, humanitarians and scientists (Frenkel–Brunswik and Sanford 1945).

The preference for an orderly authoritarian and powerful organised structure is marked by extreme patriotism, nationalism and a desire for a strong leader. Authoritarian patterns become set at an early age, especially if the child-rearing practices and educational system present the parent, teacher and social leaders as authority figures to whom submission is necessary (*ibid.*). In considering obedience to authority and authoritarian personalities, it is important to stress that most individuals in a military set-up belong to the bottom of hierarchy. Nevertheless, they are basically 'Power oriented in their personal relationships – submissive and obedient to those they consider their superiors, but contemptible and authoritarian towards those considered inferior' (Atkinson 1987). Both Adler and Nietzche described the 'will to power' as a basic human trait. What is evident is that a will to power manifests itself in extreme form in a few leaders as an intense struggle to dominate and rule, using all the means available, eliminating all obstacles in their path. These few leaders aspiring to power may then use those at the bottom of the hierarchy for their purposes, to gain and maintain power. This may entail going to war against another group or nation, labelled as the 'enemy'.

Ethnologist Konrad Lorenz describes the phenomenon of 'militant enthusiasm' that readies an organism for collective violence and killing. He says that the process of object-fixation, which usually takes place during adolescence, determines what a person in that society will live for, struggle for and, under certain circumstances, blindly go to war for:

> Every man of normally strong emotions knows, from his own experience, the subjective phenomena that go hand in hand with the response of militant enthusiasm. A shiver runs down the back. One soars elated above all ties of everyday life, one is ready to abandon all for the call of what, in the moment of this specific emotion, seems to be sacred duty. (Lorenz 1966)

He then quotes the Napoleonic soldier Heinrich Heins' poem, 'What do I care for wife or child,' before continuing:

> All obstacles in its path become unimportant, the instinctive inhibitions against hurting or killing one's fellows lose, unfortunately, much of their power. Rational considerations, criticism, and all reasonable arguments against the behaviour dictated by the militant enthusiasm are silenced by an amazing reversal of all values, making them appear not only untenable but bare and dishonourable. Men may enjoy the feeling of absolute righteousness even while they commit atrocities. Conceptual thought and moral responsibility are at their lowest ebb. As a Ukrainian proverb says: 'When the banner is unfurled, all reason is in the trumpet.'

> Anybody who has ever seen the corresponding behaviour of the male chimpanzee defending his band or family with self-sacrificing courage, will doubt the purely spiritual character of human enthusiasm... of high survival value... in a tribe of human beings. It was necessary for the individual male to forget all his other allegiances in order to be able to dedicate himself, body and soul, to the cause of communal battle. (*ibid.*)

He then lists four environmental situations that will 'release militant enthusiasm', namely:

- a social unit with which the subject identifies appears to be threatened by some external danger;
- a hateful enemy is present who emanates a threat to the values of the social unit. Both the enemy and the object to be defended are extremely variable, and demagogues are well versed in producing supra-normal dummies to release a very dangerous form of militant enthusiasm;
- inspiring leader figures; and
- the presence of others agitated by the same emotion.

Lorenz goes on to say that:

> Smaller numbers at issue with a large majority tend to obstinate defense with the emotional value of making a last stand, while very large numbers inspired by the same enthusiasm feel an urge to conquer the whole world in the name of their sacred cause. Here the laws of mass enthusiasm are strictly analogous to those of flock formation – here too, the excitation grows in proportion, perhaps even in geometrical progression, with the increasing number of individuals. This is exactly what makes militant mass enthusiasm so dangerous.

Thus it has become possible for a few leaders at the top to turn on the feeling of 'militant enthusiasm' by clever manipulation of psychological and social processes to harness it for their purposes. Where there is so-called democracy, this would entail manipulation of the mass media to convince people that war was necessary for the country. Bush, Blair and other leaders of the Anglo-Saxon world were able to do just this for the recent war in Iraq, using the excuse of weapons of mass destruction, later found never to have existed, to create enough public and political fear to justify the call to war. They were then able to set in motion the disciplined and trained institutions of the armed forces to follow orders to kill for their country (Woodward 2002 and 2004). Once a state mobilizes for war, it can appropriate its vast resources such as its bureaucracy, economy, organisation, structures and technology for mass destruction, to become a war machine (Deleuze and Guattari 1986; Kapferer 1997) – and killing, after all, is the business of war.

Many have argued with Freud that man (and not woman, as explained above) has an innate propensity for killing in war (McDougall 1968). William James (1968) argued that:

> The earlier men were hunting men, and to hunt a neighbouring tribe, kill the males loot the village, and possess the females was the most profitable, as well as the most exciting, way of living. Thus were the more martial tribes selected, and in chiefs and peoples a pure pugnacity and love of glory came to mingle with the more fundamental appetite for plunder.

However, Fromm (1973) marshalled convincing evidence to show that aggression, conflict and war were quite rare in 'primitive societies' and increased with civilisation. Andreski (1964) argues that 'the prevalence of killing within our species was made possible by the acquisition of culture', particularly the acquisition of weapons which allow mechanised killing at a distance without direct personal involvement and thus bypassing the natural inhibitory mechanism against killing. He argues:

There are reasons for doubting whether war is an absolutely necessary consequence of human nature being what it is. In every war-like policy (which means in an overwhelming majority of political formations of any kind) there are elaborate social arrangements which stimulate martial ardour by playing upon variety of emotions – fear of contempt, sexual desire, filial or fraternal attachment, loyalty to the group and other sentiments. It seems reasonable to suppose that if there was an innate propensity to war-making such stimulation would be unnecessary. (*ibid.*)

In contrast to the militarisation or brutalisation that makes killing 'easy' for some, as discussed earlier in this chapter, the reality is that this is not the most common response. Though people may be manipulated or compelled to join the forces and go to war, when they are actually required to kill, many may find it initially repulsive. Indeed, the fear of battle has been found to be so pervasive that only 25% of the combatants are able to do any firing or fighting at all (Coleman 1975). Most have to be compelled to kill, to fear the consequence of disobeying more; or to kill rather than be killed. Grossman (1996) has argued that the amazing low level of firing and killing activity in earlier wars was not due to fear but to innate inhibition to killing manifesting as laudable 'conscientious objection'. Modern armies have learned from these findings to develop classical and operant conditioning techniques to train soldiers to overcome these inhibitions to become more efficient, mechanical killers in the battlefield, with firing rates of over 90%. Some more sensitive individuals, particularly those raised with more humane values, may continue to experience revulsion when made to kill.

However, in the situation of war where killing becomes commonplace, they may not be conscious of this feeling. The cognitive dissonance and suppression of the revulsion may lead to the development of psychosomatic symptoms like vomiting (Fromm 1960). Pat Barker (1994) brilliantly explores the psychological and social reactions of combatants and civilians to war in her *Regeneration Trilogy*. The enormous long-time costs to the individual perpetrators and to society in the development of psychosocial problems like PTSD, depression, anxiety, alcohol and drug misuse, suicide, relationship problems, domestic violence, divorce, unemployment, crime and homicide are only now becoming clear (MacNair 2002; Baum 2004; Sontag and Alvarez 2008). Not only in soldiers returning from the Vietnam and Iraq wars, but even in South Sri Lanka the wave of violence and antisocial activities by deserters and ex-servicemen from the civil war are startling. Grossman (1996) estimates that 15–50%, or 400,000 to 1.5 million veterans from the 2.8 million who served in Southeast Asia, suffer from PTSD due to the Vietnam war.

This raises the important question of whether any personal responsibility can exist for killing or for having others do the killing. Can we conclude that killing is a response determined by biological and environmental conditions? That it is a behaviour sanctioned by society, legitimised by a complex set of collective beliefs and arguments? Or does any moral element to the killing exist? Is it not moral concern that makes one ask the question of why and how killing is done in the context of organised war and killing? Should the leaders who make the decisions and manipulate the system ultimately be held responsible? Should the individuals who rebel against the compelling social processes, so called 'conscientious objectors', be valued and given recognition?

Conclusions

This chapter has described the psychobiological and social factors involved in killing in the context of collective violence and war. Basic anatomical and physiological mechanisms appear to underlie aggression and its inhibition which may be involved in killing. Some well-known psychosocial stimulants like pain or the threat of pain, frustration, overcrowding, territoriality, and resources can cause aggressive behaviour. Collective aggression can be directed against a threatening out-group and result in better group cohesiveness and solidarity. Perceived injustices or manipulated emotional anger may lead to aggression. Society may then sanction killing the enemy. The emotion of militant enthusiasm can be harnessed to train people for war and killing. People can also learn to be violent and to kill from their personal experiences, their perceived need, and from the mass media.

This chapter deliberately presents a broad spectrum of psychological and other views from which readers are invited to form their own conclusions. These theories are not mutually exclusive, and synthetic, eclectic views can be adopted. Thus, one sees killing as a response determined by innate biological mechanisms interacting with environmental factors such as social learning experiences and frustrations. Collective killing can be an adaptive response, in self-defence or as a planned action, to resolve conflicts and inequities. However, leaders can manipulate these psychological needs and processes for their own pursuit of power. Can such leaders be held responsible for their actions and the destruction they cause through war? Can individuals and society be made more aware and resistant to these manipulations? Can we learn to solve our problems without resorting to violence and war?

References

Allport, G.W. (1950) 'The Role of Expectancy'. In Bramson and G. W. Goethals, eds., *War*. New York: Basic Books, New York.

Allport, G.W. (1958) *The Nature of Prejudice*. Anchor Books.

Andreski, S. (1964) 'Origins of War'. In J. D. Carthy and F. J. Ebling, eds., *The Natural History of Aggression*. London: Academic Press.

Ardrey. R. (1967) *The Territorial Imperative*. New York: Atheneum.

Arendt, H. (1963) *Eichmann in Jerusalem: a report on the Banality of Evil*. New York: Viking Press.

Atkinson, R. L., Atkinson, R. C., and Hilgard, E. R. (1983, 1987) *Introduction to Psychology*. San Diego: Harcourt Brace Jovanovich Publishers.

Bandura, A. (1973) *Aggression: A Social Learning Analysis*. New Jersey: Prentice Hall.

Barker, P. (1994) *Regeneration Trilogy*. London: Penguin Books.

Baum, D. (2004) The Price of Valor. *New Yorker*, July 12, 2004.

Bittker, T. E. (1970) 'The Choice of Collective Violence in Intergroup Conflict'. In *Violence and the Struggle for Existence*. Boston: Little, Brown & Co.

Boelkins, R. C. (1970) 'Biological Basis of Aggression'. In *Violence and the Struggle for Existence*. Boston: Little, Brown & Co.

Brown, R. (1965, 1986) *Social Psychology*. (1st & 2nd ed.). New York: Macmillan Co.

Bush, K. and Saltarelli, D. (2000) *The Two Faces of Education in Ethnic Conflict: Towards a Peacebuilding Education for Children*. Unicef Innocenti Research Centre, Florence, Italy.

Daniels, D. N., Marshall, F. G. and Ochberg, F. M., eds. (1970) *Violence and the Struggle for Existence*. Boston: Little Brown & Co.

Deleuze, G. and Guattari, F. (1986) *Nomadology: the war machine*, translated by Brian Massumi. New York: Semiotext.

Erikson, E. H. (1968) *Identity, Youth and Crisis*. London: Faber & Faber. See also Erikson (1963) *Childhood and Society*. New York: Norten & CC.I.

Frenkel-Brunswik, E. and Sanford, R.N. (1945) 'Some Personality Factors in Anti-Semitism'. *Journal of Psychology* 20: 271–91.

Freud, S. (1961) *Civilization and its Discontent*. Translated and edited by J.Strachey, New York: W. W. Norton & Co.

Fromm, E. (1973) *The Anatomy of Human Destructiveness*. Middlesex: Penguin Books.

Fromm, E. (1960) *Psychoanalysis and Zen Buddhism*. London: Unwin.

Grossman, D. (1996) *On Killing – the Psychological Cost of Learning to kill in War and Society*. Boston: Little, Brown and Company.

Ilfeld, F.W. and Metzner, R. J. (1970) 'Alternatives to Violence'. In Daniels, D.N., Marshall, F.G. & Ochberg, F.M., eds., *Violence and Struggle for Existence*, Boston: Little Brown & Co.

James, W. (1968) 'The Moral Equivalent of War'. In Bramson and G. W. Goethals, eds., *War*. New York: Basic Books, New York.

Kapferer, B. (1997) *The Feat of the Sorcerer*. Chicago: University of Chicago Press.

Lorenz, K. Z. (1966) *On Aggression*. New York: Harcourt, Brace and World Inc.

MacNair, R. M. (2002) *Perpetration-Induced Traumatic Stress – The Psychological Consequences of Killing*. Westport, Connecticut: Praeger.

Mathews, H.L. (1964) 'Overt Fighting in Mammals'. In J. D. Carthy and F. J. Ebling, eds., *The Natural History of Aggression*. London: Academic Press.

McDougal, W. (1968) 'The Instinct of Pugnacity'. In Bramson and G. W. Goethals, eds., *War*. New York: Basic Books, New York.

Megargee (1960). In Tabias and Neziroglu, below.

Milgram, S. (1974) *Obedience to Authority*. New York: Harper & Row.

Nordstrom, C. (1992). 'Backyard Front'. In C. Nordstrom and J. Martin, eds., *The Paths to Domination, Resistance and Terror*. Berkeley and London: University of California Press.

Rosenbeck, R. (1985) 'The Malignant Post-Vietnam Stress Syndrome'. *American Journal of Orthopsychiatry*, 55: 2, 319–32.

Semenuik, R. (1995). 'War Babies: The Children of the Gaza Strip.' *Equinox Magazine*, January/February.

Solomon, G. F. (1970) 'Psychodynamic Aspects of Aggression, Hostility and Violence'. In *Violence and*

Struggle for Existence, op. cit.

Somasundaram, D. J. (1998) *Scarred Minds*. New Delhi: Sage Publications.

Sontag, D. & Alvarez, L. (2008) 'Across America, Deadly Echoes of Foreign Battles', *New York Times*, January 13, 2008.

Tajfel, H. (1978) *The Social Psychology of Minorities*. The Minority Group Report No. 38. London.

Tabias, J. A. Y. and Neziroglu, F. A. (1981) 'Aggressive Behaviour, Clinical Interfaces'. In I. Vallzelli and I. Morgese (eds.), *Aggression and Violence: A Psychobiological and Clinical Approaches*. St. Vincent, Italy: Edizion.

Tinbergen, N. (1981) 'On The History of War'. In I. Vallzelli and I. Morges, eds., *Aggression and Violence: A Psychobiological and Clinical Approaches*. St. Vincent, Italy: Edizion.

Trawick, M. (2007) *Enemy Lines – Childhood, Warfare, and Play in Batticaloa*. Berkeley: University of California Press.

UNICEF (1997) State of the World's Children 1996.

Vaughan, G. M. and Hogg, M. A. (2002) *Introduction to Social Psychology*. Third Edition, Prentice Hall, Pearson Education, N. S. W., Australia.

Woodward, B. (2002) *Bush at War*. New York: Simon & Schuster.

Woodward, B. (2004) *Plan of Attack*. New York: Simon & Schuster.

Zimbardo, P. (2007) *The Lucifer Effect: How Good People Turn Evil*. London: Rider.

PROLOGUE: **GENOCIDE**

In a wider historical context, the mass slaughter of certain populations or races appears again and again. The removal of Native Americans, the Holocaust, and relatively recent violence in Uganda, the Democratic Republic of Congo and the former Yugoslavia are but a few examples. In Chapter 9, Stephen Smith examines the participation of civilians in the genocide in Rwanda, drawing on testimonies of rank and file perpetrators of genocide.

The last chapters have shifted from acts primarily against individuals to acts of killing realised through communities, namely terrorism, killing in the context of war, and now genocide. The classic pattern here is often portrayed as a shift that permits human compassion to in-group members but denial of such basic human treatment to outsiders. This 'infrahumanization' (Cortes et al. 2005), or more commonly 'dehumanization' (see Zimbardo 2007) means that out-group members are seen as less human, less worthy of equal treatment. Given the right cultural circumstances, even this does not need to be overt, as cultural mores may shift such that: '… the "other" is not seen as a person but as an object posing a threat. Once this dynamic is in place, otherwise unthinkable behavior can be justified as a means to the end of reinforcing and protecting group identity' (Kimball 2002: 134). Ignatieff (1997) describes this as a link between violence and belonging: 'The more strongly you feel the bonds of belonging to your own group, the more hostile, the more violent will your feelings be towards outsiders. You can't have this intensity of belonging without violence, because belonging of this intensity moulds the individual conscience: if a nation gives people a reason to sacrifice themselves, it also gives them a reason to kill' (p.199).

This dehumanisation is central to acts of genocide, as Dr Smith's chapter explains. Christians, for example, had a long history of dehumanising Jews before the Holocaust ever took place. Kimball (2002: 136) argues that the Holocaust '… would not have happened without the active participation of, sympathetic support of, and relative indifference exhibited by large numbers of Christians', though many other Christians opposed it (Gushee 1994). The horrifying fact is that acts of genocide often involve the compliance if not the collaboration and active participation of civilians. Cohen notes that:

> A recurrent question about perpetrators of political atrocities and serious crimes is this: how can ordinary people do terrible things, yet, during or after the event, find ways to deny the meaning of what they are doing? (2001: 15)

Alison Des Forges of Human Rights Watch comments that even the most horrific acts have been committed not by criminals or psychopaths, but by ordinary people:

> This behavior lies just under the surface of any of us. The simplified accounts of genocide allow distance between us and the perpetrators of genocide. They are so evil we couldn't ever

see ourselves doing the same thing. But if you consider the terrible pressure under which people were operating, then you automatically reassert their humanity – and that becomes alarming. You are forced to look at the situation and say, 'What would I have done? Sometimes the answer is not encouraging.' (1999: 132)

Psychologist Ervin Staub – himself a survivor of the Holocaust in the Nazi occupation of Hungary – reiterates this view, saying that:

Evil that arises out of ordinary thinking and is committed by ordinary people is the norm, not the exception… Great evil arises out of ordinary psychological processes that evolve, usually with a progression along the continuum of destruction. (1989: 126).

We may not believe we are capable of such acts, or that somehow we would behave differently from 'those people' – but history suggests otherwise.

References

Cohen, S. (2001) *States of Denial: Knowing About Atrocities and Suffering.* Cambridge: Polity Press.

Cortes, B. P., Demoulin, S., Rodriguez, R. T., Rodriguez, A. P., & Leyens, J. P. (2005) 'Infrahumanization or familiarity? Attribution of uniquely human emotions to the self, the in-group, and the out-group'. *Personality and Social Psychology Bulletin*, 31, 243–53.

Des Forges, A. (1999) *Leave None to Tell the Story: Genocide in Rwanda.* New York: Human Rights Watch.

Gushee, D. (1994) *The Righteous Gentiles of the Holocaust: A Christian Interpretation.* Minneapolis: Fortress Press.

Ignatieff, M. (1997) *The Warrior's Honor.* New York: Metropolitan Books.

Kimball, C. (2002) *When Religion Becomes Evil.* New York: HarperCollins Publishers Inc.

Staub, E. (1989) *The Roots of Evil: The Origins of Genocide and Other Group Violence.* New York: Cambridge University Press.

Zimbardo, P. (2007) *The Lucifer Effect: How Good People Turn Evil.* London: Rider.

Chapter 9

Massacre at Murambi: the Rank and File Killers of Genocide

Stephen Smith

It was still dark when the villagers gathered together just outside the school complex at Murambi Cellule, Remera Sector, Gikongoro Province, Rwanda. Their shadowy movements and low voices created an ominous presence for those inside the perimeter boundary. It was approximately 3am on 21 April 1994. Crammed onto the school site were as many as 40,000 Tutsis.[37] Some had fled there for their own safety from local towns and villages. Others had been instructed to gather there by local civic leaders, police and militia. Murambi School had become a loosely organised holding camp, guarded by Rwandan military. By 21 April, some had been awaiting their fate for over a week. They were provided with no food and little water. They were hungry, tired and very thirsty. In the coming hours, the bloodletting that would occur would be among the most violent of the genocide in Rwanda. Some 27,000 corpses are reported to have been exhumed from mass graves at the school. This would point to a minimum number murdered on site. Others would likely have been killed as they fled or, later still, found in hiding in neighbouring villages and killed in subsequent massacres.

This chapter examines the testimony of five of the civilian perpetrators of the genocide on the site of Murambi massacre. It seeks to establish the process of the massacre and the involvement of the five perpetrators – local villagers who killed their neighbours. It explores the process of their recruitment to mass murder and how they explain their own involvement in the killings. The five perpetrators were all 'rank and file' killers. They had no direct involvement in organising the killings and held no official office. They were not in the recognised uniform of either military or police units. They had no formal

---

37 Establishing the exact number of Tutsis on the site is difficult. We know that many escaped the massacre. We also know that the established body count in the mass graves numbered 26,000 when the graves were exhumed and the bodies reburied later in 1994. Estimates of the number of victims range from 30,000 to 50,000. The 40,000 figure popularly quoted is therefore an estimate.

responsibility to anyone senior, nor any junior reporting to them. Prior to the genocide in 1994, they were all peaceful, law-abiding citizens with no known previous criminal offences. All five killers were remanded and awaiting trial at the time they provided testimony. As part of an ongoing effort to establish the historical record at Murambi, the five self-confessed killers were taken back to the site at Murambi to provide eyewitness testimony. This was the first time that they had been back to the scene of the massacre. The testimony was not provided as part of any judicial process; it was audio-visual testimony taken *in situ* for historical archival purposes.[38] The prisoners (referred to by their initials) had all confessed to killing at the site as part of the Rwandan judicial system's efforts to establish justice in the wake of the genocide.

Context of the Murambi massacre

In October 1993, the Arusha accords had been signed, creating a transitional peace between the Government of Rwanda and the Rwandan Patriotic Front. The United Nations (UN) passed a resolution two days later to create UNAMIR, the United Nations Mission in Rwanda.[39] On 6 April 1994, following further meetings with the UN, President Juvénal Habyarimana was returning to Kigali from Dar-es-Salaam with Cyprien Ntaryamira, President of Burundi. As the plane carrying the two presidents approached Kigali airport, it was shot down, killing the two leaders. Almost immediately, roadblocks were set up around the city, and by that night Hutu extremists were killing Tutsis.[40] The bloodletting, which would continue for the next three months, had apparently been spontaneous. It was an apparent public outburst of rage and violence in which the Hutu majority took revenge on the Tutsi minority for several years of civil strife. But the media apparatus, which was closely linked to the Hutu leadership, had made clear for some time that the Tutsis were to be feared as 'the enemy within'.[41] Organised mass killing broke out across the country. Estimates of the number of Tutsis murdered range up to one million.

As military troops, police personnel, party leaders, mayors and a collection of local villagers gathered around the hillside of Murambi on 21 April, genocide had been in full flow in the country for two weeks. The killing

---

38 The testimonies are English translations of Kinyarwanda transcripts taken from the five audio-visual testimonies. The testimonies were recorded by the Aegis Trust in 2004 and filmed on location at the Murambi school site. The testimonies in Kinyarwanda and English translations are available at the Documentation Centre of the Kigali Memorial Centre.

39 UN Resolution 872 (1993)

40 For more detail on the unfolding of the initial killings, see Melvern (2000), Dallaire (2003), and Barnett (2002).

41 Felician Kabuga financed the hate radio station RTLM and the weekly newspaper Kangura, which spread racist ideas including, as early as 1990, the Hutu Ten Commandments, a series of anti-Tutsi 'commands' designed to create social, economic and political division (see Melvern 2000).

during the genocide included the southern province of Gikongoro, but while other provinces had many sites of mass killing, the province of Gikongoro was unusual in that mass killing was concentrated in one particular major event. Although many Tutsis were killed in their own homes and backyards, at roadblocks or in churches where they had gathered, for some reason the local leader, Laurent Bucyibaruta, the *préfet* (governor) of Gikongoro, informed Tutsis that they should congregate in public buildings. The new school complex at Murambi was a perfect collection point.

The school at Murambi is typical of most large high school complexes in Rwanda. It is a series of single-storey classrooms with plastered walls and tin roofs and one large main administration building at the entrance to the site. Two specific features made it particularly suitable as a collection point. Firstly, the topography of the site lends itself to being easily guarded. The school is perched on top of a small hill, surrounded by a natural, moat-like valley all the way around. The only exception is the wide drawbridge-like entrance area, which has no natural ravine. Secondly, construction of the school was not quite complete, which meant the site was vacant.

Recruitment and training

Genocide had been planned for some time in Gikongoro.[42] Prisoner MS (aged 33 in 1994) states that training had been conducted from 'about five months' before the genocide. He describes the process:

> They were being trained by Rusengira how to shoot using guns from the Commune… They would target aubergines and shoot them down…. Those able to shoot their target would become part of the rest of the group [of interahamwe, the Hutu paramilitary groups].

When asked who was invited for the training, he answered, 'All idle people and young men in general.' HD (aged 41 in 1994) was aware that the purpose of the training was to indoctrinate the trainees, although he had not drawn a connection between the indoctrination and the killing. He eventually agreed with the interviewer that the brainwashing was evidence that preparations had been made:

> Q: Was there any sign that genocide was going to happen before it did?
> MS: I did not notice anything. They convinced me because they were leaders. I also believed them.
> Q: But you said you used to go for training, so what did they tell you

---

42   On the training and arming of *interahamwe* militia, see Melvern (2004).

the purpose was?

MS: To exterminate the enemy.

Q: While talking to you, did they say who the enemy was?

HD: The Tutsis.

Q: …Isn't that evidence?

HD: Yes, that is evidence in fact.

The rank and file perpetrators who were trained prior to the genocide were not issued with a uniform or introduced to a formal structure. It appears that some of those trained were issued with shirts and trousers made of *bitenge* (traditional African batik material) and provided with CDR caps.[43] This informal uniform gave some of the killers the sense of being part of a group and acting under command. Only one of the five perpetrators interviewed was issued with a *bitenge* 'uniform'.

Other interviewees were not aware of training taking place and by implication had no training before the killings began. This indicates that the level of their indoctrination prior to the genocide was limited to what they had heard on the radio or among neighbours and friends.

The ways in which the five perpetrators joined the growing mob of potential killers differed. KT (aged 20 in 1994) became aware that preparations were being made when a meeting was called in the village of Sumba. HD was continuing his night watchman's job at the time:

I was a night watchman… [The] local authorities found me there and said, 'Look at this useless old man, why can't you wake up and help us? …What will you do if Inyenzi [cockroaches, the name used for Tutsis] slaughter you here?'

He describes how he and his wife had discussed the possibility of running away. Instead they prevaricated and stayed at the police station where he worked.

SC (aged 40 in 1994) had gone down to Gikongoro out of curiosity to find out what was happening because he had learned that the Tutsis were being killed. He was asked to join a force of villagers being assembled to go down to Murambi. Initially he joined the ad hoc group of would-be killers. As he walked with the group, he thought better of it because his family did not know where he was. He also expected that he could be killed or injured as he had been informed that it was a situation of war. He slipped out of the group

---

43 CDR is the *Coalition pour la Défense de la République*, a Hutu extremist party which refused to sign the Arusha accords. It was openly violent and anti-Tutsi.

at a convenient moment and returned home. He had also heard that the Tutsis were being ill-treated and held without food and water:

> I pitied them… because they had slept hungry and had spent a whole day and night without anything to eat. They told me that some had spent two days there, which upset me.

When he went to Murambi for the first time, he in fact did so in order to take food for the families gathered on the site. 'They [the guards at the site] told me I should stop bringing food to the Tutsis as no one told them to leave their homes [to come to Murambi].'

The perpetrators' conversion to killer was not instantaneous. AG (aged 40 in 1994), who was on his way to buy potatoes just after the killing had begun, confirmed this. He met a Tutsi woman who wanted to know what was happening. '… I told her, 'Since you are my neighbour, I will tell you what is going on… They are killing the Tutsis.' She thanked me and immediately left.' He then confirms that many of his neighbours fled and that some made their way to Murambi for safety.

Prior to the killings, SC was around the school site with both Tutsi and Hutu friends and neighbours. He does not distinguish which of his companions were Tutsis or Hutus. At least one of them was later killed by a grenade attack, from which it can be deduced that he was a Tutsi. Some of his other companions were convinced *genocidaires*: 'They [*interahamwe* friends] told me the war had begun, therefore I had to go with them.'

The interviewees all identify the crash of President Juvénal Habyarimana's plane as the seminal moment that triggered the killing in the area. HD recalls, 'After he died, killing began at Emujeco among Murenzi's people who were building the road joining Gasarenda to Gatare.' Emujeco was a road construction company. According to HD, Tutsi workers from Gitarama took refuge with a local judge named Nyrimenga. A fellow judge informed on the men and, according to HD, the local sector coordinator, 'Gashema Vincent killed them in the house with grenades.'

Roadblocks

Roadblocks, set up to trap fleeing Tutsis more effectively, were a major feature of the genocide. They prevented Tutsis from moving from one place to another and caught them in a controlled net. They were also points of torture and execution for those who were caught. This was the case for the roads leading to and from the site at Murambi. From Mudasomwa to Murambi, MS identifies roadblocks at Kabeza, Mata, Murangara, and four at Karamage. He denies ever manning a roadblock, but confirms that he knew of two 'religious brothers' killed on a roadblock near to his home at Mudasomwa.

AG describes his role on the roadblock as 'making light to reveal the enemy passing... It was an order from the authorities that we should hunt for the enemy.' This, he confirms, was happening in Karama Commune at the instruction of the burgomeister, Ngezahayo. It seems that 'making light' was his first role prior to killing, and that in his mind the order to 'hunt' had not yet become the order to kill.

At Taba, KT's employer asked him to assist with manning a roadblock for a single day, under the auspices of the town councillors. KT had never killed before, yet at the roadblock he took his first blood, apparently quite effortlessly. He and others on the roadblock killed at least two people on his shift. He identifies a man from the neighbourhood, whom he names as Gatake, and a boy whom he describes as 'the brother of Nyakarashi... He was thrown in the latrine, they dumped him... (pauses) We dumped him there.' Unlike AG who joined in, KT was asked to man the roadblock by his employer, one of the local ringleaders.

The meetings

Prisoner MS was the flag raiser at the CDR party office at Mudasomwa, where his uncle was the party president. He identified a meeting held at the police station in Murangara, led by Police Captain Subuhura and supported by Laurent Bucyibaruta, local Burgomaster Faustin Kanyeshyamba and François Gakuru. This meeting took place on 13 April.[44] The meeting had been arranged to brief local villagers, recruited to kill at Murambi, about the plan of action. Few details emerge, although after the meeting the organisers extended hospitality to the recruits, offering 'refreshments' at Murangara.

KT identified a similar meeting that took place in Sumba. He was night watchman at a doctor's home. The meeting was called at the house, and he was invited to attend. He does not detail who was present at the meeting but states that, after the meeting, someone he refers to as 'Simba' distributed guns to the killers at the Taba roadblocks.

Whatever the precise nature of the meetings, they were called by leaders and addressed the specifics of their plan. They gave authority to the process of mass killing and provided a justification to ease the conscience of men who would be relied upon to carry out a large-scale massacre. If the men were not convinced about the efficacy of killing beforehand, the meeting itself provided the rationale of killing in order to suppress the Tutsis before they killed the Hutus, along with instructions on how to do so.

---

44   The date of this meeting is corroborated in *African Rights* (forthcoming). This study of the genocide in Murambi recreates the steps to genocide on the site as seen by survivors and also includes further corroboration by other perpetrators on the site.

Preparing for the massacre at Murambi

Hutu villagers from a number of sectors in the region were called together. HD identifies men from Mudasomwa, Karama, Kinyamakara and Kabeza. He states that the men of Mudasomwa were already armed and that they had to find their own machetes. He then clarifies his point: 'They ordered us to look for machetes, but at that time we had them, it was wartime,' implying that machetes had been provided as part of the preparations for 'war'.

MS notes that the director of the Kitabi tea factory then provided Daihatsu cars to transport the killers and states that they began to 'track' the Tutsis. As most of the Tutsis in the region had fled, gone into hiding, or were already awaiting their fate at Murambi, the 'tracking' he refers to was presumably making their way down to Murambi, looking out for Tutsis en route.

On arrival at Murambi, they were given instructions to decorate themselves with leaves. Mudasomwa killers were to decorate themselves with *imizonobare* (a flexible willow-like plant), the 'Karama men were to wear setaria' (a tall grass eaten by cows and goats), and the rest were to wear eucalyptus leaves. AG, however, somewhat contradicts this, as he was from Karama Commune but stated that he was wearing eucalyptus. HD confirms that 'that time we went gathering that grass and put them on our foreheads and on our shoulders.' KT then confirms that 'at first we put on eucalyptus leaves, then changed to banana leaves… as we realised they had found the sign.' The Tutsis at Murambi had worked out their weak form of camouflage and had presumably started to adopt it themselves, forcing a change of tactic.

The aborted attack

The first attack on the school was orchestrated as early as 19 April. AG remembers a local leader bringing a paper round from burgomaster Ngezahayo, 'instructing everyone to get out of their houses and to hunt the enemy. He added that everyone should go with his weapon and fight the enemy in Murambi.' AG identifies some 30 men from his cell who readily joined and began to make their way to Murambi. By the time they reported to the school, they had collected a further 30 or so men along the way, including 'an interahamwe called Naganze who had a gun'. He became the self-appointed group leader.

What happened next is not clear. The Tutsis on the site appear to have grouped together to defend themselves. KT describes how their group took stones and were throwing them at the Tutsis, and that they were being stoned in return. As most of the Hutus were armed with close-contact weapons, working in a shower of stones made the massacre impossible. The Tutsis on the site successfully repelled the killers. MS states that he reported for duty to the gendarmerie but was told to come back the following day because the Tutsis had been stoning the killers that day. CS confirmed this, stating that they were asked to return the following day because of 'security concerns', and also by AG, who says that his group was told that 'it was not possible [to carry out the massacre] because we [Hutu killers] were [too] few [to succeed].'

On arriving at the site, MS saw a man he knew called Murermanzi, who had previously been his doctor. His wife acted as the nurse and was also a local teacher who had taught MS's child in primary school. He was also related by marriage to François Gakuru, one of the local leaders who attended the meeting. 'I immediately hacked his neck. He fell on the ground and K [an accomplice] saw the way I had hacked his neck off (*sic*) so speared him to death.' Having killed the man, he noted that the man had a fridge with provisions in it. He hijacked an aid-agency car to steal the fridge. 'I stopped a car that had Rwagaza written on it. I packed the fridge in the car and took it. I had done my share of the work.' Having killed Mureramanzi, he 'showed the commander who came with his daughter Kasiine Yvonne…'. He does not state who the commander was, but the revelation that the commander was there with his daughter whilst organising a massacre provides important context. Yvonne was not the only young woman to observe MS's first blood. 'There was even a girl who survived [my attack] called Maugwaneza who was there when I was killing him… but I did not kill her. I just left her and walked off.' MS had spontaneously started to kill and loot before the massacre began.

Leaders on site

A number of community leaders were identified by name on site. HD identifies the former mayor of the province Semakwavu, former sector coordinator Kamanzi and Sebuhiriri (presumably police commandant Sebuhura). AG, who was from a different commune altogether, also identifies the *interahamwe* of Mudasomwa, led by mayor Mukibaruta and commandant Sebuhura. 'I asked who they were, because I had never seen them. I was told they were the leaders of Gikongoro.' It is also not entirely clear who was in charge at the killing site. Various mayors were present at the school, including the provincial mayor, Kibaruta, whom KT identified. CS identified Havuga, vice-provincial mayor, who gave them instructions to divide into groups by cell, so that they would easily recognise each other. There did not appear to be a specific order for the slaughter to begin, or a clear plan in the first instance. Sebuhura emerges as the most significant organiser. Once the attack was called off, Sebuhura took the clear lead in reorganising the plan for an all-out attack.

The killing at Murambi

In the following two days after being repelled from the site, the leaders significantly strengthened their forces. They acquired more guns and grenades. They drafted in reinforcements from the police and army and rounded up more Hutu villagers to assist with the killing. There is no real sense of the scale of the force. But if the assumption is that the 15 Daihatsu trucks each had approximately 10 *interahamwe* from Mudasomwa, and if the men of Kamara had mustered 60 killers, we can safely assume that more than 500 killers were on site. This takes into account the many other sectors and cells that brought their own men. A complete ring of Rwandan regular army was also circling the site and preventing the Tutsis from fleeing. More than 25,000 Tutsi civilians were crammed on the school campus. It is quite conceivable that there were as many as 1,000 killers armed and ready to murder around the hillside.

The two days of interlude significantly weakened the Tutsis. The killers' leaders had purposefully been starving them and had cut off water to the site. KT is aware that 'some of them had become extremely weak' due to hunger and thirst.

The time at which the killing began is uncertain. The killers refer to different times when they arrived on site. It could be that in fact they were asked to arrive at different times. MS states that he arrived in a convoy of cars at 10am on 21 April. AG confirms that he left the site at 4am on 22 April, 'just before dawn'. KT states that he began killing at 3am on 21 April.

KT states that, 'We entered and started hacking. Sebuhura was behind us with his gun.' AG describes the process of the attack more accurately from the group he was in. He states that Sebuhura commanded his police to shoot. Grenades were then thrown by 'leaders' and 'soldiers', who were presumably from the Rwandan army. The Hutu villagers were then told to move in, using stones to subdue any resistance, before hacking and clubbing those who had survived the shooting and grenades. CS reverses the process:

> We threw stones at them… The old men were to pick up the stones, while the young ones were ordered to throw them… After some time of stoning them, policemen came and started shooting them too.

All the killers describe the same set of weapons used during the massacre. These include grenades, guns, machetes, clubs and stones.

What emerges is a confused picture of frenzied bloodshed. Grenades were thrown into small crowds of people and these were followed by machete-wielding villagers, creating a scene of screaming anguish. KT describes his involvement:

> KT: It was dark when I entered … There was a lady whose thigh was cut off [by me] and she died… [There were] cries of agony everywhere…
>
> Q: How many people did you kill yourself?
>
> KT: I am sure you can imagine there were a great many people. We could not tell their number but there were many, so many people died there.

Q: Explain how you killed them…
KT: I just hacked because I had a machete.

KT's honesty about his involvement adds credibility to his story. He is the only killer who admits to losing track of how many people he actually 'hacked'. His unique observation that the leaders had a 'Katyusha', a Soviet multiple-head rocket launcher, mounted in one of the buildings, must be taken seriously. The possibility that it was an actual 'Katyusha' is very unlikely. However, he is obviously referring to some kind of launched ballistic used to fire into the crowds, which is quite possible, particularly as the army were on site to support the massacre. It is uncertain how many rounds they fired from the rocket launcher and what its impact was on the civilian population lying and sitting on the ground, but the damage must have been severe, if it was used. It appears that the local leadership had acquired the launcher from somewhere following the aborted attack. KT claims to have been there the earliest, at 3am on 21 April, so the others may not have witnessed the use of the rocket device because they arrived later in the day.

A picture emerges of all-out desperate warfare and human carnage. The Hutu killers were frantically firing into groups of people and slashing helpless victims. The Tutsi victims occasionally mounted small pockets of resistance, using stones, or they simply tried to flee the cordon, only to be shot, cut or clubbed on the way through several rings of killers. The killers worked from the outside of the site, moving inward, being careful to kill as they went. CS relates that 'when the soldiers arrived, they started shooting. Then I saw a soldier taking a grenade and throwing it at someone. It crashed [into] him, his inner parts came out and he died there.'

Admissions of murder

MS admits killing the one man with the fridge. However, this took place outside the main school compound. Once he was in the school, he only admitted to 'slashing' victims. He was 'slashing' with a machete. As most people died of fatal machete cuts, it can only be assumed that MS did kill more than one man, but he is only prepared to admit that one murder.

AG confirms that he killed two people with his club, shortly before dawn. His description is brief and to the point. 'I hit him with a club and he died right away. The same with other one. I hit him with the club and he died immediately.' As with MS, AG seems to minimise his activity on the site at the time of the massacre. If he killed two people 'in a few minutes' interval', this calls into question what he was doing there through the rest of the day. He was conceivably posted to the perimeter circle, where he would have to wait for Tutsis to be fleeing the site, but he does not state this.

CS describes a moment towards the end of the massacre. His Hutu neighbour was standing over his Tutsi son-in-law who had just been murdered. At that moment a Tutsi passed by, presumably fleeing the scene. CS relates that:

> …he saw someone passing. 'Look! That is a Tutsi passing!' he said. …as he was still in mourning for his son-in-law, I went and killed [the Tutsi man]… When I hit him with the club, he immediately laid down due to starvation… I hit him with the club, I felt like my heart was sobbing.

Whilst they are prepared to admit murder and describe the scene at the massacre site, there appears to be a gap between their confession of involvement and the actual extent of their participation. Any Hutu on site at the time would have had to work quite hard only to kill two people in several hours, unless the army with its ballistic support was carrying out most of the killing. However, the evidence of the prisoners themselves states that it was a combined effort and that the Hutu villagers had an active and equal role in the killings.

After the massacre

The five interviewees had started to kill at Murambi and continued thereafter. HD recalls that he arrived home after the massacre to be greeted by his stepmother, who ran out to meet him, telling him that his (Hutu) father had been killed down in the valley. He relates that he took a stretcher to fetch his father's body. On his return to the house, he found his younger brother 'hacking' his stepmother. When asked why his brother was killing their stepmother, HD replies, 'because she was a Tutsi'. He confesses to her murder too, 'because I did nothing to stop my brother'.

After the Murambi massacre, AG went on to kill other Tutsis in his own neighbourhood. He describes one instance where he killed the child of a Hutu woman, who had been married to a Tutsi. KT went home to Taba and also continued to kill. He admits to killing local neighbours, including a man called Xavery, a young person who was 'the child Mukabaramba' and his own church pastor, whom he killed in the presence of 'Karekeze', his sector coordinator. Oddly, KT also assisted a Tutsi stonemason and helped him to hide. 'I took him to a man called Jude's, it's where he hid.' When French troops arrived in the area, he took the man from his hiding place and, wielding his machete, marched him down the road, appearing to be taking him to kill him. He then handed him over to the safety of the French soldiers. He also saved another woman who was married to a Hutu man:

> Whenever attackers would want to kill them (sic), we would reject the idea, saying that if they killed them, we should kill all those Tutsis married to Hutu men or women. That is how she survived.

CS describes how, after his return from the Murambi massacre, two children were caught hiding in neighbours' houses. He had been a friend of the two boys. One of the children addressed him directly as he was about to be killed, saying, 'I am going to die but please give Munyaneza two of the rabbits that you have been keeping for me.' CS relates his reaction: 'I felt so sad. He was like a son to me... I knew I could not go ahead and kill him... I left before the child was killed. He was killed afterwards.' However, later that same day, CS was responsible for finding Murekezi, the father of these two boys. After he had been flushed out of a neighbour's house, Murekezi was killed by another Hutu villager in the ensuing chase. CS counts Murekezi among those he killed, as he was responsible for exposing him.

For genocide to succeed in Rwanda, rank and file killers were essential. They did the work of the ideologues. They knew who lived where, in their sector and cell, and they could accurately carry out the genocide at local level. The Government was simultaneously fighting a war with the Rwandan Patriotic Front and needed its army for that purpose. What is not clear is how and why the Rwandan Government was so successful in recruiting so many people of previous good character to hunt and kill their neighbours.

Creating the enemy

HD is convinced that the creation of the enemy was essential to his participation in the killing:

Q: When you participated, did you really believe those people were enemies?

HD   Yes, of course! Otherwise I could not have participated. I considered them my enemies.

Q: Did you really believe it? Did they force that into your head?

HD: Yes, they did. Nothing could have withdrawn it.

The creation of a virtual enemy was essential in order to distance the killers from their victims. If they were enemies, they had to be fought and killed. There was clearly a sense that the Hutu villagers were about to enter a battlefield as they prepared to kill during the early hours of 21 April. As they put on their eucalyptus and banana leaves, they were creating pseudo-camouflage. The fact that they were merely ensuring their own protection during the carnage was not important. They felt that they were dressing to enter the theatre of war.

A state of war was certainly created in the minds of the killers. When AG describes the 'written order from the mayor which was saying we had to go to Murambi to save our people', he is convinced that he is involved in an act of liberation. The conditioning of the populace to believe they were involved in repelling an uprising in an act of necessary civil war was an element of the leadership's plan. Repeatedly in their interviews, the killers refer to 'war', 'fighting', and the 'enemy'.

The heroic act of self-defence mounted by the Tutsi men, defending their helpless families with the pile of stones, only heightened that sense of warfare. The would-be killers had arrived on 19 April, ready to carry out their bloody task, only to be told that they had been repelled. Although most of them did not engage with the Tutsis that day, they knew the Hutus had been forced to retreat. Clearly, the 'enemy' was prepared to fight them.

KT is clear that he was told at the meeting that the people gathered at Murambi 'were to be fought at any cost because they had killed Habyarimana and crashed his helicopter (sic)'. He was asked to clarify whether there was really a fight or a massacre of innocents:

Q: You keep on saying 'we fought'. Were you really fighting or did you attack them?
KT: We were fighting.
Q: Did you kill them and vice versa?
KT: We were able to kill them because we were stronger than they were, so we entered [the site] and killed them, that is what happened.

However, KT does provide a clue to a deeper-held animosity behind the killing instinct. 'When we were young … they used to tell me that when my Mum was carrying me, the Tutsis almost caused her a miscarriage… that is even before I was born.' This is the only time that one of the interviewees relates the rationale of killing to deeper, longer-held fears and animosity. The overriding sense given of the Hutu/Tutsi relationship prior to the genocide is that of people living alongside each other, with no stated reason to hate or to kill.

Motivation

MS confirmed that he had been trained in Mudasomwa, and that the men of Mudasomwa were the most motivated. It is not easy to decipher from these five testimonies whether association to a trained group made any significant difference to the willingness to participate. What does come through is that the men of Mudasomwa were well equipped, had the Daihatsu cars from the factory, were eager to participate, and immediately left Murambi and proceeded to Cyanika to carry out a further massacre.

HD's father was killed by Tutsis fleeing Murambi. Initially in the interview, he blames the Tutsis for his father's death and uses the incident to justify watching his brother killing their stepmother. However, it then transpires that his father had actually gone to ambush the fleeing Tutsis. The ambush went wrong, leaving his father at the mercy of his would-be victims. HD sums up the complex relationships between groups, families and individuals: 'What I know is that my father was a victim of the war, and my brother killed my stepmother because she was Tutsi and I did not prevent him from killing her.' Somewhere in that sentence is his own justification for continuing to kill with a relatively clear conscience.

One of the stated motives was self-defence. The propaganda campaign had not only created the conditions of civil war but also of heightened fear that the Tutsis had a plan to kill the Hutus and could not be trusted. To kill a Tutsi was therefore an act of self-defence. AG states unequivocally that 'They [the leadership] said, 'There is only one enemy and you must kill him or her, and if you do not, you yourself shall be killed [by the Tutsi]'.' He is insistent that this was his main motive for involvement. AG's sister was married to a Tutsi, and before the genocide he had considered his Tutsi neighbours and friends as 'relatives'. He is clear in his own mind that 'We never had any conflicts between us. In fact, I would not have killed them if it were not for the fact [that] they told us that if we did not kill them, they would definitely kill us.' But whatever his attitude to Tutsis in his close circle before the genocide, and whatever his rational justification for beginning the killing as an act of self-defence, something more primal took over once the first blood was drawn. When asked why he killed a particular child, AG answers, 'I had wild thoughts that made me think we were hunting… Wherever I saw a Tutsi, I would kill.'

Leadership

Throughout the interviews, all the interviewees are insistent that 'the leadership' were to blame. KT goes as far as to accuse the leaders of 'exterminating us'. Although he is the only one to refer to the long and bitter suspicion of the Tutsis, he clarifies that 'We always shared the local beer together. How come they had never been bad to us?... That is when some leaders started…' He implies that the leaders would sow their rumours through social gatherings, undermining their relationships and eroding the last threads of trust that existed between individual people.

HD is more outraged about the leaders, believing they have evaded justice. He wanted the interviewer to report to the Prosecutor General that 'no intellectuals and those who read law books have admitted to actions during the genocide.' He accuses Councillor Mureramanzi of cutting the water taps at Murambi and erecting two roadblocks, one of which was at Murambi. He also identifies him at Murambi, throwing grenades and using a car to fetch ammunition. As Mureramanzi had not confessed or stood trial at the time of his interview, HD feels less culpable for the massacre, even though he has confessed to killing.

HD also admits that he had not been entirely honest because he had not previously identified his physician, Dr N., in his witness file because, 'I was afraid he could give me a lethal injection.' Dr N. apparently helped HD write his submission to the court on condition that he did not include Dr N.'s actions in his witness statement:

> However, I still accuse him, because he was using grenades, even though he denies it. He convinced us to accept what we did, and at the same time, they deny it. Poor peasants! What will be our fate if the educated deny their participation?

Resentment about the leadership runs deep. Not only do the interviewees feel that they were misled during the genocide, but that now they are also bearing the brunt of the legal process. HD puts his resentment succinctly, 'Big persons don't comply, but the poor accept [their crimes].' He cites several examples of local leaders and educated people who participated at Murambi, who have escaped justice:

> Look at Callixte! He was the one that provided the tractor that dug the mass graves...He does not confess, but we were there together. Today he is eating eggs and rice, while I am only eating maize...

They are sharply critical of the fact that the senior leaders are tried in Arusha on the grounds that they cannot testify against them. They say that Kigali would be a better location for the major trials because 'even an old lady can crawl for one week [and make it] to Kigali and say, "My son, didn't you kill my family?!"'

AG was apparently 'arrested' by the same councillor who had gathered the villagers together to form the group to conduct the killings at Murambi. His frustration is palpable as he blames the community lay leaders for inciting them, then leaving them to bear the consequences. He states, 'If I were given [the] opportunity, I would go back to my area, I would go pointing out the people we were with [at Murambi] and even though there is a leader among them, I would name him too.'

MS expressed resentment that at the time of interview, Semakwavu was in Belgium because, 'He was leader of the commune and attended all the meetings.' Similarly, KT is angry that Sebuhura escaped to France. He suggests that the French took him by plane immediately after the massacre.

Evading responsibility

The interviewees refer to their admissions of guilt on many occasions. They are adamant that they have admitted their crimes in full, and have done so without prompting. However, they appear to have overriding considerations.

They are acutely aware that the admission of guilt will result in lighter sentencing. They are also aware of the politics of reconciliation. They place themselves carefully in the various intersections of the politics of justice post-genocide. They reinforce the fact that they have admitted their guilt, while many killers are at liberty who have avoided any confession. They thereby create a relative moral high ground from which to state that, in confessing, they have somehow bought the right to freedom and a guilt-free future.

MS appears to take his responsibility fully:

> We put ourselves in the victims' shoes and apologise to the survivors and the citizens of Rwanda, and after that, if people will forgive us, the Government will take the final decision [about our fate].

He describes his personal feeling as being like 'a scar in my heart'. He also appears to see this as a long-term commitment as he hopes that 'my offspring should always apologise [so that] it will never happen again, as it is very bad'. But this apparently open acceptance of responsibility evades the real choices he made at the time of the genocide and the punishment due to him. He states that 'everything was organised by the Government... the previous Government put a cross on our shoulders.' He also appears to use the confession of guilt as a direct means to mitigate the full force of his sentence:

> Prisoners accept that they committed a crime and this makes the Government's job easier. Not only that, but our punishments are reduced, as mine was reduced from category one to category two.

MS is content to blame the previous leadership for his crimes and satisfied with the downgrading of his prosecution category – which virtually secures his early release. He thereby squares the circle by facing justice, evading much of his sentence, feeling sufficiently contrite, but never accepting culpability.

HD has similarly 'seen the advantage of pleading guilty'. He states that 'When you are guilty of something, you always live with a heavy burden on your heart, but after saying the truth, I feel as strong as a rock.' It seems that this strength is linked to salving his sense of guilt and providing a way through it for him. He goes on: 'Whoever admits what they did, will have their penalty reduced.'

However, not all of the interviewees evade the personal choices they made at the time. AG confirms that 'No one forced me, it was out of my own will...' In actual fact, he takes responsibility for the murder of one man, when his role was that of bystander:

> AG: We took the boy... and Ntankirutimana Cyrpien... tied [him] his

with ropes... and drowned him in the river.

Q: What do you mean when you say you killed him? You told us other people drowned him...

AG: People took him and killed him while I was there, which means if they did not kill him, I would have killed him myself.

Q: In other words you did not do anything to him...?

AG: I neither tied him nor drowned him, but I witnessed the whole event.

Of the five interviewees, AG is the only one aware that he created a fantasy 'enemy' out of innocent people. He also reached the conclusion that his decision not to act decisively to assist Tutsi neighbours contributed to their deaths. He states, 'Instead of hiding them, I killed them!'

Forgiveness

HD refers to the Government Commission 'that was put in place to teach people to accept their crimes so that they can be forgiven'. The killers appear to want forgiveness for their crimes. They also expect it in return for their confessions.

MS took steps to seek forgiveness for the murder of Mureramanzi by going to Butare to see his surviving daughter and ask her forgiveness. According to his statement, she accepted his request to visit her to ask for forgiveness. He reports that she told him, 'Let the Government do whatever they want, but for me, I have forgiven you.' That said, MS still looks for spiritual answers to his sense of guilt: 'Only God who is mighty can forgive us. The unity Government wants to grant forgiveness, [but] we don't deserve any mercy.' He does suggest that the killers should be used at the memorial sites to demonstrate ongoing penitence for the benefit of education. 'We [will] sit [at the memorial site] and recall what we did. This will enable us to see [that] what we did is beyond imagination.'

In attempting to apologise, AG does not know to whom to apologise. He does not know most of the people he killed and also opts to plead to higher authority: 'I have already apologised to the people I know, but those I don't know, I would like to apologise to the Government and to ask God to forgive me.' AG reinforces the link between confession and amnesty and has little sense of asking the victims for forgiveness directly:

I suggest the Government forgives me because I am trying to simplify its work by confessing and convicting those who do not admit their participation. Therefore the Government should forgive me, because I say the truth about what happened without giving them a hard time.

Pressed further, it transpired that he did talk to one survivor and told her he had killed her relatives. While doing so, he asked for her forgiveness for his wider participation in the genocide. 'She appreciated me and said, "You say the truth, keep it up and don't change!"' Taking this as meaning she has forgiven him, he then states, '…we can ask them to forgive us and in return they will forgive us. Thereafter we will live together in peace as before.'

Surprisingly, there is almost an expectation that forgiveness will follow confession as a right. KT makes that clear:

KT: According to what I did, depending on their hearts, they [the genocide survivors] can pardon me, because I was used. I never did those things on my own.

Q: What if they do not pardon you?

KT: Then there would be no difference between them and those who killed.

He then goes on to place himself squarely as a victim too: 'We all died, but the Tutsis were innocent.'

Conclusions

More questions remain unresolved than answered. How important was the propaganda in creating the context for persuading rank and file killers to participate? To what extent did leadership really influence the decisions of ordinary people to kill? What part did the conditions of civil war play in encouraging vigilantism in close neighbourhoods? What proportion of the population killed or collaborated? Was it really a mass movement or was it a select group of activists and those who were easily persuaded?

These five interviewees give us a small glimpse into the minds of rank and file killers across Rwanda. Murambi is a useful case study as it was a specific site with a specific process for recruitment, and it involved leaders, meetings, military and police personnel, as well as rank and file killers.

It becomes clear from the interviews that long-existing hatreds were significant as background, and the propaganda worked well to create the sense of threat. The leadership recruited effectively and created a clear rationale of self-defence. Leaders organised events relatively effectively and gave the sense of structure. The justification of 'fighting' was necessary and persuasive, even though the killers were totally aware that the 'enemy' was weak and defenceless. Once the rank and file began to kill, they became committed to the cause, but at times their conscience persuaded them to stand back from active killing, to walk away or even to save someone while killing another. The confession of responsibility is the alter-ego of the evasion of responsibility; the killers want to be forgiven, they expect to be forgiven.

Understanding more about the rank and file killers of Rwanda's genocide is essential to understanding this specific genocide and genocidal killers more generally. Whether they killed two people, twenty people or two hundred, without HD, KT, MS, AG and SC, genocide in Rwanda would still have occurred. But, it would not have succeeded without the likes of them in large numbers. Genocidal massacre is an increasing feature in the landscape of killing.

In recent years, the International Criminal Tribunal for Rwanda (ICTR) and the International Criminal Tribunal for the former Yugoslavia (ICTY) have successfully indicted and convicted some of the ideologues and organisers of genocide. In future, the International Criminal Court (ICC) is expected to do the same, but the key to the prevention of such killing lies elsewhere. We need to understand better the mechanisms that convince rank and file killers to wield the machetes that kill.

References

African Rights (forthcoming) *'Go! If You Die, Perhaps I Will Live': A Collective Account of Genocide and Survival in Murambi*, Gikongoro. Kigali: African Rights.

Barnett, M. (2002) *Eyewitness to a Genocide: The United Nations and Rwanda*. New York: Cornell University Press.

Dallaire, R. (2003) *Shake Hands with the Devil; The Failure of Humanity in Rwanda*. Toronto: Random House.

Melvern, L. (2000) *A People Betrayed; The Role of the West in Rwanda's Genocide*. London: Zed Books.

Melvern, L. (2004) *Conspiracy to Murder; The Rwanda Genocide*. London: Verso.

Epilogue

Why We Kill

Nancy Loucks, Sally Smith Holt and Joanna R. Adler

Whilst reading these chapters, we may agree or disagree with certain or all the types of killing discussed. We will find some easier to accept than others, and we will impose our own experiences, beliefs, and attitudes onto how we interpret the content herein. Exactly which chapters trigger feelings of revulsion or empathy will vary but are unlikely to be unique to any individual:

> ... accounts are learnt by ordinary cultural transmission, and are drawn from a well-established, collectively available pool. An account is adopted because of its public acceptability. Socialization teaches us which motives are acceptable for which actions. (Cohen 2001: 59)

Redefinition and euphemisms for killing are perhaps the most repeated theme in the book. We do not kill, we protect the family's honour. We do not kill, we punish the perpetrator. We do not kill, we are taking the most humane course of action (for the unborn child, for the pregnant mother, for the terminally ill, for ourselves). We do not kill, we fight for freedom. Such language masks, sanitises, and confers respectability (Cohen 2001). Cohen notes that 'An entire language of denial has been constructed in order to evade thinking about the unthinkable' (*ibid.*: 11; also Lifton and Markusen 1990). Cohen found that people could learn to accept even highly disturbing information through the process of redefinition and denial:

> One common thread runs through the many different stories of denial: people, organizations, governments or whole societies are presented with information that is too disturbing, threatening or anomalous to be fully absorbed or openly acknowledged. The information is therefore somehow repressed, disavowed, pushed aside or reinterpreted. Or else the information 'registers' well enough, but its implications – cognitive, emotional or moral – are evaded, neutralized or rationalized away. (2001: 1)

Zimbardo comments on this behaviour as well, noting the tendency for humans to '"explain away" our personal responsibility for the damage we cause by our role-based actions', to the extreme that Nazi SS leaders can claim they were "only following orders"' (2007: 218).

One question the book raises is how different the various types of killing actually are. Obviously the ultimate outcome is the same, but the similarities can stretch further. For example, Keith Soothill's chapter on serial killers notes that '… the distinction between killings by terrorists and multiple killings with no evident political motive is becoming increasingly blurred.' Perhaps even more controversially, similarities in the impact of homicide and capital punishment in terms of secondary victimisation arguably draw those types of killing together as well:

> Both families experience suffering as a result of the homicide, one through loss of a loved one, the other through the imminent loss by execution, and neither through any 'fault' of their own. Both sets of families have similar needs and concerns and therefore, we argue, should be recognised as 'victims'. (p.73)

This book was not written to attribute blame, nor to evoke sympathy for one perspective over another. Rather, it was written to stimulate debate as to how and why we justify our beliefs and perhaps better to understand the beliefs of others, even those with which we disagree. Lawrence Hinman commented in his chapter on abortion that such issues '… [pose] most clearly to us as a society the question of how we can live together with deep moral differences.'

As human beings, and indeed as social animals who grow up within a particular context, we will continue to explain and justify, to sanitise and deny, rather than to acknowledge that we too may kill, that we too are capable of such behaviour, even where we do not define it as wrong:

Normal people know how to deny things; they are not immobilized by intrusive thoughts about how terrible everything is. They sustain themselves precisely by the denials and self-deceptions they so easily condemn in others. (Cohen: 57)

Zimbardo notes that 'attempting to understand the situational and systemic contributions to any individual's behaviour does not excuse the person or absolve him or her from responsibility in engaging in immoral, illegal, or evil deeds' (2007: xi). It does, however, help us work towards preventing such acts.

Cohen, S. (2001) *States of Denial: Knowing About Atrocities and Suffering.* Cambridge: Polity Press.
Lifton, R. J. and Markusen, E. (1990) *The Genocidal Mentality.* New York: Basic Books.